FINANCIAL FREEDOM MASTERY 2.0

3 BOOKS IN 1:
THE BEST STRATEGIES TO INCREASE YOUR ON-LINE BUSINESS AND CREATE PASSIVE INCOME, BECOMING AN EXPERT IN NETWORK MARKETING, AFFILIATE MARKETING AND COPYWRITING

PAUL J. ABRAMAH

Financial Freedom Mastery 2.0

© Copyright 2020 - All rights reserved.

The content contained within this book may not be reproduced, duplicated or transmitted without direct written permission from the author or the publisher. Under no circumstances will any blame or legal responsibility be held against the publisher, or author, for any damages, reparation, or monetary loss due to the information contained within this book. Either directly or indirectly.

Legal Notice:

This book is copyright protected. This book is only for personal use. You cannot amend, distribute, sell, use, quote or paraphrase any part, or the content within this book, without the consent of the author or publisher.

Disclaimer Notice:

Please note the information contained within this document is for educational and entertainment purposes only. All effort has been executed to present accurate, up to date, and reliable, complete information. No warranties of any kind are declared or implied. Readers acknowledge that the author is not engaging in the rendering of legal, financial, medical or professional advice. The content within this book has been derived from various sources. Please consult a licensed professional before attempting any techniques outlined in this book.

By reading this document, the reader agrees that under no circumstances is the author responsible for any losses, direct or indirect, which are incurred as a result of the use of information contained within this document, including, but not limited to, — errors, omissions, or inaccuracies.

TABLE OF CONTENTS
AFFILIATE MARKETING 2020

INTRODUCTION 10

CHAPTER 1 WHAT IS AFFILIATE MARKETING? 14

CHAPTER 2 CHOSE RIGHT NICHE 20

CHAPTER 3 LOW TICKET VS. HIGH TICKET 24

CHAPTER 4 HOW TO COME AN AFFILIATE MARKETER 28

CHAPTER 5 SURVEYING THE AFFILIATE LANDSCAPE; PROGRAMS AND NETWORKS 34

CHAPTER 6 KEYWORD RESEARCH AND PRODUCT SELECTION 42

CHAPTER 7 TOP AFFILIATE MARKETING PROGRAMS 50

CHAPTER 8 HOW TO CHOOSE AFFILIATE MARKETING PROGRAM 56

CHAPTER 9 SEO: SEARCH ENGINE OPTIMIZATION 59

CHAPTER 10 EMAIL MARKETING 64

CHAPTER 11 EMAIL LIST 68

CHAPTER 12 SALES FUNNELS STRATEGIES 72

CHAPTER 13 TOOLS AND RESOURCES FOR AFFILIATES 78

CHAPTER 14 WRITING CONTENT FOR AFFILIATE MARKETING 86

CHAPTER 15 USING SOCIAL MEDIA PLATFORMS FOR AFFILIATE MARKETING 94

CHAPTER 16 MISTAKES MAKE ON AFFILIATE MARKETING 102

CHAPTER 17 STRATEGIES 108

CHAPTER 18 TRICKS AND TIPS 114

CONCLUSION 120

TABLE OF CONTENTS
NETWORK MARKETING AND SOCIAL MEDIA 2020

INTRODUCTION **126**

CHAPTER 1 WHAT IS NETWORK MARKETING? **130**

CHAPTER 2 CHOOSING THE RIGHT COMPANY **136**

CHAPTER 3 HOW TO FIND PROSPECT **144**

CHAPTER 4 THE ART OF INVITATION **154**

CHAPTER 5 PRESENTING AND PROSPECT **164**

CHAPTER 6 HOW TO PROMOTE YOUR PRODUCTS AND EVENTS? **172**

CHAPTER 7 MINDSET TO BECAME A BEST NETWORKER **180**

CHAPTER 8 RELATIONSHIP MARKETING **190**

CHAPTER 9 MISTAKES NEW NETWORKER MADE **200**

CHAPTER 10 DEVELOP YOUR LEADERSHIP **210**

CHAPTER 11 ABSORB BEST STRATEGIES AND TRICKS FROM TOP NETWORK MARKETERS ON THE MARKET **218**

CHAPTER 12 EXPLODING THE REACH OF YOUR NETWORK **230**

CHAPTER 13 OPPORTUNITIES OR SCAM **236**

CHAPTER 14 IMPORTANT SOCIAL NETWORKS **244**

CHAPTER 15 THE TOOLS YOU REALLY NEED **252**

CHAPTER 16 7 STEPS TO EFFECTIVE MENTORING AND TRAINING ... **260**

CHAPTER 17 THE THREE BUSINESS BUILDING PHASES OF NETWORK MARKETING **268**

CONCLUSION **276**

TABLE OF CONTENTS
COPYWRITING 2020

INTRODUCTION 282

CHAPTER 1 WHAT'S IS COPYWRITING? 286

CHAPTER 2 THE BEST PLATFORMS WHERE TO LEARN FROM/EXAMPLES OF EXPERTS 290

CHAPTER 3 TRANSFORMING THE WORLD'S WORST SENTENCE INTO INCREDIBLY CAPTIVATING COPY 296

CHAPTER 4 SEO AND HOW TO RANK ON GOOGLE 302

CHAPTER 5 BEST NICHES TO COPYWRITING FOR PROFIT 310

CHAPTER 6 COPYWRITING FOR SOCIAL MEDIA ADS 316

CHAPTER 7 COPYWRITING FOR EMAIL MARKETING 324

CHAPTER 8 MAKING DECISION TO WRITE 334

CHAPTER 9 SELLING THE CONCEPT NOT THE PRODUCT 340

CHAPTER 10 HOW MUCH COPY SHOULD YOU WRITE? 346

CHAPTER 11 ART OF PERSONAL COMMUNICATION 352

CHAPTER 12 COPY 356

CHAPTER 13 EDITING PROCESS 362

CHAPTER 14 THE PSYCHOLOGICAL TRIGGERS 366

CHAPTER 15 HOW MUCH MONEY CAN YOU MAKE COPYWRITING? 372

CHAPTER 16 WHAT DOES IT TAKE TO BECOME A COPYWRITER? 378

CHAPTER 17 THE BASICS OF COPYWRITING 386

CHAPTER 18 COPYWRITING TECHNIQUES 390

CHAPTER 19 HOW TO AVOID THE MOST COMMON COPYWRITING MISTAKES? 394

CHAPTER 20 COPYWRITING ETHICS: STAYING TRUE TO YOUR VALUES 400

CHAPTER 21 ESSENTIAL QUESTIONS FOR YOUR COPY 404

CONCLUSION 410

AFFILIATE MARKETING 2020

A BEGINNERS GUIDE TO UNDERSTAND SEO FROM HOME AND A STEP BY STEP GUIDE FOR INCREASE PASSIVE INCOME WITH AFFILIATIONS AND ONLINE SELLING

PAUL J. ABRAMAH

Introduction

Affiliate marketing is among the most popular ways to produce passive income online. And it doesn't always require any financial expense, though it can be helpful to invest in building your website, in article marketing, and advertising. Selling services or products as an affiliate marketer involves promoting them and finding a flat rate commission or percentage of income from each sale created from your link. Essentially, the company offers you a personalized link that you tell your audience, whether it be on a blog, a contact list, a site, or a web store. When readers or viewers click through your hyperlink and make an obtain the ongoing company you're working with, you get paid.

It's generally best to let your visitors know that you're an affiliate marketer and may profit from their purchase, so it's important to build a relationship with your viewers where they trust your opinion when you vouch for a brand. If your target audience thinks you're selling them products so you can profit just, they'll be less likely to buy through your link. Aiming to help customers better their lives will constantly sell better than pushing something at them.

You can incorporate internet affiliate marketing into your already-established online presence. Links can be shared in your site posts, on your website, or through your email list using different methods to attract clients toward the products you're recommending. In the event that you don't already have a blog page or website, it's smart to begin one if you want to pursue affiliate marketing to obtain passive income. You can create a Shopify store also. Whatever avenue you choose to make use of in posting your links, you'll have to build a status or brand in a niche in order to become a credible expert in your niche.

In order to select a niche, make a list of topics you're already educated or passionate about and cross-reference that with a list of profitable niches. An excellent niche is one that has a popular for products and is not overly saturated with online marketers already. You need area to grow your business.

However, you do wish at least some competition in your niche and that means you know that it is already profitable more than enough to draw additional online business owners. You'll also wish to look for a niche which has a large amount of product vendors so the selection of products you can share is larger, rather than all the affiliates will be marketing the same items. Ensure there is a demand for the merchandise in your market by checking Best Sellers lists on Amazon and additional retailers more specific to your niche.

Before you select an affiliate network, you'll have to have a real way to talk about your links with your audience. To build your website, you'll require a domain. If you don't currently have a name for your brand or store, choose your name predicated on what domain can be available, purchase your domain, buy and setup hosting then. Your domain is like your actual business, and the hosting is like the virtual real estate where your business lives.

Once you have your domain and hosting secured, install WordPress and choose a theme. There are plenty of free themes to select from and they're all very customizable. You can create your own site without any coding knowledge, or you can outsource this step to a freelancer if you would like to end up being sure your site looks nice. It should be basic, clean looking, and easy to get around. You don't want your readers to become bombarded with ads, crazy colors, or an overwhelmingly cluttered site.

Also be sure your website includes a professional logo together with your business's or brand's name onto it, and that it's mobile friendly. This site will be used to share your affiliate links, but in order to build trust and credibility together with your audience, you'll also have to offer something more.

Informative posts about studies and trends which come up in your niche can help drive traffic to your website and build your audience, but you don't need to take up a blog necessarily. Your site can host guest bloggers or content material creators in your market so that your target audience has one central spot to find the various content they're thinking about. Videos and blog posts are most likely to get organic traffic by showing up in searches.

The important thing to keep in mind is that your visitors must trust and respect that the suggestions coming from your site will be the reliable suggestions of an authority in your niche. You may also create a product page on your own site where you feature your affiliate marketer products with links to buy them.

Blogging and creating your very own content is one of the best methods to build the reputation and credibility you should be a successful affiliate marketer. Producing high-quality content frequently allows your viewers and readers to be accustomed to your content, grow a relationship with your blog page, and continue coming back to see what you have to offer.

You should certainly share your affiliate links in these blogs in order to expose your audience to the products you're representing, but make sure your posts aren't commercial and not all centered around promoting products. Some types of articles that can be a good asset to your site are how-to guides, "Top 10" style lists, and posts addressing common queries and concerns that people in your market have regarding certain aspects of your niche; or latest events and trends which have come up.

Your audience wants to read authentic content that they'll want to talk about with their family and friends. If your specific niche market is beauty and health, you can cite latest studies that show the ultimate way to wash your face in the early morning, or you can share the best way to use a spray establishing on your own makeup. Presenting this kind of content allows your viewers to begin with viewing you as a specialist in your field, so when you begin mixing in product critiques or brand comparisons which contain your affiliate links they'll become more likely to trust your recommendations and buy through your link.

Whenever a consumer receives free information that they find valuable, they will reciprocate the action simply by purchasing your products. This is called the theory of reciprocity, and it's very important to many ways of creating passive income online.

Once a website is had by you or a blog to share your links on, you need to ensure that your site gets visitors. Because the internet is filled with websites, bloggers, shops, cat videos, and social press influencers, you can't depend on organic traffic only to bring audiences to your content. You'll have to increase engagement, ensure that your content shows up in queries, and build relationships together with your audience that maintain them coming back.

Collect email addresses from your own audience so you can compile an email set of people in your market. This email list is one of the greatest resources an on-line entrepreneur can have when making passive income. You can build yours by adding a sign-up package to your website's homepage with a location to enter their email address and another to enter their name. Be sure to include a free call-to-actions like "sign-up for our free newsletter" or "get linked to us" to inspire people to partake in this feature.

Offering free information products in the form of PDF files or short eBooks is also a way to gather email addresses. Customers prefer to receive free products, so they'll enter their email addresses to allow them to be sent the info. This helps you grow your email list, as well as raising the reader's openness to buying your products due to the principle of reciprocity.

Chapter 1 What Is Affiliate Marketing?

Although making money can be quite a challenge nowadays, this still does not change the fact that it is but essential especially given the current state of the economy. People must work doubly hard in order to earn enough income to cover all their day to day expenses. And perhaps one of the consolations here is the fact that there are a couple of ways on how to generate income today, thanks to the Internet and information age.

The Internet has opened a lot of doors of money-making opportunities to the public. And among the most popular of which today is affiliate marketing—which will be the center of discussion of this book.

What is affiliate marketing?

As Wikipedia put it, it is a marketing practice wherein a business or company rewards its affiliates for every visitor or customer that it can bring through marketing means.

So essentially, this means that if you work as an affiliate, your main goal will be to promote the products, services or brand of a certain business via the Internet. You will just to serve as the link or connection between the consumer and the seller. There is no need to create new products or service.

And if your marketing efforts are successful based on your ability to generate traffic to the website of your host company or business or a purchase, you will be given commission or pay according to the set terms.

Nonetheless, even though it sounds quite simple, it can still be quite tricky. Notice here that although this may be among the quickest and easiest ways, there is no mention of it being one of the easiest.

This is because affiliate marketing is a highly performance-driven type of marketing strategy. At the same time, the competition can be quite stiff especially given the intense competition among the businesses themselves, as well as the proliferation of other affiliate marketers who are contending for the same consumers.

There are also a couple of participants involved in the affiliate marketing process. To begin with, there is the merchant or company that hires the affiliate marketers in order to boost their sales and profits. Then there is you, the affiliate or publisher. You will be the one in charge of product, service or brand promotion. You will receive salary or commission depending on the results of your affiliate work.

In certain cases, will be the network. It serves as the intermediate connection between the merchant and you, the affiliate. It processes the payments and provides various tools as well as offers.

Then last but certainly not least, there is the customer. He or she is your target market. Your goal is to make him or her buy the product of your host business after he or she has read the ad, or you have posted in your affiliate site.

The bottom lines

Having said all that, the bottom line here is that affiliate marketing is all about product and brand promotion via the Internet. Ever since the latter has become an integral part of the lifestyle of the consumers in this generation, it has also become vital for the businesses to establish and maintain a strong presence in the World Wide Web. And one of the many ways to do this is through affiliate marketing.

As an affiliate marketer, your task will be to use your affiliate site to promote the products, services and brand of your host company. Although it may sound easy, it can be a bit tricky especially given the fact that there is a whole lot of other Internet marketers like you who are competing to get the attention of online shoppers.

Hence, you must think about your own marketing tactic or strategy in order to stay ahead of the game. Since this is performance-based, the harder you work, the more money you will be able to earn.

How Do I Get Started?

Now that you have a general idea about what affiliate marketing is, the next step would be to know how it works. This will be the center of on this.

The first step to be an affiliate is choosing the affiliate program you want to be part of. In this area, there are lots to choose from especially since businesses are already appreciating the value of the internet in the success of their sales and profits. If you have a company in mind, just go straight to its site and see the requirements and processes for registration.

On the other hand, if you are still searching for possible choices, you can check out the Internet. Just use the search engines to look for affiliate programs and see the options in the search results page.

After you have chosen the business or company you prefer to work for, the next step would be to register your affiliate site or page. In some companies, this can be done for free, while others charge a certain fee.

Once your application has been approved, you can already pick out the products that you want to sell or market. Your host business will then provide you with an affiliate code that is unique for you. You will then use this to refer traffic to their website. This code will give them the signal that a customer made a purchase via your affiliate work. This will then be reflected in your performance and assessment for payment.

Ready-made promotional materials are also usually given by host companies. Most of the time, these are the same across all their affiliates to give a uniform look and branding. This way, they can instill brand recall among the consumers.

The promotional materials consist of text links, banners along with other types of creative copies. When you get them, all you must do is copy the code and put it in your affiliate site. This is where traffic generation and referral will stem from.

So, when your site visitors click on the links from your host site, they will be redirected to the latter. And when they make a purchase or subscription, the company will know that your affiliate site made the referral. Hence, you get commission.

As for performance monitoring of their affiliates, host businesses generate their own affiliate ID and affiliate software. An example of the latter will be the WP Affiliate Platform. At the same time, you will also be given a full and real time access to all the statistics related to sales and commission.

With all that, you already have everything that you need to do your affiliate work. Some companies can even provide custom-made creative materials for you. Just give them the specifics. This is usually done by those who wish to customize the promotional materials to fit the theme and elements of their affiliate site. This way, they can be more appealing and appropriate as well to the site's audience.

Once the creative materials have been provided for you, all that is left for you to do is plan an appropriate marketing strategy to reach your target market and persuade them to make a purchase, or just even show interest by clicking the link you have in your affiliate site.

Yes, there are times that you do not need to make a sale in order to get commission. Some host businesses provide different terms of payment. To give you an idea, here are some examples of affiliate payment terms:

Pay per sale. For one, there is the pay per sale option. Here, your merchant will pay you a certain percentage from the sale price once a client from your site completes a purchase. In this type, actual purchase from your referred client is necessary. Otherwise, you will have no commission.

Pay per click. For this type, no actual sale is necessary. You will get commission once a visitor from your site clicks one of the ads or links from your host company. So, the more users clicking and being redirected to the site of your host company, the larger amount you will be paid.

Pay per lead. Lastly, affiliates can also get payment once they are able to refer a visitor to the host site and get them to fill out a contact form. All you must do is lead them to your host company's website and have them register and fill out a contact form. Once that process is completed, you will receive commission. Again, there is no need to make a sale.

Chapter 2 Chose Right Niche

Identifying Your Niche

Regarding identifying your product niche, you want to start by considering what industries you are most passionate about or interested in learning about. Many people underestimate the value of picking a niche that interests you, but true marketing masters know that this is the key to find a niche that you are going to be able to grow in. When you are passionate about, or at least interested in a certain subject, you are more likely to invest in learning about it and understand what it is that you are learning about. With marketing, this means that you are going to be far more intuitive about what types of trends are ideal for you to partake in, what products are going to succeed in your industry, and how you can grow your business effectively.

After you have identified about 3-5 passions or interests that you could pursue as a business venture, you want to start brainstorming all the possible products and product lines that you could offer in each niche. Write those potential products or product lines down under each possible niche. In addition to writing down possible product lines, consider areas that you could branch out into as your business grew, too. For example, let us say you wanted to offer graphic t-shirts for women in a product line as your primary product line or the one that you would be starting in. Possible extensions of this could be to add male graphic t-shirts, child graphic t-shirts, and even graphic t-shirts for dogs. Alternatively, you could venture into offering graphic canvas bags, totes, and other female-oriented accessories if you wanted to maintain a female niche.

Getting a clear idea of what you could offer and how you could extend your offers is important, as this is your earliest opportunity to validate that your possible chosen niche would not only be strong in the beginning, but would also have plenty of room for growth. Make sure that you take the time to really consider how these products would fit into your possible niche and whether they would make logical sense with your business. It is important that you are honest and concise when you validate possible product niches in order to feel confident that the route you have chosen is going to be a strong one. Now is not the time to be idealistic, but instead to be realistic, as you are going to be placing a lot of weight into this decision and you want to make sure that you minimize the risk as much as possible by validating it as honestly as possible right away.

Next, you need to start narrowing down your possible product niches into ones that are as specific as possible. While you do not want to niche down too hard to the point where you have almost nothing left to offer, you do want to niche down to the point where what you are offering is clear and easily groups together. For example, rather than saying "Gardening supplies" which is too broad or "gardening rakes" which is too specific, you might offer "designer flowerpots as a niche. This way, there are plenty of different product lines that you can incorporate, ranging from modern and sleek to flowery and feminine, yet it is still a clear niche that you are serving.

At this point, you can identify whether or not a niche is ideal based on your level of passion in that niche, the room for growth that it has, and the way that you might be able to narrow it down into a more specific category. All that is left to do is validate your niche with the outside world to ensure that the niche you pick is one that will interest other people, which will ensure that you are likely to earn sales from it. Nothing would be more disappointing than validating a niche with yourself, only to launch it to the public and find that it is something that not too many people are interested in.

When it comes to validating your niche, you can do so by researching your chosen niche on platforms like Google Trends. You can also do basic research on social media for your chosen niche by searching up hashtags or keywords relating to your niche and seeing just how popular those terms are. Ideally, you want a niche that has 2-5 million people interested in it so that you have plenty of room for growth. If there is any more than that, you might be attempting to tap into a niche that is far too broad for you to make any level of success in. If you pick one that has a smaller audience, you are not going to have enough people to market to and you will find yourself marketing to no one.

Chapter 3 Low Ticket vs. High Ticket

Affiliate Marketing offers a great income opportunity for people who want to make money online. It is a win-win situation for both merchants and affiliates alike. When affiliates promote a product or service through their websites, blogs, YouTube videos, or any other marketing channel, they do not get paid unless their efforts lead to additional traffic or a sale.

Therefore, for merchants, Affiliate Marketing is an efficient and affordable form of marketing. Affiliates, on the other hand, simply need to promote the product or service through whatever means, because an increase in traffic or sales is a sure increase on his or her pay. Affiliate marketers do not need to produce a good, stock it, handle it, or deal with any other operational issue, they just must introduce the potential clients to the actual sellers.

However, it is up to an affiliate to choose the products and/or services he or she wishes to promote because he or she can consider some products not worth promoting and others well worth his or her time. Therefore, an affiliate marketer will need to understand the following:

1. High Ticket affiliate product or service
2. Low Ticket affiliate product or service

High Ticket Affiliate Products or Services

Salespeople who receive a commission and affiliate marketers sell tons of products online, products that carry price tags ranging from a few dollars to thousands of dollars. Some products such as diamond jewelry, HD televisions, fine watches, and other upscale products sell for thousands of dollars through affiliate marketers, and this means that it is possible for these affiliates to make a good commission from the sale of one product. Commissions may range from less than 10% to as high as 50%, depending on the affiliate program an affiliate has signed up for. Therefore, when it comes to High Ticket Affiliate Marketing, shrewd marketing is the secret to making good money, since these opportunities might not come by often.

Choosing a High-Ticket Product or Service

It is important to choose a product or service that the marketer is familiar with and an affiliate program that is reputable and dependable. High Ticket products are usually sold by name-brand businesses through respected online stores, which is why consumers feel comfortable ordering. Affiliates planning to promote such products should first check product from the online store's website and choose those that have a solid reputation.

Research the Niche

Affiliates cannot promote a product effectively unless they understand their target market. High Ticket items often require consumers with substantial credit and discretionary income. However, some consumers consider high-ticket products as investments. Such consumers may not have a large income, but they often have the credit needed to serve their interests.

Build an Online Presence

Affiliates selling big-ticket items should create a large and targeted online presence through social media accounts, websites, and blogs. They should also create solid content that presents them as experts in their field. For example, those promoting expensive watches should have a blog that different watches and accessories. They should also stress the benefits of the product they are promoting, in addition to the features of the product. For example, how the price of a product will appreciate with time, making it a good investment.

Drive Traffic to his or her Site

It is important for High Ticket affiliate marketers to try out different marketing strategies, such as AdSense, social network marketing, email marketing, and Banners, to find the ones that work best. However, the best advertising strategies should funnel potential big-ticket customers to the affiliate's website first, rather than the product's website.

Benefits of High-Ticket Affiliate Marketing include:

1. High Ticket consumers tend to be repeat customers, if an affiliate marketer builds trust with them.
2. Affiliates who sell High Ticket items can become their own brand.
3. One sale can set a marketer up for a month, or even several months.

Low Ticket Affiliate Marketing

There are tons of Low-Ticket items to promote from websites. Some include training sites, Clickbank, Amazon, book sites, fashion sites, and anything else one can think of. Low Ticket affiliate products usually range from about $50 to a few hundred dollars. Affiliates who deal in such products usually earn a commission ranging from 5% to 40%.

Low Ticket Affiliate Marketing is ideal for people who are just starting out because they can easily promote low-cost items through social media, blogs, and email marketing, without too much effort. However, in order to make a good income, they need to sell many products, which in turn requires a large online following.

Selling Low Ticket affiliate products and services requires a disciplined approach to the Affiliate Marketing business. When affiliates sell low priced items, they lack the same margin of error that High Ticket affiliates enjoy. However, if they manage their expenses, they can leverage the large market for low-cost items to generate more revenue through volume.

In addition, promoting Low Ticket items profitably requires a strategy that lowers an individual's customer acquisition costs. Therefore, paying $2 per click for advertising will not be profitable if he or she is promoting $20 items. Using SEO and social media marketing, on the other hand, will likely drive traffic to an individual's site at a much lower cost?

It is a fact that Low Ticket items are easier to sell, which is why most affiliate programs are Low Ticket programs. However, Affiliate Marketing is like a basket of eggs, and the number of eggs an individual can promote is limitless. In this case, the eggs are products and/or services. Few people can afford High Ticket products and services; therefore, it is wise to have a variety of products and/or services for the audience that visits the site to browse through. Making money is important; however, affiliates should not forget about their audience. Essentially, they need to meet their audiences' needs, whether High Ticket or Low Ticket.

Chapter 4 How to Come an Affiliate Marketer

Most people with corporate jobs are trapped in a rat race. They almost have no time for themselves. The biggest advantage of being an affiliate marketer is the fact that you are now free to work under your own terms. If you are feeling unwell, you can sleep in and work the following day. Conversely, if you are energetic, you may channel all your energies into marketing and boost your earnings. In the corporate world, you could work as hard as possible, but still, your salary remains the same while your employer enjoys the fruits of your hard work. The following are some of the other great reasons why being an affiliate marketer is a great thing.

- It's a diverse billion-dollar industry

Think about any product or niche, and chances are there's an affiliate program catering to it. You will have more success by promoting products and services that you take great interest in. When you sign up to an affiliate network, you can select your favorite program from diverse offers. This ensures that you are making money while promoting products that you are passionate about.

- Low-cost

Commonly, when people decide to escape their corporate job and achieve financial freedom, often, they are looking to set up their own business. But then setting up and running a successful business is not an easy thing, for you need tremendous capital, which might very easily lead you down the path of debts, and the fact that upwards of 80% of startups fail within five years doesn't make the idea any more appealing. But when it comes to affiliate marketing, you don't need a lot to get started. In fact, with just an internet connection and an active social media account, you could be well on the way to receiving your first commission in a week's time.

- Expertise is not a necessity

Think about being a surgeon. You must go to school and get certified before you can start to practice. If you were found operating on someone's brain without a license, it would land you in trouble, right? These regulations are great. But when it comes to affiliate marketing, the results are the only thing that matters. You might not be very great at marketing a certain product, but if you are putting an effort to achieve your marketing goals, that's fine. You'd be surprised that most successful affiliate marketers have a background in totally unrelated fields.

- Passive income

When you are an accountant with a big pharmaceutical, you must always show up to work to earn a salary. If you stay away from work, you presumably don't get the salary. But when it comes to affiliate marketing, you have a perfect opportunity to earn while you sleep. Of course, this won't happen automatically. You must put in tremendous initial work so that you may be able to earn passively. For instance, if you own a blog, you must generate valuable content so that the search engines will keep directing traffic to your blog, and the visitors will heed to your various Calls to Action. In this way, you will be earning passively. This is exactly why you see many affiliate marketers affording to tour the world and living in exotic places. They might be traveling, but they are also earning, so the party doesn't stop.

- You become a thought leader

People seem to trust people that demonstrate competence. When you have been marketing a product or service for a while, you will acquire more knowledge about the product and service, and it will show in your marketing message. In that case, you qualify to become a thought leader, and people will start looking to you for guidance where that product or service is involved. Being a thought leader boosts your earning potential as you can influence more people, and you also have the luxury of setting higher prices than the norm. But then again you must be careful that you don't abuse your power else people will become vicious with you.

- How to Become A Successful Affiliate Marketer

Some people imagine that just because they have a great ad budget, they are automatically going to succeed in affiliate marketing. Having a great budget and even selecting great programs is fine, but that's not the end all be all to affiliate marketing. There are various factors you must consider in order to succeed as an affiliate marketer.

- Learn to specialize

One of the biggest rookies mistakes most affiliate marketers are prone to make is the tendency of chewing more than one can swallow. Just because affiliate networks are chock full of affiliate programs doesn't mean that you are at liberty to promote every one of them. The programs are mainly diverse for the purpose of letting you choose from a wide array. Thus, always ensure that you are promoting a few products that are centered on your circle of competence. When you promote too many programs, you are bound to become overwhelmed and lose motivation. Also, you could lose a lot of time and money. But when you specialize in a certain niche, you can maximize your earnings, and possibly become a thought leader.

- Use several traffic sources

Some affiliate marketers seem to have a fixed mindset as to which traffic sources are the best. Maybe they ran a successful campaign using native ads and developed a fondness toward native ads, so much, so they always use native ads for all campaigns. As an affiliate marketer, you must have an adventurous spirit and test out the effectiveness of various traffic sources. Of course, you may lose some money, but in the end, you will gain great insight as to what types of traffic sources are the best for various offers.

- Track your affiliate campaign

If you are not careful, you could lose a lot of money, especially when you engage in media buying. Don't just throw your affiliate link and pray that the commissions should start rolling in. You want to track your campaign results and ensure that there are no glitches, and should you find one, waste no time in correcting it.

- Research

Common sense dictates that you stand the best chances of making a profit when you promote a product in high demand. But then you can only understand the popularity of a product by conducting research. Some marketers rush into promoting shiny products only to make losses. Always ensure that you engage in research so that you maximize your earnings.

- Stay aware

The marketing trends of the early 2000s are not like marketing trends today. The only thing constant in life is change. In the world of affiliate marketing, you must keep an eye on the changing trends and learn to adapt, or else you will lose out to your competition. You don't want to be in a position that you are forced to change. You want to discern the changes and make yourself flexible. This ensures that you are always ahead of the pack. And it guarantees that you are always running profitable campaigns.

- Be creative

In as much as it is important to keep up with the marketing trends, it is just as important to be creative. When we talk about creativity, we don't mean to say that you should invent the next commercially successful computer. But creativity means that you should deliver your marketing message from a creative angle. People are extremely responsive to creativity. A creative message triggers certain emotion in your target audience and increases the likelihood of them converting into customers.

- Select the right merchants

You can only become successful in affiliate marketing when you are dealing with a trustworthy affiliate network or merchant. You'd be amazed by the fraudulent practices of various brands and affiliate networks. When you fall in the hands of a scamming merchant, your hard work will go down the drain, and you won't be compensated. Thus, ensure that you perform some research before you decide to work with a network or merchant. In this age of the internet, it is easy to learn about businesses, thanks to sites. If a merchant or an affiliate network scammed someone before, chances are the victim was so bitter and decided to alert other unsuspecting people through posting a negative. You certainly want to stay away from a merchant or affiliate network that has earned plenty of negative.

- Use tools

We have made considerable advancements in technology. There are tools to help us execute various functions in almost every area of our life. When it comes to affiliate marketing, there are many tools both paid and free, that make our work easier. Ensure that you are using these tools in order to lighten your workload and increase your profits.

The Players Involved in Affiliate Marketing and Their Roles

One of the first things an individual must strive to understand as he or she thinks about getting into a field of business is the players in that business. This knowledge will help such an individual to have a better picture of the entire business process and to consider the best place to get in if indeed there are options for this. Knowing the different players, their roles, and possibly the amount of money each of them makes in comparison to the amount of time and effort they put in is perfect for setting goals as to where an individual would set his or her sights.

Therefore, an individual who is new to affiliate marketing must know the people or businesses he or she will be dealing with on a day-to-day basis, and what he or she will need to do to get paid. Some of the most successful affiliate marketers go even further to know the people they are competing with, for them to take advantage of current trends and look for ways to beat everyone else.

Chapter 5 Surveying the Affiliate Landscape; Programs and Networks

The idea of affiliate marketing is brilliant if not genius. It spreads the responsibility of distributing a product or service to various people, in different places and to people who have a vested interest in spreading the product or service. At the end of the day, everyone will receive a share of the profits depending on his or her efforts.

Affiliate Networks

There are four key parties involved in affiliate marketing. These are:

1. The Merchant or Seller

The merchant sometimes referred to as a seller, creator, retail or vendor can be an individual, a company or a business with a product or service that they want to sell. This person may or may not be involved in the marketing of the product. He can leave the marketing entirely to the affiliates or he may employ affiliates to assist with other ongoing marketing tactics.

2. The Affiliate/Advertiser/ Publisher

Making money online has become so easy that people can now work in the comfort of their home, without having to sit through traffic, without having to wake up at ungodly hours or without having to work very late in the evening. An affiliate simply earns commissions by promoting other people's products. Again, an affiliate can be an individual or a company. Affiliate marketing can be a business on its own. The work of an affiliate is to find and convince customers to purchase a certain product or service. He or she can advertise products through their social networks, blogs, and websites. They can sell or recommend a product directly or publish of the products.

3. The Consumer

The consumers of a product or the customers are the end-users or recipients of the products.

They are essential because they are the ones who complete the circle. Without them, the merchants cannot make any money and without money, they cannot pay affiliates. Once they make a payment for a product or service or complete a certain action the merchant makes money and in turn, the affiliate makes money too.

4. The Network

An affiliate network encompasses the merchant and the affiliates as well as any other intermediaries between the merchant and the affiliate like a company that facilitates payments from the merchant to the affiliate. The network is where affiliates find merchants and vice versa and it is a place where affiliates can select products to promote. Amazon is one of the biggest affiliate networks. It connects merchants to affiliates. Affiliates must sign into their affiliate program to get a link for advertising. If a customer purchases an item through an affiliate's link, then the affiliate earns a piece of the pie.

Affiliate Programs

A merchant and an affiliate deal with each other through an affiliate program. In most cases, the affiliate is the one who applies to join an affiliate program. Most programs do not have a joining fee. An affiliate program can be defined as the precise arrangement between a merchant and an affiliate. The program dictates how much a merchant is supposed to pay an affiliate.

A merchant can agree to pay an affiliate commission based on:
- The traffic they send to the merchant
- The number of completed actions like having visitors leave their contact information or download something
- The complete sale of a product or service

Examples of well-known affiliate programs include

1. Amazon

Amazon runs an affiliate program under the name Amazon Associates that lets affiliates pick and advertises items sold on Amazon. Whenever a customer clicks on the affiliate's link, they get redirected to Amazon. If the customer goes ahead and buys an item, the affiliate automatically gets a commission.

2. eBay Partners

eBay is another shopping website with millions of products where affiliates can make money. Once an affiliate signs up on eBay partners, he or she can advertise any product of his or her choice on his or her social media pages, blogs or websites. If a sale is generated using the affiliate's link, the affiliate receives the payment according to a predetermined commission.

3. Share Sale Affiliates

ShareASale is another trusted affiliate network. The merchants who have their products displayed on the program are big names so as an affiliate you have the assurance that you will generate sales. The site is also user-friendly, and the affiliates have access to fast user support whenever they need it.

4. ClickBank

Just like the above sites, ClickBank offers a wide range of products that are popular across the globe and therefore easy for affiliates to sell and make money. Probably what makes ClickBank very popular among affiliates is the fact that the commissions paid to affiliates are very high and that they receive payment on a regular basis.

5. CJ Affiliate Publisher's Program

CJ Affiliate Publisher's Program is a bit more advanced and stricter but with years of experience, an affiliate can greatly benefit from it. It showcases attractive brands and their yearly increase in commission is very attractive to affiliates.

Engaging in affiliate marketing can be rewarding for a business in several ways:

1. Affiliate marketing helps a business grow through the effort of an affiliate. The affiliate attracts potential customers to a business as well as brings business to a merchant

2. A merchant does not have to spend a lot of time and energy advertising their products, he or she leaves all the work to the affiliate

3. The merchant only spends money if the marketing strategy is effective

4. It is easy to gauge the performance of the marketing strategy

5. Merchants who make use of affiliate marketing can reach a wider pool of consumers

Search Marketing and Affiliate Marketing have a common goal, to generate more sales for a business. If a business carries these out effectively then it is sure to grow to heights beyond what anyone could have dreamed of.

Where to Find Affiliate Networks

Affiliate Marketing

As mentioned earlier, affiliate marketing is a business that is all about earning an income by influencing others. It typically involves introducing people to a product or service in a creative way and if they buy because of your effort, you earn a commission.

Affiliates do this by building traffic towards a website, with the hope that the people they direct to the website buy the products. Affiliate marketing is based on revenue sharing and four players are involved, the network, the merchant, the publisher and the customer.

1. The merchant is usually the creator of the product, the seller, the retailer or the vendors. A good example of a merchant is Samsung, a company that produces a variety of technology products

2. The affiliate also referred to as the publisher, is the player that in charge of marketing the merchant's products. The affiliate can use all kinds of marketing strategies to promote the product. For example, it can run its online or acquire the services of different types of marketers.

3. The customers or consumers are the people who buy the product or service produced by the merchant after the affiliates have done their job.

4. The network usually works as an intermediary between the affiliate and the merchant.

Affiliate Networks

Affiliate networks act as intermediaries who connect affiliates and merchants. They act as intermediaries between the people in charge of marketing and the product owners. Companies use affiliate networks when they want to increase their market reach and penetration, where they do not have a substantial advertising platform, or where they want to tap into a new industry.

Examples of affiliate networks include eBay Partner Network (EPN), Click bank and ShareASale with the biggest affiliate network being Amazon Associates. Amazon allows anyone to sign in and generate a custom affiliate link to Amazon products. If a customer buys through the affiliate's link, the affiliate makes his or her commission. Successful affiliate networks ensure a win-win situation for all core players.

Most affiliate networks create a database for products where affiliate marketers come and choose which ones to promote.

Why do you need an affiliate network?

There are several reasons why people need an affiliate network:

1. People use affiliate networks to handle tracking, recruitment, reporting and billing affiliates
2. All successful affiliates are linked to a network making recruitment to your product easier
3. Affiliate networks put a lot of money to improve their technology, if one deal with the affiliates directly, they do not get such benefits
4. Affiliate networks have done away with manual processes and use many automated processes.
5. Affiliate networks allow businesses to focus on their core competencies

6. Affiliate networks are real, and they do work. A good number of company's secure business with affiliates

Where do you find affiliate networks? There are hundreds of thousand affiliate networks online with new ones coming up daily. An easy way to find affiliate networks is to visit affiliate platforms or use the Google search engine. Look for top-performing affiliate networks in line with your business.

In order to find an affiliate network, you need to know these three things:

1. What affiliate network works best for your business
2. Find out which ones are most successful in your line of business
3. Which affiliate networks bring more customer traffic?

After evaluating the above questions, use these five pointers to help you further identify the best affiliate network.

1. Identify the list of merchants linked to an affiliate network. You do not want to run on the same affiliate network as your biggest competitor
2. What payment models are in use in an affiliate network? Find out what advertising models attracts affiliates to that network
3. What type of payout model is most successful in that affiliate network? If as a merchant you do not allow affiliates to use the cost-per-action (CPA) payout on your products, a network using CPA might not be for you
4. Does that affiliate network have experience monitoring fraud? Find out how they deal with fraudsters in the network

5. Find out what support that affiliate network gives to its clients

6. How much they charge for set up if joining as a merchant

Affiliate networks do not have one size fits all. The best affiliate network is the one that aligns with your business in all directions. It can be one of the top networks or even the small ones if it aligns with your business.

For an individual venturing in affiliate marketing, terms such as search marketing, affiliate marketing, and affiliate programs should never be foreign to him or her. In a generation where the Internet has made it possible for people to buy products from their comfortable couch at home, or during a five-minute break at work, knowing how to optimize your business for search marketing is critical. Clients want to find you with the greatest of ease when they are looking for an opportunity to buy something, or even stumble across your advertisements on social media when taking time off to catch up with what is trending.

Furthermore, you will need to work with an affiliate network that not only pays well but also pays through your most convenient methods. This means you will have to learn whether you prefer to be paid using Pay Per Sale (PPS), Cost Per Action (CPA), or Cost Per Click (CPC), since each network will have its most preferred way of paying out the commissions.

Chapter 6 Keyword Research and Product Selection

Keyword research

Keywords are keywords with which both webmasters and users associate an Internet presence. These must therefore be chosen with care. Furthermore, web designers slip into the role of their website visitors during keyword research. They locate phrases and keywords that users enter in search engines. Then they place them in a clever way in their online presence in order to appear as high as possible in the organic (unpaid) search results. The challenge, however, is to find the right keywords that are popular with users but stand out from the competition.

Types of keywords

There are different types of keywords. About the intention of the users, keywords can be divided into three different groups. These consist of commercial, informative and navigating keywords.

Commercial keywords enter the users who have a purchase intention. A classic example of this would be "Buying a Travel Guide to the USA". Those who sell the product they are looking for should choose their keywords carefully and always be careful to signal the intention to buy.

When choosing the keywords "Travel Tips USA", however, users who enter these terms have the intention of receiving free travel tips. Thus, the main intention of this user is not to visit a paid travel guide. However, providers who offer an article with free travel tips for the USA and want to advertise their travel guide at the end of the text can use this keyword. Users searching for information on a specific topic use informative keyword. The question: "How big is the Eiffel Tower?" is a classic example of the use of informative keywords. Such questions are also ideal for Voice SEO. Webmasters who use these keywords will not find any users who have a purchase intention.

Short or head tail keywords consist of only one term. Even though this keyword species is a non-specific genus, it covers a huge spectrum. Mid tail key words mainly contain two to three terms and represent the middle of the extremely unspecific short tail and specific long tail keywords.

Long tail keywords usually contain more than four terms. This keyword is a specific type of keyword that becomes more and more exact thanks to the addition of additional terms.

An example of a short or head tail keyword would be the term "bread". The mid tail keyword extension could be "bake bread". The final long tail keyword might be "bake bread at home".

Finding the right keywords for successful search engine optimization

The keyword research of search engine optimization stands for the search for a suitable keyword to a website. Users use the selected keyword to locate the page on the Internet. Accordingly, the choice of the keyword plays the leading role. However, this should not only match the website content, but should also be searched for by the selected target group. However, the term keyword does not only stand for a single keyword, but also defines a text unit that can either be found in the text or briefly represents the content of the text as a suitable keyword. Accordingly, keywords are created from several terms and numbers. They are representatives for terms, about which a text is found at best with Google as well as further search engines. The biggest challenge for webmasters lies in their ability to put themselves in their target group. In practice, it often happens that websites are optimized for unsuitable keywords because the target group uses completely different names than the website operator. The aim of keyword research is to find the words that most of the target group members are looking for.

The distinction between good and bad keywords

Before the instructions for a successful keyword search are dealt with, the distinction between good and bad keywords is made.

An online retailer who sells outerwear such as T-shirts, jackets or pullovers would probably at first glance choose the keyword "outerwear", which is theoretically perfectly correct, but in practice less well received by the searcher. The question is whether the target group is looking for "outerwear". The answer is rather no. The keyword "outerwear" is a Head Tail Keyword, which is not commercial. Even if it could achieve a high search volume, the number of connections would be extremely low because this keyword is too inaccurate. The keywords "T-shirt" or "jacket" do not represent a suitable alternative either, because they do not indicate which target the searchers are aiming for, because they are not a commercial keyword. If the individuals want to make a purchase, they will rather enter the keywords "buy jacket" (commercial keyword). Online merchants who only rank their shop for the term "jacket" by no means address their desired target group directly. The keyword research thus aims at a precise formulation and exact alignment of the keywords.

In general, the principle applies: "The more general a keyword is, the greater the number of suitable pages Google will find". At the same time, this leads to enormous competition. As a result, the online retailer's chance of getting to the first page, who only ranked his shop after the keyword "jacket", drops considerably. Therefore, a keyword, which describes the respective offer of the side as exactly as possible, should be the main goal. However, it should be a commercial keyword. In this way, entrepreneurs reach their target group with significantly less effort.

Recommendation of keyword species

In order to find suitable keywords, the knowledge of the correct keyword type is necessary. At times, long tail keywords dominated search engine optimization. This is partly due to the small number of competitors. That is why website operators can quickly move up to the top rank of search queries. However, the problem with long tail keywords lies in their search volume. A search volume of 100 is not enough to be successful with a website. For this reason, an optimization of similar long tail keywords and related texts takes place using different keywords. Therefore, it is not recommended that a page presents five individual web pages with the same topic but optimized with different long tail keywords. This increases the search volume. However, this strategy has had its day. Google is now extremely clever and recognizes these tricks. This strategy came to an end at the latest with the so-called Panda Update. For this reason, website operators rank only as a single long tail keyword, which however reduces the search volume. The following overview summarizes the disadvantages of long tail keywords.

Latest updates prevent Google ranking of different pages on the same topic.

The search volume is extremely small.

Contributions of inferior quality have a negative impact on the authority of the website.

Due to the mentioned disadvantages it is worthwhile to switch to Mid Tail Keywords. Even if these are highly competitive, with a good choice and consistent content promotion, they can quickly catapult a website into the top ranks.

However, the competition is the greatest with short tail keywords. But webmasters reach the largest number of users with this keyword type. However, practice has proven that short tail keywords are not the right choice. Therefore, Mid Tail Keywords are best suited. Their competition is limited. This is partly because they are not as general as short tail keywords. In addition, they increase the probability of a financial statement.

A carefully conducted keyword research saves the webmasters not only time, but also money. A suitable keyword is the prerequisite for earning money. Unsuitable keywords that do not match the website content do not provide added value for the searcher. In addition, careful webmasters with a good keyword research can find keywords that competitors do not use. In this way, webmasters benefit from the comparative competitive advantages. Suitable methods and structured procedures for keyword research

The following keyword search can be done with Google. Webmasters do not need any tools with costs for this manual. Accordingly, the displayed keyword research is free of charge.

Keyword brainstorming

Write down keywords that match the website in question

The keyword is surrounded by a cloud with matching additional terms

If the example keyword is "baking bread", other terms such as gluten-free, whole meal flour, sunflower bread or baguette can surround the main keyword.

In order to be able to better understand and apply these measures, the techniques described are carried out using the keyword "baking bread" as an example.

Keyword Input into a suitable keyword tool

The following instructions are for a successful keyword search, which is carried out with Google. The Google Keyword Planner can help. Webmasters can also use other keyword tools, which they can use for free. After the tool has been selected, the keyword is entered the selected tool. Those who want to do the keyword research with AdWords only need a Google account. The webmasters then simply enter their main term in the Keyword Planner Tool under "Search for new keywords using a phrase, a web page and a category". When you click on Ideas Retrieve, different ones are displayed.

Sorting the list in keyword search according to the respective search volume

As a result, users receive a whole list of keyword suggestions that correspond to the main term. With a click on the field called "Average search queries per month" webmasters can arrange them from large too small. The keywords that stand out due to the highest search volume appear in the upper rank. At the end or on the last result pages of this list, keywords with a small search volume are mentioned. Usually these are long tail keywords. The middle ranks are important for webmasters, as most mid tail keywords are placed here. Based on this ad, website operators select a keyword that best matches the content of their online presence. It is advisable to look at the column called "Competition" and to inspect the climbing pages for the respective mid tail keyword. However, since the Google Keyword Planner is an AdWords tool, the competition does not refer to the display of search results, but to general ads. For this reason, webmasters may not neglect the climbing web pages to the respective keyword.

Competitive intelligence

At this step, webmasters analyze their competitors to a keyword. There are different indicators for this. The competition can serve both as an indication of how powerful the competition is and the "interrupted bid". The higher the bid, the higher the competition. However, website designers do not rely solely on this information. This is because a certain keyword is extremely expensive to display and enjoys great popularity but is not very successful in organic search results. In order to find out how big the competition for the selected keyword is, it is worth applying the following techniques.

Enter the URL, the domain metrics, and a check of the backlinks.

Control of ON-Page Optimization

Check the respective search results on question-answer pages or in forums

Inspect content quality more closely

In order to better understand and apply these measures, the techniques described are carried out using the example keyword "baking bread".

Input of the URL, the domain metrics as well as a check of the backlinks

In this step, webmasters use a tool that presents them with important metrics. The free tool called "SEO Toolbar" of the developer named MOZ can be helpful. It requires an installation. After the successful setup of the toolbar, the keyword input takes place at Google. Among the current results, the toolbar with all the metrics for the matching page and domain now appears without further ado. Webmasters are particularly interested in the values URL Rating, Backlinks / Linking Domains to the Website, Domain Rating and Backlinks / Linking Domains to the Complete Page.

Chapter 7 Top Affiliate Marketing Programs

The best way to describe affiliate marketing would be to use an analogy. Let us say you are the president of your university and every single student in that university listens to your voice. Since you are the president of this university, most of the people in that university follows your advice and recommendations. When suddenly a professor of the university offers you sell his textbook, and in return, you get a commission or a percentage of the textbook sale by promoting the professor's book to your audience or following.

So, this would be an example of affiliate marketing. Simply what you must do to get sales would be first to create a big following and then promote a product to that audience. Simple enough, right? Well, there are some tricks involved in this method, to become successful in affiliate marketing. Now there are a lot of ways you can start to market a product to make a commission; we will be talking about how to do so by using the best methods for you to start affiliate marketing.

Now, the methods which will help you to start making money with the affiliate market will be YouTube, blogging, Instagram/Facebook page. Now, these three are the best ways to get started with your affiliate marketing business. There are some pros and cons to each of these tools; you might have to try out all three methods before you can see which one works for you and which one doesn't. Now without further ado, let's begin with YouTube.

- **Amazon**

As we know by now, Amazon is the biggest online store right now. So whatever sells in Amazon sells anywhere, so if your goal is to find a niche that will make you money and is profitable, then you need to Amazons products?

If you have been to Amazon's website to purchase a product or anything of that matter, bellow you will see the best sellers rank under the product description. What that bestseller lists symbolized is how much the product is being bought, this is very important for you to note. If the product is not selling on Amazon, which is the biggest e-commerce store in the world, it will not sell anywhere. Now here is what you are going to do to find a product that sells.

The very first thing you are going to do is get on your computer and go to Amazon's website, and now I want you to do is go on to the best seller's page on Amazon. This page will give you a rough idea of what sells and what doesn't, also will show you the niche products which are selling already. Anything in Amazon's best sellers' page will most likely sell that is if you can offer it at a lower price. Regardless of which platform you will be using for your Affiliate business if Amazon has the same product for sale as you do, it will have it for the same price or cheaper than you would. This is the case most of the time, but if you can sell it for less expensive than your competitors meaning Amazon, then you have a winning product! Congrats.

Now if that's not the case, it is out time to find an untapped niche. So, go to the best sellers' page on Amazon and look at the top 100 on that list carefully, if you see similar products from the same niche then this niche is profitable. But it could be hard to penetrate that specific market or niche, and this is where we find a micro-niche. So, for example, if the slot is iPhone accessories and there are multiple iPhone accessories on the best sellers list, what we will do is search up iPhone accessories on Amazon search bar. Then we will go through the top six products and check to see their best sellers list if the best sellers list showcases a number below 50,000 for all six items, then this niche is profitable.

- **YouTube**

YouTube was founded on February 14th, 2005, established by three past PayPal employees-Chad Hurley, Steve Chen, and Jawed Karim. YouTube at first was created by the founders to share videos easily without facing any problems while doing so, fast forward to November 2006 when YouTube was sold to Google for USD 1.65. Ever since then, YouTube has not stopped growing. According to some sources, there is at least 1 billion hours' worth of videos are being watched every day on YouTube. That goes to show how big YouTube is, now you might be wondering since this website is so popular you could quickly start promoting affiliate products and earn some high commissions.

Well, there are some tricks involved to do so, although there are a lot of videos watched on YouTube on any given the time of day there is still some things you need to make sure is in check from your end before you can start to promote your product on this website. Don't worry, it isn't hard, just like any business it will take some time and effort to get started.

The first thing you will need is to create a niche. Think about what you are interested in. For example, if you are interested in fitness, then make a fitness channel. If you are interested in science, make a Science channel. The primary thing you need to consider before you start your very own YouTube channel is to make sure that whatever your channel is about, it needs to be something you are genuinely interested in. This is the reason why people can see through everything these days. If you hate fitness and you decide to make a fitness channel, they can tell that you don't like fitness-related stuff and therefore won't subscribe to your channel. Making sure you have love and passion for the circuit you will be building on YouTube is imperative.

- **Blogging**

Let us talk about blogging and using it to market products and earn affiliate marketing commissions. Just like YouTube, blogging is a great way to make affiliate marketing commissions. You can say blogging is the godfather of affiliate marketing, as that's what started this whole "affiliate marketing" trend. Just like YouTube, you need to get steady traffic to your blog before you can begin to make some money from it.

Now, there are a lot of ways to drive traffic to your blog, and they are quite like YouTube's way of attracting traffic, but we will only discuss the main three methods you can use to start advertising your blogs right now.

The first method is getting free traffic from other blogs and forums. Let's say your blog is related to fitness. What you will do is find a popular blog and its discussions online. If it is a forum, then it's recommended that you truly become a part of the forum and start asking questions and answering questions. Once you truly begin to feel like you are becoming a part of the conference, then slowly start to link your blogs into the forum post which will help you get more traffic to your blog. You see, doing this will help you get more traffic to your blog where you will start to promote your products. Now if it is a blog, then I would recommend you put a link to your blog in the comment of the more significant, more popular blog. This will also help you get traffic.

- **Instagram/Facebook Page**

This is also a fantastic technique to start earning those affiliate commissions. So how this works is quite like YouTube. You will first need to attract a following to your page, and then you can start to promote your products slowly. Now to explain this process instead is this: no audience = no sales. Therefore, our primary goal is to start getting our Instagram page bigger, which would equate to more affiliate commission.

The first method would be setting up a Facebook page, which would be specific to your niche. Now, after you have created an Instagram account and a Facebook page, start promoting both pages only by purchasing shootouts from more prominent pages related to your niche. After that is done, you will slowly begin to grow your Instagram/Facebook page, but one thing to remember is that you don't want to stop posting content on your Instagram/Facebook page as it will result in a drop of followers and engagement rate.

The second method to grow your Instagram page is to use a technique known as "follow-unfollow." It is self-explanatory. What you must do is follow users hoping that they would follow you back and then eventually unfollow them. This technique works if your goal is to gain some following quickly. That said, this is not the best way for long-term growth, so keep that in mind. Start following people and unfollow them after three days or so.

Finally, let us talk about how to make money with affiliate marketing on Instagram. So, after you have a following off around 100k, you will then start to notice people will pay you cash to have their product on your page. You can also do affiliate marketing with ClickBank, but it just works better when you promote on Instagram using the "shootout" technique.

Using all three at once

Now, ideally, this is how it should be. Using YouTube, Blogging, and Instagram, all at once will yield you the best results. So, if you want to make some serious cash with affiliate marketing, here is how you do it. You will first create a brand. For example, if you're into fitness, you will create a YouTube channel, blog, and Instagram/Facebook account with a brand name that you came up with.

THE TOP 20 AFFILIATE MARKETING EDUCATIONAL PROGRAMS:

1. Click Bank University 2.0

2. John Crestani's Super Affiliate Program

3. GetResponse Pro

4. Aweber

5. Classified Ad Submissions

6. Cool Marketing Software

7. Unique Domain Names

8. SquadHelp

9. R.A. Wealth JV Program

10. FREE Online Business Training

11. Wesley "Billion Dollar" Virgin Super Affiliate

12. The "12 Minute Affiliate" Super Affiliate Program

13. SALEHOO #1 Affiliate Program in 2019

14. The Rich Dad Summit- by Robert Kiyosaki

15. Kindle Money Mastery 2.0

16. YouTube Secrets Revealed

17. Affiliate Bots $900/day Affiliate Software

18. Digital Private Label Rights Products for Rebranding

19. Millionaire Society

20. Long Tail Pro- #1 Keyword Research Software

Chapter 8 How to Choose Affiliate Marketing Program

First, let's begin by defining affiliate marketing you earn commission from the people that purchase the product through your site. For example, if you write an article about travel and you talk about where to find cheap flights. Link the text to a flights comparison page that has an affiliate marketing program that you have already signed up for. If someone clicks on the link in your article and buys a flight from that a page, you will earn a portion of that total sale.

To use affiliate marketing, you need to check the website has a program and if it does, sign up for it. You will receive a special affiliate code that you put into your articles that trace back any sales from your site to you. This is how you earn money. You can also track your performance on the site's affiliate marketing page.

The three main types of affiliate marketing are:

- Pay per sale where you receive a commission for each sale you make through your blog.
- Pay per click where you receive a commission for every time a visitor clicks on an ad.
- Pay per lead where you earn commission from several leads you get from another company.

Which Affiliate Program Should You Use?

Several companies offer affiliate program. Check some companies within your niche and check their websites to see if they have information for affiliates. The two most universal and popular affiliate marketing program are Amazon and ClickBank.

Amazon is easy to set up, and it gives you thousands of items that you can link to from your site. For example, if you have a blog about camping, you can write articles about the essential equipment for a weekend camping in the rain. In your article, you can mention some of the best products that people would need and link these to Amazon. If a visitor clicks on the link and decides to purchase the product, you will make a commission from that sale. Amazon uses cookies on its affiliate program. What does this mean? It means that if someone clicks on a link from your site, you will still receive a commission even if that person buys the item within a 90-day period.

To use the Amazon affiliate program, you need to sign up to it and fill out your business or blog details plus your bank details. Then you will receive your unique affiliate ID that will be connected to the links of the products you use from the Amazon site. It's worth noting that Amazon is strict with their affiliate program and you must follow their rules and conditions. If not, you face losing your account. These rules include making sure you use a disclosure in each article that says you are using affiliate links in any articles where you do use them. Be sure to read through Amazon's terms and conditions to make sure you avoid any issues.

Another popular affiliate program is ClickBank which has a similar concept to Amazon. It's free to use, and like Amazon, it has a vast range of items for sale. To use ClickBank, register for the affiliate program and then find the product you want to promote on your blog. Copy your unique link that will be coded with your affiliate ID and add to your article. When visitors click on the link, they will be redirected to the product's sale page, and they will have the opportunity to purchase it.

There are other affiliate programs you can use. Hotels is great for travel websites that talk about accommodation. You can add links to articles to specific hotels that you mention to earn a commission from every person that books a stay at the hotel. Other sites include Get Your Guide which has an affiliate program for the hundreds of different excursions and activities they provide in dozens of cities across the world.

Here are some of the significant advantages of using affiliate marketing to monetize your blog.

- If you have a site that has a high volume of traffic, this is a great and simple way of earning a comfortable passive income stream.
- There are no fees at all for affiliate program. You simply need to sign up and add the links to your article. Then, if successful, you will start earning commission from the links.
- Your only concern needs to be creating engaging content that will bring a high volume of traffic. Issues such as customer support, shipping, and storage of the product are the concern of the company.
- Affiliate marketing reaches a global audience, so you have a potentially huge audience.
- In this, we looked at how you can use affiliate marketing to monetize your blog.
- Affiliate marketing is when you promote a company's products or services on your site and if this turns into a conversion and the visitor pays a product, you will earn a commission. You promote the product or service through a link added into a text where visitors can click on it and can buy the product.
- There are hundreds of affiliate program, and it pays to look around for what is available in your niche. However, the two most popular program are Amazon and Click Bank.
- Using affiliate marketing is an excellent way of making a potentially highly profitable passive income stream, especially if your blog has high volumes of traffic.

Chapter 9 SEO: Search Engine Optimization

Search Engine Optimization (SEO) is increasingly becoming a more integral part of any business's marketing strategy as easy visibility from a basic Google or Bing search remains the simplest and most effective way to draw in new customers. SEO can be difficult for those running a small business to begin using without some prior training as there are several different facets required to use them effectively. For example, SEO is just as much about what content you use to populate your site as it is about the way your entire website is structured.

While other means, including having an active social media presence, will help to generate some additional traffic for your site, they are much more effective when used as a way that maximizes SEO at the same time. As such, it is important to take the time to ensure that the content from your website, as well as the website itself, is as readily available to the relevant databases as possible. While this process may seem difficult and time consuming at first, the results will always far outweigh the costs. What's more, improving your SEO is free marketing, not committing to it fully is akin to leaving money on the table.

Search engines such as Bing or Google work by sending out automated programs known as crawlers to follow the links to various URLs for every website that is currently online. The crawlers then track relevant data from each page before sending that information to databases which compile it before sending the results to users when queried. Due to the amount of data being parsed, keywords were originally used to make things easier to handle.

As knowledge and understanding of how to game the system grew, simple keywords were no longer enough and now there are a wide variety of different factors including popularity, backlinks, descriptions and more that help users to return reliable results in seconds. This is what makes SEO as crucial as failing in all areas can often be akin to failing at all as your site will be passed over by sites who are firing on all cylinders.

Therefore, common terms that potential users might employ carry such weight as targeting the right type of search engine traffic can be the difference between success and failure for your fledgling affiliate marketing business. What's worse, filling in the right boxes with wrong details can burry your completely competent site under inferior results to ensure that practically no one will ever be able to find it?

While SEO is a hotly debated subject, the good news is that you can get by without hiring an expert if you are willing to do the leg work yourself and keep up with it in the long-term. While this won't have you leading the pack, it will at least keep you in the running. When it comes to getting started improving your SEO by yourself, the biggest cost is going to come in terms of the time commitment that you put forth in improving your website's SEO. The following tips will help you get started on the right foot.

Choosing keywords

When it comes to choosing the best keywords for your website, your first thoughts are going to be words that will see the greatest number of hits overall. Truly successful keywords go beyond this, however, and reflect how a website or company pictures itself at a fundamental level.

Focus on key phrases: In hopes of finding more useful details, keywords have grown into key phrases over the years and finding the right one for you is crucial to your long-term success. While it can be easy to overthink the process, the goal should be to find something that isn't too broad to be useful or too narrow to generate reasonable results. For example, if your website sells nutritionally conscious dog food, then on their own the words food and dog will not get you where you need to be. Instead, a better choice would be to choose words that relate to the specialty ingredients your dog foods contain.

Ideally, you are going to want to choose key phrases that are between 2 and 4 words that relate to your website in the most general terms possible. This means it is best to do some additional research up front as you may be surprised to find some common phrases are quite unpopular for whatever reason. The fewer search results you return when testing out these words, the less popular the phrase is with the public. Again, your goal should be able to find key phrases that are popular enough to see use without generating so many hits that it is completely ineffective.

Don't think of them as a contest: While it can be tempting to go at top search results by trying to compete for the same keywords directly, this is rarely going to work in your favor. As the new website on the totem pole, your results are automatically going to be lower than a website that has had time to establish itself in the market. Rather than going to the king directly, instead, try developing your own following around a related keyword before dipping your toes in the more competitive space.

While finding yourself at the top of that search can provide an ego boost, the odds of it happening are rarely in favor of anyone other than major corporations or sites that include the keyword in their name. It is therefore almost always better to go with something more precisely tailored to your business while still being a reasonable thing for someone to type into a search engine.

Pop some tags

Metadata tags are like keywords and key phrases in that they make it more likely that your pages ae going to show up within relevant search results. Unlike with keywords, however, they do not typically show up on the pages themselves and are typically only visible within the code of the pages in question. You can think of metadata tags as the keywords of the underlying data. Meta data tags can be viewed on any page by simply right clicking on it and then selecting the option to view page source. The meta tag specifics will be found near the top of the screen. Meta tags can be altered by anyone with a basic understanding of HTML, or, from the appropriate menu option from the backend of your website.

There are four primary types of meta tags that you are going to want to use when it comes to trying to improve your SEO, meta attribute keywords are those that are related to the current page specifically, the title tag is the name that the search engine displays when the page is referenced and the meta attribute description is the description that comes up as part of the search result. Finally, the robots meta attribute is used to ensure that crawlers know to document the page.

Due to the glut of keyword stuffing over the past decade, the keyword attribute has decreased in value when compared to the other attributes, nevertheless, it will still give you a small SEO bump when compared to those websites that don't use it at all. The most important meta tag these days is the title tag which is why it is important to always take the time to ensure that it is formatted properly on each one of your pages. It is important to choose a title tag that clearly indicates what the content in question contains while also including at least one key phrase if possible. Remember, the title is what is going to show up in all your search results, so it is important that it is a good one.

If you manage to make it to the top page of Google results but you aren't at the top of the top, then it is going to most likely be the description attribute that pushes you over the edge. You have 20 words to sway potential visitors to your site that your link is going to provide them with the details they need, while also telling Google how to classify your page. Take some time to think about it and make those 20 words as impactful as possible.

If you aren't sure where to start, a good place is by trying to include as many relevant key phrases into this as you can manage. While their use here won't directly improve your SEO, studies show that seeing the words they are looking for in a description makes potential viewers more likely to choose one search result over another. Just make sure you do more than list a bunch of keywords, a legible sentence of text is key to proving your site is full of viable content as well.

Robot Attribute: The robot attribute is perhaps the most straightforward of all the modifiable attributes as there are only two options you can choose from. The index/no index option tells various search engines whether you want your page to be returned from basic search results. The follow/unfollow option, on the other hand, tells crawlers whether they are supposed to follow links on your pages to their destinations or not. In most instances, you should choose index and follow respectively.

Chapter 10 Email Marketing

Email marketing continues to be a popular marketing resource for people, although it is becoming increasingly apparent that this marketing style is optional. In the past, if you did not have an email list, you were irrelevant and probably not running a successful business. These days, people can successfully run a business without an email list and often do. An email list is still crucial, as it provides you with a level of security that no other marketing strategy can provide you with.

If you want to be successful with email marketing in 2020, the key is to use this strategy sparingly. Many people are receiving 1+ email per day from a single company, causing them to ignore most email marketing campaigns. If you attempt to market through email too consistently, recent studies show that you may train your audience to delete your emails rather than look at them because they are tired of having them show up. The simple fact is virtually no one in your audience wants to hear from you in their email inbox every day. Some don't even want to hear from you more than once a week. Keeping your email newsletters more modest ensures that when your emails show up, people get curious about what you have shared and so they open them.

Many businesses aren't even doing that, though.

Many businesses are building email lists and emailing their list just 1-2 times per month, or even less. The reason why they are even bothering to build their lists in the first place is simple: it offers security. In the summer of 2019, we have already seen Facebook and Instagram crash twice, with pictures, status updates, comments, and messenger features not working or only working here and there for many users. While these crashes only lasted one day, they proved to be extremely detrimental to business owners. Think about it: if Facebook or Instagram were to go down for a week, could you make any money? Probably not, because you would not have a way to reach your audience unless you had invested time in building an email list. An email list cannot be taken away from you, nor can it "crash." So, if your primary platforms go down, having that email list you built will still give you an opportunity to connect with your audience. Even if you do not plan on emailing your audience frequently, build a list. You will be grateful that you did.

Online PR

PR means that you are gaining coverage on your business from other people. For example, if you launch your business, and a popular blog writes about it, you are gaining PR. Online PR is an important opportunity for you to market your business and establish credibility and authority, while also reaching the eyes of new possible consumers. You want to take advantage of this marketing style so that you can increase your reach and become more recognizable to the people in your audience.

Hiring affiliates to help you market your business is one great way to market using online PR, but there are other strategies, too. One way is to reach out to reporters and journalists and let them know about your business to encourage them to do an interview with your company. However, remember that many other people are doing this too, so you need to do it in the right way if you are going to spark their interest, receive an interview, and maintain credibility while also boosting the reputation of your company. Attempting to contact them in a pushy or impolite manner can result in you being unprofessional or rude, which can possibly tarnish your business. Remember: they have a large pull in the community!

Other ways that you can engage in online PR include engaging with of your company and engaging with comments made on your website. You can also personally comment or respond back to any comments or emails that come into your business, allowing you to establish yourself and add a personal touch. Any way that you can personally engage with your audience, especially if it is going to be spotlighted in some way for others to see, is a great opportunity for you to take advantage of online PR.

Inbound Marketing

Inbound marketing is more frequently known as "attraction marketing" in the modern era, and it is an incredibly powerful marketing strategy that you can use to help you get more people coming to you for the products or services that you offer. The biggest benefit of attraction marketing is that you are not pushing customers to buy from you; you are encouraging them to come to the decision of buying from you on their own. In other words, you are attracting them to your business without having to use any form of "used car salesman" tactics.

Inbound marketing is a strategy that uses a series of tools to encourage people to do business with you. When you are using this strategy, rather than asking for the sale, you are offering multiple opportunities for the customer to ask you for the sale. For example, using a blog to build interest in your business, creating videos that show off how awesome your products or services are, and using email as a point of contact rather than a constant source of marketing with newsletters are all ways to use inbound marketing. If you use tools like this, you will be sure to spark an interest in your audience and encourage them to want to buy from you, rather than pushing for them to buy from you. The difference is that your sales are a lot easier to make, and your reputation improves tenfold because you are someone that people want to buy from, rather than someone that people feel pressured to buy from. In 2020, this marketing strategy is expected to grow even more popular than it already has in recent years, so expect to take advantage of it in your own marketing strategy if you want to succeed!

Chapter 11 Email List

If you are a blogger with an e-commerce store selling a product or service of any kind through your blog, an email list or a newsletter subscription is an integral part of your marketing arsenal. Why? Because it is a powerful sales tool that can drive your business and engagement. An email list is a direct way to keep your subscribers updated about the products and services offered on your blog, and more importantly, alert them about any new products or services that are now available.

Optimizing your email lists and the type of information you send out to your subscribers is easy enough. Remember that the people who are reading your emails are people who could possibly be potential customers if they aren't already, and if you're serious about monetizing your blog, you are going to need to make your customers your lifeline.

When your readers read your email list, they want to feel that whatever you have put down in there is speaking to them directly, and not just a generic email blast with no specific group or target in mind. Readers like to feel exclusive and special, so make them feel that way and construct your emails like you would as if you were speaking to your readers face to face instead of over the internet. Make your reader feel important like you have specifically tailored your product or service to meet their needs, make them feel special, and they will keep coming back to your blog for more.

And the most important thing to remember is to always respond to any of your readers who reply to your emails. Always.

Building an Effective Email List

With the right strategies in place, you could have your email list up and running in no time. Remember an email list means more blog traffic for you in return, especially if your readers subscribe to your list and keep visiting your blog each time, they get an update about something new that is happening on your site. To really maximize on your email list, the following methods will help you give your subscription numbers a boost:

- Pop-Ups – Pop-ups are annoying yes, but on some level, they do work, especially if the reader is already showing a keen interest in your blog and is a frequent visitor. Many blogs incorporate the use of pop-up encouraging readers to sign up for their newsletter or subscribe to their blog. You've seen it if you've visited other blogs yourself. Annoying at times, yes, but there is a reason many blogs are using this. Because they work.

- Freebies – People are sometimes reluctant to give away their email address for fear of being spammed annoying in their inboxes by unwanted emails. Unless there was a good enough incentive and reason for them to do so. Everyone loves to receive a little gift for free, so why not try that tactic to entice your readers to sign up for your newsletter when they visit your blog? Depending on the nature of your blog, try to provide a giveaway that is going to be something of value to your readers, something they would be excited to receive in their inbox. Perhaps a discount to one of your products or services, for example.

- Subscribe Pages – Your readers can't subscribe to your blog if there isn't a subscribe page available. To be effective with you subscribe pages, it is a good idea to include multiple sign-up boxes for your readers to choose from and provide the readers with as much detail as possible about what they can come to expect when they subscribe to your blog.

- Promote Your Blog on Social Media – It is highly likely that you have your own social media accounts, but are you using these platforms to market your blog? If you aren't, then you should! Social media is everywhere, there is no escaping it, so imagine the huge audience potential you are missing out if you're not leveraging this platform to your blog's advantage. Use your social media account to highlight the exciting features on your email list, updated regularly, and update often so your social media followers have no chance of forgetting it.

And then we come to the million-dollar question.

How to Monetize Your Email List

- Directing traffic to your site

Do you have AdSense on your blog already? Then you're going to want to tap into the email list potential to get readers heading your blog's way. An email list is an indirect way of monetizing your blog, but you should grab every opportunity you can to link back to your site or even link to a post on your site that has the potential to generate money on its own, then that is what you should do. The more traffic that gets directed to your site, the more potential there is to earn an income from your blog.

- Using Affiliate links

The second way is using affiliated links. Do you have a product or service that you are happy with and you have written a shining about on your blog? Include them in the email that you are going to send out to your subscribers. If your blog has been around for a while, there's going to be a lot of posts and content in it, and sometimes readers just don't have the time to sift through all of that before they find what they are looking for. Why not make things easy for them? Include the affiliate link in that email along with your, and if you're on your blog is enough to convince them to buy that product or service, you'll get a cut of the sale. Money in your pocket, all thanks to your blog and email list. You're going to be glad you've got an email list on hand when you want to promote a new book, a new product or a new service because this is one of the best platforms to start building up interest among your subscribers before the launch of the new product or service takes place.

Chapter 12 Sales Funnels Strategies

To understand what a sales funnel is, let's use a physical funnel to demonstrate it. A funnel is a plastic or metal object that has two open ends – a wider upper end and a narrower bottom end. Funnels are normally used to channel fluid into containers that have smaller openings. Typically, the funnel's smaller bottom end is inserted into the container that needs to be filled with fluid. The fluid is then poured into the bigger upper end of the funnel.

The major aim of using a funnel to channel fluid into a container that has a small opening is to avoid leakage or wastage. If you attempt to pour a liquid into a container that has a small opening without a funnel, you might end up spilling the entire liquid or half of it on the ground. Another characteristic thing about funnels is that a huge amount of liquid goes in through the upper part and trickles out into a receiving container through the smaller end of the funnel.

Now, when it comes to sales and marketing, funnels are used to perform a similar function. Their main function in marketing is to guide a large audience of potential buyers through what is called a customer journey until they are ready to buy. Just like the physical funnel, a huge audience will go into a sales funnel, but only those who are interested in a product will make it through the narrow lower end.

So, a sales funnel is used to channel potential customers through the buying process until they are ready to become actual or paying customers. When buyers are passed through a sales funnel, they are nurtured, and those who are not really interested in the product in question will be placed in a different segment. Those who are interested in the product will be segmented differently and then shown how they could proceed to buy the product.

In affiliate marketing (using the working affiliate marketing model) and online business space, sales funnels play a huge and important role. It is used to guide the buyer through the entire buying process until they are finally ready to buy.

One of the reasons why a sales funnel is important is that today's average customer does not buy a product the very first time they hear or know about it. Usually, the customer goes through what is known as a customer journey during which they must consider ways of paying for the product.

Typically, if you want today's average customer to buy from you, you need to keep in touch with them as they go through the customer journey. And the only way through which you might keep in touch with them is through sending emails – email marketing is an integral part of the sales funnel process.

Another reason why a funnel is important is that it helps you to build a good relationship with your audience. If you have a good relationship with your potential customers, they would often want to buy from you. Yes, this happens because the average customer purchases products based on emotions and justifiable logistics and evidence.

Have you ever noticed that friends often tend to patronize each other? The reason is that people attach emotions to the buying process. When you nurture a relationship with your audience to the point that they begin to see you as a friend – if you market or promote a product to them, they would be glad to buy from you.

Additionally, no matter the type of product or service you want to sell or promote, there are already thousands of other people selling the same product or service. The big question then becomes, how do you convince your potential customer to abandon the other options before them and patronize you? To convince them, you would need to build a relationship with them, and having a sales funnel will help to do that.

Parts of a sales funnel

A typical sales funnel has three essential parts – these three parts could then be developed into several, depending on the individual, their target audience, and the type of product that is being promoted.

Attract

As mentioned earlier, a typical customer passes through several paths before they finally decide to buy a product, especially if the product is a high-ticket offer. Now, if you want to walk your ideal client through the various steps they need to go through before buying your product. The first part or step is to attract them to whatever it is you want to sell.

This first part is where you run ad campaigns or create a blog post to draw the attention of the potential buyer to your affiliate offer or product. For instance, if you are promoting a back-pain management product, and you have created a perfect buyer persona, the things you could do in this first step of your sales funnel creation include the following:

- Create an ad campaign on Facebook. The title of the campaign could go like this, "discover how a 55-year-old factory worker is managing his back pain." The aim of the campaign is to draw the attention of your ideal potential buyer to click on the "read more" button. When they click on the read more button, then they are taken to the next part of the funnel.

- If you want to use free traffic, you could create a blog post on your blog that talks about some of the benefits of the product you want to promote. Then ask readers to click a link that would give them more information. When they click on the link, they are then taken to the next stage of the funnel.

- You could also consider creating a post on social media to draw attention to the product you want to promote.

Basically, this first part of the sales funnel is mostly concerned with piquing the interest of the potential buyer. Things you do in this first part are majorly centered on the creation of ads on social media, creation of posts on blogs, or other traffic methods.

You want to gain the attention of potential customers, so you could give them more information about your product.

Typically, when you have drawn the attention of the potential buyer, you need to convince them to get to the second stage of the process. To do that, you need to provide them with something of value in exchange for their email. Lead magnets or tripwires are normally used at this stage to lure the potential customer to leave their email with you.

Remember, the ad post you created on Facebook, Google, etc. will have a link to your landing page. It is on the landing page that you will collect the email of those who want to download your free lead magnet.

A landing page is simply a one-page webpage that is used to collect email of prospects. The emails collected using a landing page is then added to your email list. You can create a landing page using various autoresponders like MailChimp, Aweber, Click Funnels, etc.

Delight

At this stage, the potential buyer has provided you with their email; they have downloaded their copy of the lead magnet that you are giving away. They have probably read the lead magnet and are waiting to hear back from you on what they are to do next.

If the lead magnet you gave them for free earlier was insightful and full of valuable information, then this second stage of the sales funnel should not be hard for you. It is at this stage that you begin to send the potential customer a series of emails. The emails are meant to help warm up the buyer and introduce the product you want to promote to them.

For instance, if you are promoting a weight loss product, you could educate your subscribers or prospects on some of the reasons why they have not achieved success with their other weight loss efforts. Ideally, if you know about three reasons why people fail to lose weight, you could divide them into three different emails and send them individually to your prospects.

With these emails, you are gradually nurturing a relationship with your audience. It has been observed by avid internet marketers that you need to send at least seven warm-up messages to your prospects before they are ready to buy whatever you are selling or promoting. It is important that at this second stage, you should not introduce the product you are selling or promoting yet.

Interest

This part is where you begin to pique the interest of the prospect in whatever it is you are selling or promoting. At this point, you might have sent them a few emails meant to nurture them. You are going to gradually start introducing your prospects to the product you want to promote – all these you have to do with emails.

The first email you should send in this series should introduce the new product you are promoting. Then subsequent emails should talk about the major selling points of the product and why it is better than whatever the prospect is already used to. Remember, the potential customer is not just going to take your words for it; they need you to show them proof that the product works.

To prove the efficacy of the product, you need to show your prospects some testimonials which would serve as social proof. How do you get testimonials since you have probably never used the product yourself? It is simple – head on to the product's page on the vendor's website.

You will find or testimonials left on the product by users. Screenshot some of the glowing and include them in your emails. Make sure you throw in as many such testimonials as possible in your emails – it helps to build up your credibility and that of the product you are selling or promoting.

Action

What you do in stage two and three of the sales funnel process is called nurturing prospects or warming up of prospects. You are basically preparing them to be ready for the product you want to introduce to them. If you are good at what you do, before you are even done with stage 3, most of your prospects would already be asking you to introduce them to the product you want to sell.

The last part of your sales funnel should be where you show your prospects how to get the product you have been pitching to them all along. It is as simple as sending an email to prospects with an affiliate link to the product you have been promoting. As mentioned earlier, if you have done a good job in both part two and part three, then you should have no problem with this last phase of the funnel.

Note: a funnel may have many parts, and some of the parts mentioned above could be compressed into just two parts. It all depends on you, your audience, and the product you are promoting. Using a sales funnel to market a product is an art on its own and you need to dedicate time to learn it.

Some of the things you would want to learn as it regards creating a functional sales funnel include the following:

- How to use emotional triggers to get potential customers to subscribe to your email list.
- How to send the right types of emails to subscribers and convert them from cold leads into warm buyers.
- How to create a high converting lead magnet, tripwire and landing page.
- How to segment your email list and make sure that you only send emails to the right audience.
- How to position yourself as an authority in your niche.

Chapter 13 Tools and Resources for Affiliates

Tools help you make the best of your time and effort when it comes to marketing. We will look at the tools to help you make full use of your time, efficiently market your site and promote, your affiliations online. Most tools listed here give you a free version (with limited capabilities) or a trial version before requiring you to purchase the full license to use.

If you feel like this tool has met your needs, then sign up for a full package.

- Flippa

This essential tool can help you get into the process of building a sustainable and successful affiliate site from scratch. This site is created as a bidding marketplace for people to buy and sell websites. For affiliate marketers especially, you get to buy sites that already come with strong backlinks and an optimized SEO growth. Keep in mind that you need to conduct a full backlink audit before you purchase a domain from Flippa to ensure that the domain isn't inflated by unethical SEO practices.

- CJ Affiliate

Affiliate marketing begins with a strong partnership with sites that need sales. CJ Affiliates is a number one resource for affiliate partnerships as it connects affiliates with merchants wanting to drive up sales for their products. Affiliates get paid for each phone call, or lead, or website when visitors peruse a merchant's site from the affiliate links discovered. CJ Affiliate is a great starting point if you want to seek partnerships.

- SEMRush

If you are looking for keyword research, competition analysis and even fixing SEO errors then SEMRush is a tool needed in your affiliate marketing arsenal. This tool is a favorite among marketers who want to understand what kind or type of content drives the highest ROI for their competitors as well as analyze on-page SEO issues. What's more, you can use SEMRush to monitor press mentions.

- Ahrefs

Ahrefs is another keyword research tool that you can use just like SEMRush. It also provides on-page audits and competitive content analysis. What's different with Ahrefs is that it places a deeper emphasis on backlinks than on-page SEO. Ahrefs gives marketers insights about lost as well as new backlinks as well as sites that are linked to broken pages on your site. Marketers will find it useful to use Ahrefs for new and lost backlinks, assessing competitor link profiles, and obtaining new link building opportunities.

You can also use Ahrefs to find sites that are linked to broken pages and of course finding top-performing competitor content. You can try out both SEMRush as well as Ahref's to build on your SEO optimization. If you can invest in both- great but if you cannot then think about what you really want to track first. If you are an industry leader in your niche, SEMRush would prove to be worthwhile. Since both SEMRush and Ahref have trial periods for their software, you can use both and see which works best for you.

- Yoast SEO

Yoast SEO gives you advanced SEO functionality in each page which includes the title tag and meta description which you can customize, canonical link customization, sitemap customization as well as meta robot's customization. Yoast is a free tool; but if you want 24/7 support, then you can go for the paid version. They also have a redirect manager in the paid version that allows you to redirect broken pages or pages that you want to be removed from search results.

- Grammarly

This example exemplifies another useful tool to have if you are publishing content on a regular basis. It is good to have a tool that can check your spelling, grammar as well as plagiarism all in one go. All in all, it makes your written content even better.

- Duplichecker

If you are part of the content team for your website, then running your article through Duplichecker will help you spot any kind of plagiarism. Of course, Grammarly also does this task, but if your intention is only to check plagiarism, then Duplichecker is a good investment tool. Accidental cases of plagiarism can prove to be a painful legal issue, so it's best to get your content checked.

- Hemingway

Another amazing content tool, Hemingway, helps you to simplify your writing. It is based off the writing style of Ernest Hemingway, hence the name of the software. Whatever content you write, especially the ones that go on the Internet, needs to be simple, straightforward and easy to understand. Your readers what the point to come across fast and their want insights, which means you do not want fluff tossed into your content just to make your sound intelligent. With the Hemingway software, you can simplify complex sentence, and it also points out complex words and adverbs that you can replace with simple ones.

- Sumo

One of the main things you want your site to do is attract visitors and with Sumo, you turn your visitors into customers. Most website visitors are not ready to open their wallets and make a purchase with their credit cards when they reach your site, especially if it is their first time visiting. How can you possibly get money from them? You sell them things that they are ready to buy. The best way most successful affiliate marketers do is to scale to build their email list. This enables marketers to drive repeat visitors back to their site and to purchase products over a period. With Sumo, you can have easy to install email capture forms on your site.

- Google AdSense

Earning money for each referral you get is wonderful isn't it? Want to elevate this experience? Use Google AdSense! With Google AdSense, you get a second revenue stream as you continue to scale your business. AdSense basically allows you to create ad blocks that you can use throughout your site that other sites can pay to utilize. You can also select payments based on per ad in a variety of manners such as through CPM. Applying this method, you get paid a flat fee per thousand website pageviews for a specific ad. The rates can range between $1 to $3 and this rate can go higher based on niche categories. Another way which you can do this is through CPC which is cost-per-click. This way, you get paid each time an ad is clicked on your site. The rates for this vary between one industry to the other.

- AdThrive

Getting money from AdSense is slightly tough, but if you have a good website, AdSense can give you a second revenue stream no doubt. What if you're only making a few dollars in ads and only have about 1,000 website visitors? You can also use AdThrive to optimize your ads, so you get better performance. AdThrive delves deep into your analytics to understand the advertisers who have the best performance on your site. From this, you can see higher CTRs on your ads and this will enable you to generate more revenue.

- InfusionSoft

InfusionSoft is a paid software and a little on the pricey end, but it is a powerful tool to use for any marketer and manager. Its finest feature is the automation that makes extremely efficient marketing campaigns for you. InfusionSoft is a robust yet costly email marketing tool that would benefit any small business looking towards reaching out to a bigger audience. The startup fee for this software is at $2,000. After this, maintenance would cost anywhere between $199 to $599 a month depending on the package you choose.

In brief, InfusionSoft saves you plenty of time. For first time users, it takes a little while to learn how to use the system and set it up according to your needs. But once setup is completed, you are pretty much set up for a smooth ride. InfusionSoft is renowned for its high deliverability rates and its ability to scale no matter what the size of the campaign.

- Keyhole

Keyhole offers a detailed analysis of the hashtags that you use for your marketing campaign. Instead of randomly using hashtags with your campaigns, Keyhole enables you to track and analyze hashtags in real time, shows you how influential it is, as well as its engagement, reach and popularity. The trial is free, but paid versions start at $132 to $799 a month. Let's face it- marketing campaigns nowadays thrive on hashtags. Not only can you track hashtags, but you can also get analytics by account, keywords, mentions and URL. This is a useful tool to have if you are always working on marketing campaigns targeting heavy social media users.

- Buzzsumo

Buzzsumo enables marketers to source the most shared content on specific topics and websites. Marketers can also refine lists according to the type of content such as blog posts, news items, or just infographics. The advanced feature includes 'monitoring' and 'influencers' that marketers can use to get ahead of the competition. The free version of Buzzsumo gives you limited results. However, the pro version starter plan is ideal for small businesses and bloggers, as it costs $99/month. But if you want something deeper and significant, then the advanced feature at $299/month comes with API access and many more incredible features.

Content marketers would love this because it helps in searching for trending topics and subjects on the internet easier and plus, it allows content creators to analyze headlines for their effectiveness. Buzzsumo helps content marketers understand how to create the next viral topic.

- CoSchedule

CoSchedule is a software that helps you plan, organize and manage your marketing campaigns, your content and your strategies. Any marketing campaign needs to be planned and executed according to schedule, and with CoSchedule, you can streamline this process easily. CoSchedule works great with Chrome, Google Docs, WordPress and Evernote too! CoSchedule ranges from $15 per month for personal use to $600 per month for larger agency users. CoSchedule allows you to stay organized and it saves time. It is excellent for large companies or small agencies to manage deadlines, share notes, stay up on to their day to day tasks and get updates on campaign progress. Timelines are easier to manage; any alerts are prompted by CoSchedule.

- Pingdom Website Speed Test

Website speed is a crucial element in retaining a user's visit to your site. Website speed is one of the fastest ways to improve your SEO rankings and increase conversion rates. With Pingdom's, marketers can test their website speed, and it also gives a free report that gives you an in-depth analysis of your site as well as tips to improve it. The test itself is free however for a full-on website monitoring service; it will cost you anywhere from $13.95 to $454 per month.

Full-time monitoring is essential and useful for large websites that receive plenty of traffic. A few more minutes of downtime or crash can cost you revenue as well as traffic. You can save a lot of money by investing in a monthly plan with Pingdom to continuously check your websites' status, give you alerts and monitor and report on site speed.

- Canva

With easy to use designing software available to us, most of our company's basic design materials can be made ourselves because let's face it: not everyone can afford a graphic designer on a retainer basis. If Adobe Photoshop and Illustrator is too complicated to us, then Canva is an easier alternative that makes design easy and fast. Canva has templates that are created especially for social media sharing and posting, and these templates are stunning. A few clicks here and there and you have eye-popping visual.

Chapter 14 Writing Content for Affiliate Marketing

Starting a blog can be done in less than an hour if you want to do things fast and furious; however, doing it in a hurry won't always make you earn money in the long run. Creating a blog, let alone a successful blog, takes lots of time thinking about a plan that can satisfy both your personal interests and the audience you're looking to reach for. If you search all over the internet, most people would agree to say there are tons of ways to create a blog.

To build a blog, you can always hire someone to do it for you or do it by yourself, but you can also make it for free or pay for a hosting service to run the site for you. Either way, each blog has its own charm and every blogger needs to know a thing or two about different disciplines if he or she is on the look to make money blogging.

Nonetheless, there's nothing more vital for this than knowing what will the blog be about? How are you going to address your target niche? And most important, do you even know what a niche is?

How to Know Who Your Target Audience Is

In order to know who your target audience is and what your blog will be about, there are two main concepts you need to know and be wary of the difference between them.

Niche

In marketing, a niche is every market a product or brand is focused on or oriented to. The niche will help you define who are you talking to, the target audience's age, the price of the products offered, the quality level of the product, and more variables involved in marketing an idea.

Target Audience

On the same page, a target audience refers to the market niche's group of people a campaign or product is intended to, as they are the end-consumers of a product or service.

Both terms seem to be the same thing, right? Don't worry, they're not. The difference is simple. A target audience represents the people you are focusing the blog on while a niche is the market containing the target audience. For example, selling sports-related items for left-handed people is your selected niche while left-handed people are your target audience.

Ok, ok. Learning the concepts is a great thing, but how do you select a profitable niche to start your blog once and for all?

Is Your Niche Profitable?

Knowing which the most profitable niches are will help you sort this out and help you finally define your niche. To know if a niche is profitable enough to make you earn money, it must follow a few simple principles:

Is Your Goal Clear?

Do you want to start a blog just to make money or to share your passion and interest in a niche? Providing yourself with an honest answer to this question will help you see things a lot clearer, as it will define the true nature of your blog. Writing about topics or products you don't feel passionate about isn't the way to go, as your lack of interest and knowledge will translate into your writing, and people usually don't follow a gold-digger.

Are You Solving A Problem or Providing Help for Your Audience?

To find a profitable niche it's crucial to know if your content will help someone else out there. Problem-solving is a must-have quality everyone should have in life, especially if you are a blogger, as you are basically posting everything you know and love on the internet for the world to see. Besides, if your end goal is to create a profitable blog, providing useful and trustworthy advice is recommended.

Is Your Product Unique?

If the way you approach your blog and the product is unique, people will feel it as well. A unique product refers to a proposal you don't regularly see online, and these specific niches are a great source of money. The more specific your niche is, the more money you can earn in return.

Is It Suitable for A Long-Term Business?

A profitable niche will always leave room for improvement and will let you evolve and expand to new markets and audiences without losing your focus on the core niche you've started with.

What Are the Most Popular Profitable Niches Online?

Among the infinite number of niches available in the world, there are always a few that stand out, whether they're marketed online or not. These are the most used niches to make a profit by blogging.

Health and Fitness/Weight Loss

Blogging about illnesses of every kind, diseases, medical-related tips, fitness advice, and weight loss programs, among others, are some of the most common niches people blog about. The reason is that everyone wants to take care of his or her health in some way or the other. This niche also includes healthy cooking and baking blogs.

Finance and Money

Someone I heard before told me, "Money brings more money your way," and in this case, it's completely true. Blogging about finance and money-related issues bring people together somehow and blogging about making money by blogging is certainly a million-dollar idea. This niche includes forex exchange, passive income tips, how to grow your business, budgeting, investment tips, and more.

Hobbies

This niche could easily contain any and every other niche in it, as it opens a wide world of opportunities and topics to blog about. With this niche, you can blog about music, sports, arts, or any hobby that requires people to spend a bit of money to do it. Fishing, golfing, snowboarding, and photography are among the most profitable, as they will help you add affiliate links or sponsors more easily.

Home Improvement/DIY Projects

Everything that includes fast and DIY projects can fit these niches. From home improvement tips to DIY projects for kids to do in class, how to fix basic electrical stuff at home, or ways to revamp your living space will make you earn money.

Fashion/Beauty

These niches are mostly intertwined and can sometimes be mixed up with DIY, health, hobbies, lifestyle, and more. However, fashion and beauty are extremely profitable, as they will allow you to link several products to draw traffic to your blog. From pieces of garment to makeup, skincare, and hair care products are suitable for these niches.

Lifestyle/Travel

The same goes for lifestyle and travel niches, as most of the bloggers who devote their content to lifestyle end up sharing about their trips and adventures abroad, their fashion style, what they eat, essential tips to handle everyday problems, parenthood advice, and more.

How to Use Web-Builders

Once you've chosen your niche, it's time to build the blog. As easy as it sounds, the internet is flooded with countless web building apps and services everyone should try. But first, some basic terms.

Web Builder

A website builder is simply a digital tool that allows you to build, edit, and manage any type of website without requiring any coding, programming, nor design skills whatsoever. Although some web-builders out there offer a wide variety of features that range from free templates to fully customizable templates and drag-and-drop editors, most web-builders lack coding and programming panel features for more experienced users.

Some website builders are used offline while other work only when connected to the internet.

Offline web builders are applications you install on your computer, which allows you to create your entire website completely offline. After you've finished your work, you'll then have to upload the website files to the World Wide Web. The downside for this kind of website builder is that it requires you to get a hosting service provider to run the website without problems.

Online web builders are the complete opposite. Often, if not most, loaded with a user-friendly interface and drag-and-drop editor, this kind of website building platform lets you create a website in minutes instead of hours or days. Filled with countless templates, themes, and pictures to choose from, online website builders have proven to be the most popular among website owners.

Website Host

A web host is a service, which gathers all your website information (copy, images, links, ads, style, and more) and stores them in big servers to make the site available for everyone on the web. Web hosts can be shared or dedicated.

A shared host refers to a big server, which runs and stores countless websites within. Most websites on the internet use shared hosts to run their content, including blogs.

On the other hand, a dedicated host refers to a server that only runs and stores one single website, providing the site with better features, dedicated attention to security, and is mostly cloud-based. Large companies that don't want to risk the privacy of their data or the stability of their website use this kind of web hosting service.

How Do Web-Builders Work

As most website builders have a drag-and-drop editor, anyone can build a blog in a few minutes. These tools showcase a wide variety of features including predefined themes, templates, image galleries, fonts, customization settings, animation features for buttons and pictures, and eCommerce and payment options for a well-rounded website.

When creating a blog, it's crucial for people to have a name and niche on their head to speed up the process. Then, choose a template, customize it to fit your needs, select all the features you'd like your blog to have (eCommerce, PayPal, shopping carts, comments, and newsletter forms, among others), write the content you want to share, and hit publish to end the process.

What Is the Best Web-Builders Available?

On the internet their hundreds of website building options available to offer bloggers their best features. They also offer free and paid plans to fit your needs and preferences.

To pick the best option for you, it's important to consider how expensive it is to access the platform, how easy is to use it, how much can the platform scale and grow with your blog, if it's easy to maintain the blog, and how many monetization options does the web-builder offers you to include money-making strategies on the site.

WordPress

WordPress has become the most-used platform to create blogs in the past decade. Since it was created, WordPress is home for more than 30% of the websites currently on the web, and almost 70% of them are blogs. Hosting services and domain capabilities are offered on their paid plans.

Weebly

Weebly integrates Google analytics, SEO strategies, and pre-upload features on their editor, which permits people to set their goals and prepare their content to generate traffic right from the get-go. Its web browser-based platform invites users to drag, drop, and move items from one side of the screen to the other and see their blog take share before their eyes.

Blogger

Blogger is the OG blogger's platform. This web-builder was created in 1999 and revamped in 2003 after Google bought the company. Blogger allows people to create a blog page in minutes, has comment-tracking features, mobile-friendly templates, and hosting and maintenance features are taken care of by the company instead of you doing the work.

Squarespace

Widely known all over the world, Squarespace offers users the tools and features they need to create a blog of their dreams right from scratch. Squarespace allows bloggers to drag and drop elements to build a blog, and include several plans to add eCommerce features, and domain and hosting services.

Now that the web-building process is out of the way, how is your site going to stay up online? You'll need to get yourself a hosting service.

Chapter 15 Using Social Media Platforms for Affiliate Marketing

So, your company has been on Facebook and Instagram since the time it formed and now, you're looking into other platforms to attract new audiences to your brand. Or maybe, you want to close one or two platforms which you feel is not getting the kind of traction you want and venture into something new. Whatever the case, you need to continue your social media presence, but in 2019, it's a matter of understanding which of these platforms are still lucrative and worth your time and money and which are not.

Plenty of social media strategies fail because companies prioritize the wrong platforms. If you open an account simply because other people are doing it, but if it is not pulling in the traction you want, you are wasting your time. Social media is fickle, so staying on top of the best practices and platforms takes time, a good strategy, as well as dedication.

So which platforms do you continue your efforts in, and which should you call quits? Before you list on your social media platforms, you should ask yourself three key questions:

- Are you a B2C company, a B2B, or do you do both?
- Who is your target audience?
- What is your overall objective?

The answers to these questions are your focus. When you have the answers to these questions, it will be a lot easier to flesh things out, so you can decide a minimum of two to a maximum of three platforms that you can dedicate to reaching out to your customers.

A solid two or three is ideal but if you have the support of a strong and active social media team, then, go ahead and branch out to other platforms. But if you don't have this kind of luxury, better just stick to a maximum of 3 channels. Each chosen channel will take time to grow and develop. Think of it as a plant that you need to nurture, water, and fertilize to see fruitful results.

In this, we'll examine at the best five social media platforms of 2019, their main audiences as well as the top industries for each of these channels.

1. Facebook
2. Twitter
3. Instagram
4. LinkedIn
5. Pinterest

Once you have the answers to the questions above, you're on your way towards crafting a successful social media strategy. If, however, you're still not sure or if you want a definite answer to your social media concerns, then you should get a social media audit done. Most of it is free, and it gives you a more personalized and immersive idea on data and recommendations.

1. Which one are you- B2C or B2B?

Identifying your company focus will impact the way you position your social media. The way social media is used in today's world is primarily for engagement. Where products and services are concerned, social media is used mainly to check out, tutorials, finding out what's being talked about a certain product or service, how-tos, and so on. Those opting for social media are at the very top of the sales funnel, which means for marketing, you could be targeting your ads at the wrong stage in the buying process. Unless your product is in the impulse buy category, the possibility of users traveling down the sales funnel instead of going to the next post is next to none.

Identifying if you are B2C or B2B will help you aim your social media strategies. For instance, B2B strategies are usually geared towards increasing leads and generating interest in a brand.

2. Do you know who your target audience is?

Have you ever seen an ad that is so irrelevant to you? You probably would have if you are on social media. You get ads for pregnant moms when you are not pregnant; you get ads for herbal remedies for men when you aren't male. Whatever the ad may be, you can bet that there were times when you were the receiver of an ill-targeted ad. You're probably thinking I) these businesses just wasted money on me and ii) whoever oversees these ads needs to get a social media targeting lesson.

And you're right- these businesses are wasting their money. If they wrongly targeted you, they could have wrongly targeted many other users. So, how do you know who to target when you create your own strategies? Take out a piece of paper and answer these following questions:

- Where does your audience live?
- What is their age?
- Are they mostly females or males?
- How much do they usually earn?
- Do they own a house?
- What do they like to do?
- What are their jobs and where do they work?
- Do they have kids?
- What kind of problems do they face?
- What are their main sources of information?
- Who are the top paying customers and who are the most loyal?

From answering these questions, guess what- you've just created a profile of your average buyer. To help you a little bit more, you can use this simple tool by Facebook to profile your target audience: Facebook Audience Insights.

1. What is your main goal?

Are your goals aligned with your company's goals? When you talk about goals, do both teams and departments have the same idea of these goals?

When crafting your goals for social media specifically, you need to remind yourself that social media is an extremely visual platform. People go to these platforms to SEE things and not DO things. Just like how you purchase this book not to read it but to LEARN something.

The Top 6 Social Media Sites Best for Businesses in 2019

The table below gives you a brief idea of what each social media is about and who should post what kind of content.

These are some of the most popular social media, but there are plenty more out there such as Tumblr, Snapchat, Periscope, and so on.

It is always a good idea to explore each of these platforms because each is unique in one way or another. However, for more traction, audience reach, and access, Facebook, Twitter, and Instagram should be your top priority.

Platform	Who Should Use It?
Facebook	Everyone, of course! Even baby-boomers are at it.
Twitter	Everyone – from individuals, small businesses to large multinational corporations

Instagram	Food, Fashion, Fitness, Lifestyle, food, personalities, advocates, and luxury brands
LinkedIn	Businesses, influencers, Recruiters, and Job-Seekers
YouTube	Brands with video content and ads, anyone giving explanations or sharing expertise
Pinterest	Fashion, Travel, food, design, home décor, makeup, and DIY- audience ratio is female.

FACEBOOK

Great for: B2C as well as some B2B

Age and Gender: Between 25 – 55+, both men and women

At the end of 2018, at least 1.5 billion Facebook users logged on to Facebook daily with the most common age being 25 to 34-year-olds. Whether you despise Facebook for your personal profile, you still need one for your company even if it is not the main platform you choose to market on. You need a Facebook account simply because Facebook provides the local SEO signal. In other words, search engines look for your Facebook business profile to put out other local searches. The Facebook business profile pings your business to SEO.

TWITTER

Great for: B2C as well as for some B2B

Age and Gender:18 – 29, both men and women

Plenty of people thought Twitter was dying and heading in the same direction as Myspace. But thanks to plenty of events such as the US presidential elections , the solar eclipse of 2017, the Royal Weddings, the World Cup, and natural disasters, Twitter has proven time and again that it is an invaluable tool, especially for news and information and political rants all in 280 characters or less. Twitter is also proving itself to be an invaluable tool for brands to be used for customer service. Nike, Wendy's, Virgin Airlines, and even the British Royal Museum use Twitter to tweet their businesses and respond to customer service issues.

Twitter is an excellent tool to connect with the movers and shakers of your industry, thought leaders, politicians, and business owners at a more elegant scale and to give your brand a unique personality that reflects your products, your brand, and your creativity.

INSTAGRAM

Great for: Works extremely well for B2C, so you can try it on B2B, provided you have the right angle

Age and Gender: 18 – 35, mostly men and women

If you have a visual product, then Instagram is your best friend. Instagram is everything you like on Facebook but without the fluff.

Instagram is in its very essence, a photo app. When it first began, Instagram users randomly uploaded images to share but as Instagram becomes more sophisticated, so did its users. Now, you see curated, high-res photos, carefully timed and placed on the grid. With high-impact images, brand captures the imagination, the personality, and the spirit of their target audience through stunning visuals, hashtags, and stories. Facebook, as we all know, owns Instagram and you're required to have a Facebook account to open an Instagram account. This also means Instagram shares the same features and ad targeting options that you would find on Facebook which makes it an incredibly excellent option for brand engagement and awareness. To tell a story, you want high-quality images-nothing less, and please, stay away from stock photos. Nobody in 2019 is going to buy that. If you're going to post on

Instagram, you'd better have access to high-quality photos that showcase your company and your brand and its people.

PINTEREST

Great for: B2CAge and Gender: 18 – 45, mostly women, but men are increasingly becoming part.

Pinterest begins as a hobbyist's platform to 'pin' inspiration from all over the internet. Whether you are planning a wedding, remodeling your car, starting out on your hydroponic garden, or learning to cook, there is a pinboard for you to explore. Most people have a Pinterest account even when they aren't planning anything or learning something- it's just a great place to have all your internet clippings nicely organized in virtual boards, which you can access anytime!

Again, Pinterest is very much a visual platform: so, if you a visual product or you offer services that involve visual planning- such as remodeling a car or even run a health and fitness business, this platform can inspire, and vice versa! It is the beehive of social media.

So which social media platform should you choose for your business in 2019?

The answers to the three questions posed to you at the beginning of this should already give you a direction of which platform to open and concentrate your efforts in. However, sometimes, the most unconventional of platforms seem to work for some business provided they've found a niche content they'd like to target. For example, Instagram can be used to showcase a company's culture. Pinterest is mainly for motivational quotes and inspiration.

If you've found an angle for your content, then go ahead and experiment with the social platforms you choose. However, if you don't see it bring in the kind of traction you want, end it.

You need to monitor, post, and respond on your platforms, so using platforms such as Hootsuite and Sprout will make this easier.

On the other hand, you can also employ a large enough social media team to curate, create, post, monitor, and respond for your company's brand or you could also outsource this task to a social media marketing agency to do help you.

In sum, remember that social media platforms are exactly that- to be social. Keep this in mind when you strategize, or you'll just cause a social media suicide for your brand.

Chapter 16 Mistakes Make on Affiliate Marketing

Everyone makes mistakes and so can affiliate marketers. But this lists some of the most common mistakes which can be avoided if you learn about them. Mistakes are more common when you are just a beginner because that is the stage when you perform all the trial and error experiments with your campaigns and strategies. And that is exactly how you become a pro gradually. It is true that a mistake is what makes you wise but at times, these mistakes can be a costly affair and so are better off avoided. So, here are some of the common mistakes that every budding affiliate marketer is bound to make and the also speaks about what you can do to prevent them.

Mistake – Wrong product choice

Affiliate marketing campaigns cover every possible product on this plant and the product need not always be something physical. It can be digital too. But with so many options also come the need to make the right choice. But can making the wrong choice impact your affiliate marketing strategy? Yes, it can. And so, you need to be careful while selecting the product as this is one of your basic steps as an affiliate marketer. This can be your defining moment towards success, so don't rush it.

Your niche should be something that will drive you and inspire you to make good content. You shouldn't be forcing yourself to sit in front of your laptop and do research on products to promote. It should be your passion. When you are inspired from your niche, you can easily devise several other marketing strategies and activities around it. Moreover, the passion might take you to such a level that your work becomes even more authentic and unique and that is exactly what will help you to stand out from the rest of the affiliate marketers. A simple search on Google about ideas on affiliate marketing niches will bring you thousands of results but picking something randomly never works.

One very common mistake that several budding affiliate marketers make is choosing a niche just because it brings more money. You need to understand one very simple thing. No matter how prominent or cool the niche is, you will never be able to make it big if you yourself are not interested in it. Believe it or not, nobody in the world is a natural when it comes to affiliate marketer. Every big affiliate marketer of today started out with something they love and then they spent days and nights researching and sharpening their skills. But if the product choice is wrong, you will just feel like a slave doing this just for the sake of money and not because you really want to.

Mistake – Promoting too many products right from the beginning
This is another mistake which people make but don't really see the fault in it. When you are just starting out in this field, there will be a temptation to include as many products as you can and start promoting all of them. Don't do that. The default approach towards affiliate marketing for any new person in this field is being over-enthusiastic and over-ambitious. But this will ultimately lead to stress and demotivation when you must figure out proper strategies for all these products. You will quickly become less and less enthusiastic and drop the entire strategy altogether. It is easy to get distracted when you have too much on your plate and you will not have any time for yourself or for your family.

The value you are putting in starts lowering down and this, ultimately, brings down the number of sales. So, if you want to be smart, then focus less on the quantity and more on the quality because that is how you climb the ladder of success. Pick a handful of products which you personally feel good about and would love to promote. Research extensively on them and focus all your energy onto those products. When you commit your brainstorming capacity and focus on a single product at a time, you will come up with better ideas and statistics show that you will also find it easier to convert your promotions into actual sales.

If you are thinking that approaching affiliate marketing in this manner will do you no good and will only shun your growth, then think again. There is no harm in proceeding one product at a time. Why cause havoc by trying your hand out at many things when you can make each product a success and then proceed? Every campaign is different from all aspects and thus, they need individual attention. So, you need to provide the campaigns with what they need, and success is not far.

Mistake – Only trying to sell and not help
With affiliate marketing, people often develop a mindset that is all about selling and not actually helping the audience with any information. If this continues, you will gradually start losing the audience that you have. Don't let sales become your only priority. Yes, you will have the tendency to do it, but remind yourself about long-term profitability. The mindset of making profits only will not give you poor results but also generate mediocre content. Good-quality content is what you should focus on. When your content is good, audience will follow and so will the sales.

Your writing should be focused on how the readers can benefit from it. Every feature should be explained in detail and think about all the probable questions that might pop up in the minds of the readers. Once you have figured the questions out, make a separate FAQ with every piece of content and answer those questions there so that your audience is not left with any confusion. Keep friction at bay. The placement of banner ads can be sometimes frustrating to the audience. So, place them accordingly so that they do not drive your readers so angry that they have reached a point of no-return.

Whenever you implement some sort of outbound sales tactic, some consequence will come. It is up to you to decide which ones you really want, and which ones are not worth the hassle.

Mistake – Poor quality website

This is another mistake that affiliate marketers make. Your content is important, but your content is not all about what you write. It is also about the platform. When your website quality is low, you will notice your traffic decreasing which results in a low volume of sales. If you are not an experienced web designer, don't worry because you don't have to be. No one is telling you to be perfect from the beginning. But with the resources that are available in today's world, making a good website is way easier than ever before. WordPress is one of the best places to start because of their user-friendly approach.

User experience matters a lot if you want to retain your audience. If there are too many ads on your webpage or if the page is not responsive enough, then your audience might simply migrate to some other page providing the same information. A messy template is also one of the many reasons which can scare off your visitors because your website might appear to be too complex for them. When you lose audience because of these cases, there are very low chances of gaining them back because no matter how much improvement you make, those people will remember your website for the bad experience they had.

You can understand this well when you compare it with shopping. Shoppers always prefer those shops which are clean and tidy and have everything arranged in a proper manner. They are even likely to spend more in such shops. But they will not visit an overcrowded mall because they cannot figure out anything over there. So, some of the things that you should make sure while building the website are –

- The website should be easily navigated
- Every should be properly categorized and easy to find
- The website should be responsive
- The calls to action should be prominent and clear
- Every page should have only one call to action
- The on-site elements should be properly highlighted on the webpages and the design should be chosen accordingly

It's true that building a website can be overwhelming but when done with patience, it is not something impossible.

Mistake – Content that is regular and of high-quality

Have you every though about what your product is as an affiliate marketer? Well, the answer is quite simple – it is your content. Every affiliate marketer wants to get more sales but in order to make your audience, you will first need to have good content. If readers find your content to be credible and valuable, they will automatically want to rely on your advice when they want to buy a product. The common misconception that almost every affiliate marketer has is that if you have 10 mediocre posts then it is equivalent to one great post. But this is a lie. It never happens that way.

No matter what type of content you produce, whether they are posts on product comparisons or product, your sales will be directly or indirectly affected by the quality of your content. If your content is not actionable or insightful, then there is no use of publishing content at all. Consider yourself as the buyer every time you compose a new post and then think about the fact whether the post would have been useful to you or not. The universal rule of getting any person hooked to your writing is to make your content interesting.

The first step to composing a new post is to decide the topic. Once that is done, you need to research keywords. Find keywords that are relevant to your topic and have less competition. This must be done if you want to outrank the competition that is already present. You should also check the word count of the posts that are ranking high on the first-page results. Then, set that word count as a benchmark for your own posts. Don't forget to include images in your posts because it is normally seen that posts with images automatically rank higher than posts that do not have any images at all. Lastly, be regular with your posts and don't make your audience wait too long for the next post.

Mistake – Not keeping an eye on the performance of your website

Not making use of a tracking tool is another of the common mistakes made by affiliate marketers. You cannot simply have a glance at your website and say whether it is performing good or bad. You need to have access to advanced tools with which you can study the metrics. If you do not track your data, you will not be able to optimize it and without these two things marketing is simply nothing. Whatever strategies you are implementing or whatever tweaks you are making to your strategies or campaigns will have an effect and these tracking tools will help you study that effect. You need to be able to recognize all the patterns that are working out in your favor. Google Analytics is the best tool to monitor all aspects of the website performance but if you want, you can use any such similar tool as well.

Does your website have a good speed? This is another important aspect that is highly overlooked. Studies have proved that whenever a website takes longer than 2 seconds to load, the audience bounce rate automatically increases by a whopping 50%. You must keep it in mind that everyone is impatient. Everyone wants to see the content now or never. If you keep your audience waiting, they will simply find another site that won't be delaying them.

Chapter 17 Strategies

Consider your content strategy

It doesn't matter what your desired niche is or how you plan on showing your passion for it. What does matter is that you choose content creation ideas that you are naturally drawn to and that you can keep up with in the long-term? Make no mistake, when you start content marketing you are getting into something that is a marathon, not a sprint, slow and steady wins the race.

Creating a small amount of content, even if it is extremely useful and well thought out content, isn't going to do much to generate the types of returns that you are looking for, it is important to choose a content creating strategy that you can stick within the long-term while also generating new content on a weekly or even a daily basis. Getting started on a content creation program and then giving up after a short period of time is even worse than not generating any content as all as when people visit your website or wherever else your content is posted and only see things that are outdated it promotes the idea that you don't care about what it is that you are promoting or that nothing new is likely to be provided which makes it less likely they will return again in the future.

To this end, it is important to generate the type of content that plays to the strengths of your brand, product, or services as well as catering to the content consumption habits of your target audience. It is important that you resist the urge to try and be all things to all people both when it comes to targeting viewers outside of your target audience as well as with the content you provide.

A poorly made piece of content isn't going to win you any new followers and may even because some otherwise interested individuals to go elsewhere. A better choice is to instead train your target audience to expect a specific type of content from you and then work on making that content into the best version of itself that it can possibly be.

Be a leader in your field: The general idea here is that you need to do everything in your power to show that you aren't just doing what everyone else in your niche is going to be doing, if you want to generate new customers then you need to prove to them that you are ahead of the curve in whatever market you have chosen for yourself. This is accomplished by creating content that is based around the issues of the moment, getting your name out there among leading authorities that your target audience is going to recognize and getting known names to contribute their content to your site.

Create a mix of long-form and short-form content: While regular and reliable production of single-serving content such as blog posts or videos are crucial to growing your audience, you are also going to want to brainstorm options for something that is more long-form such as an eBook or a video series exploring a socially relevant topic that your target audience is sure to relate to. Social media posts are at the other end of the spectrum and can fill the role of daily content to ensure that you are never far from your target audiences' thoughts.

While short-form content should strive to be as immediately relevant as possible, it is perfectly acceptable for long-form content to be of a more evergreen nature. There is no reason that you should have to constantly be updating an eBook, for example, that you created if you choose a topic that is likely to remain relevant to your audience for the foreseeable future. Neither do you need to rush into this type of content as a well-considered topic is going to be much more effective in pushing your brand as opposed to something that you came up within the span of just a few days?

Today's audiences are more media savvy than ever and if you didn't spend the time to create something that is legitimately worth their time they will know; and what's worse, they will make sure all their friends know not to bother with you as well. If you aren't careful, generating subpar content can be even worse than remaining silent as it can send the wrong type of message to your target audience that can be as difficult to get rid of as a particularly nasty stain on your favorite shirt.

Make a calendar and stick with it: While this is not something that you are going to need to do right away, once you are comfortable with the type of content that you are going to be creating on a regular basis as well as who your target audience for said content is, you are going to want to set a schedule for when new content is being created and stick with it. The specifics of the calendar are up to you, the crucial thing here is that you are going to want to produce content on the type of basis that your target audience can count on and that you can easily keep up with over a prolonged period of time.

While it will take weeks, if not months, for individuals to get into the habit of checking out your content on a regular basis, it will only take a fraction of the time to lose all your hard-won work. Don't let this happen to you, make it a point of only starting to create content that you can reliably produce on a regular basis.

Be prepared to track your results: The current tools that are going to be available to you when it comes to monitoring who is interacting with the content that you are providing as well as if they are sharing it with their friends, how long they are spending doing so and more are more detailed and easier to use than ever before. Unfortunately, they won't do you any good if you don't take the time to learn how to make the most of them and to utilize them on a regular basis. Good content marketing requires quite a bit of effort and by analyzing the various types of analytics that are available for the taking you will be able to determine if your hard work is paying off.

Don't rest on your laurels, it won't do you any good to collect all the various types of data that is available to you if you don't then try to utilize it as effectively as possible. Specifically, you are going to want to be aware of which pieces of your content people are responding to most vigorously as well as that which they are avoiding like the plague. Furthermore, once you have generated a healthy amount of traffic from all of your hard work you will be able to focus in even more and determine what type of content is going to generate sales of the products or services that you are ultimately trying to sell.

Product reviews

One of the most important types of content that you will be creating will fall under the broad category of product. A is a great way to slip in past the natural defenses that many people have against outright sales pitches as it contains practically all the same information and none of the stigma. A is a helpful way for customers to avoid bad products, a sales page is little more than a pushy ad. This strategy requires that you have a blog in addition to your Instagram so that you can write longer affiliate content. The pictures you post on Instagram will then act as a funnel to this type of content.

The most productive formula that many affiliates regularly use is one that looks at a specific product with a critical eye. It is important to point out any weaknesses in the product, as well as its strengths as you want your readers to assume that you are being as unbiased as possible. This means you cannot give each product you focus on a complete pass; otherwise, readers will not return the next time they are looking for helpful reviews. The most important part of every review post you create is to include at least two links where readers can go to find out more about the product in question, and hopefully buy it.

Broad strokes review: Depending on the type of niche you have found for yourself, you may be able to utilize simple, brief reviews that include a single picture and talk about the product as a whole for a few paragraphs before including a rating as well as a link to purchase. The goal with these types of posts is for readers to be able to quickly see which products have received the highest rating which means they are best for less expensive products which customers are typically looking for detailed information regarding.

Broad strokes reviews are effective partially because of their brevity, for more information the customer has no choice, but to click through which might be enough to get your commission, or it might even push them towards a sale. The more products that are included in each individual post the better as the goal should be to make it clear which few options are truly the best. Finally, readers are more likely to scroll through an entire page of brief reviews rather than read one that is in-depth as it appears to be a more productive use of time.

Comprehensive reviews: Depending on the type of audience you are looking for and the type of brand you are building; comprehensive reviews may be a better choice than short reviews. As the name implies, these reviews go more in depth about the product in question and are best used when it comes to food-based blogs that include a detailed explanation of the ingredients in questions all the way through the meal is finished and ready to eat. They are also useful if you have built yourself up as an authority in a specific niche for a higher priced item. You will also want to consider comprehensive reviews if, after viewing the sales page of the merchant in question you feel as though they could use a little help making the sale.

Comparisons: If the product that you are marketing stands up well when compared with other similar products, you don't need to worry about writing too much about it and can instead simply compare several products based on their obvious strengths and weaknesses as well as feature parity. The best use of this type of is when you are an affiliate for all the products in question as there is literally no way to lose. If this is the case, then you will want to go out of your way to ensure that each product has both strengths and weakness to prevent one or two products from looking like total duds. The more types of products you include on this type of review the better, if you do it properly you can attract plenty of additional traffic simply because you are a good resource.

Negative Reviews: Many people are naturally contrarian by nature which is something you can use to your advantage when writing certain types of reviews. While you won't want to turn potential customers off to a product entirely, you should phrase the review with a negative slant. The end of the review should then include a caveat about the product only being recommended for those who are an expert in the niche in question, for only the most serious, most devoted etc. You will find that you get many extra click-throughs from people who are anxious to prove you wrong.

Chapter 18 Tricks and Tips

As you begin working your drop shipping business, you are going to begin to learn your own tips and tricks to help you master the business. However, to help you get started, we have compiled a list of some of the best tips and tricks you should pay attention to when you are starting your drop shipping business. Having this knowledge under your belt now and applying them immediately will ensure that you are prepared for everything that is to come and that you come out of the gates strong.

It is a good idea to keep a book handy so that as you learn your own tips and tricks in the industry, you can write them down. While you may remember some due to using them on a regular basis, having them written down can help you remember what works in the situations you don't tend to experience as often, such as specific situations with certain vendors. Make sure that you keep this notebook handy and that you use it whenever you need in order to make sure that you are running your business smoothly and efficiently.

Reputation

As with any business, your reputation is highly important. You need to recognize what goes into creating a solid reputation and how you can use your reputation to positively impact your business performance. Your reputation is closely attached to your brand, but it is not your brand itself. Instead, it is the way people think about your brand.

Take a moment to think about a company that you haven't had such a good experience with. It is likely that many people haven't had a good experience, and for you and the rest of the population, their reputation is tarnished. People may continue to shop there, but it does not equate to them gaining as much business as they could if they had a positive reputation.

Now, think about a business that you love shopping with. Think about how positive they make you feel and the type of experience you have when you do business with them. Also, think about how other people tend to talk about that business. Since their overall reputation is more positive and they are known to serve their customers effectively, it is likely that their reputation is excellent.

With your own business, you want to be the one with the reputation that has people eager to work with you. People should be aware of how positive your business is and the type of experience they can expect to have with you well before the first time they ever do business with you. When people run into issues with their service, they should be able to rely on the fact that your company will rectify the situation quickly and in a justified manner. The customer needs to know that you are always going to look out for their best interest and do everything you can to serve them to the highest of your abilities.

Clear Communication

Many drop shippers fail to notify their customers about the nature of their business. Customers are led to believe that the retailer holds all the supplies and that they are independently responsible for all inventory-related operations when they are not. This can lead to miscommunication with the customer and can create a lack of trust in the business. It is important that you are always clear and up front with your customers that they are purchasing from a drop shipping retailer and that you do not have any involvement with the inventory that your store stocks.

When you do this, you maintain a transparency with your customers that earns their trust. You also relieve some of the pressure from your own business if something goes wrong. When people are aware that you work with dropship suppliers, they gain the ability to realize that some troubles may be experienced that will take you slightly longer to rectify due to the outsourced suppliers. It gives you the opportunity to have some slack from your customers.

Tracking Numbers

It is extremely important that you obtain tracking numbers from your suppliers whenever they ship products for your customers. Make sure that all your suppliers offer tracking numbers and that you utilize them with your shipping process. Tracking numbers are important for protecting not only yourself but your customer as well.

When you get tracking numbers, it adds a level of convenience to the system for your suppliers. It also adds security for you and your business. Since you will be able to track the products as they are being shipped, you will be able to tell where they may have gotten lost if that happens, or if the order has been delivered but someone claims it hasn't been. It is important that you have tracking numbers associated with every single shipment.

Delivery Time

When you are working on getting suppliers, it is vital that you understand what their delivery time is. Various companies will have different shipping lengths so try and find an average length and then look for companies who can work within' this average. Then, you can also provide this average on your website. When you are letting people know approximately how long shipping takes, always be sure to under promise and over deliver. What that means is: if the average shipping time with your suppliers is 7 to 14 days, tell your customers it will be 12 to 17 days. That way if the product arrives in less than 7 days, they will be pleasantly surprised, but if it goes into the longer shipping times, your customer won't feel as though they have been lied to about shipping periods.

Warranties

Depending on what value your products are, you may want to consider offering a warranty for your products. Offering warranties on high valued items can make it easier for you to sell the item because people feel as though their investment has been protected. It also shows that you are committed to customer satisfaction.

How you choose to construct your warranty will be entirely up to you. You want to make sure that your warranty will protect your customer without it costing you a large amount of money. Because of this you also want to make sure that your suppliers are providing you with high-quality products that won't be likely to break down. Having a proper warranty in place is important if you are going to provide one, so take some time to research what similar warranties look like and how they are constructed for the customer and the business so you can get an idea of how your own warranty should look. Make sure you advertise the warranty on the product page as it is a great selling point for many products, especially those that are high value.

Samples

Before you commit to using any drop shipping company you always want to make sure that you are testing out samples of their products first. Any good quality drop shipping supplier will allow you to purchase a couple of samples of their products so that you can test the quality of their products. It allows you to see if you like what they have to offer and if it reflects the type of quality you want to provide for your customers.

If a company does not allow you to purchase samples from them, you can almost always find an alternative that will allow you to. If you absolutely must go through a specific company, you might consider purchasing one of their units from a company that already dropships their products. While you will pay an inflated fee for the sample, it will allow you to test out the product and see what you think of the quality and value it offers to your own customers.

Modest Start

When you are starting a new company you always want to start modestly. No matter how much research you conduct before starting your company, nothing will ever compare to hands-on experience. Allowing yourself to start modestly will give you the opportunity to learn everything along the way and develop a strong understanding of your business so that when you expand you are prepared to handle the developments and you are clear on your role in the business.

Learning these tips and tricks before you officially kick off your business will help you start ahead of the game. While you will still need hands-on experience to make sure that you master your own business, being able to have this knowledge in mind beforehand will set you up for success in the long run. Make sure that you keep a notebook on hand so you can jot down your own lessons along the way so that you are always prepared for each situation and you can refer to your notes in difficult situations.

Conclusion

Now you know that Affiliate Marketing is a way of making money as an intermediary. Marketers make a commission from a sale or a referral when a visitor to their site clicks on a link that directs them to a product or page online. Furthermore, contrary to what most people would think, Affiliate Marketing has been around for a very long time and did not start after the invention of the Internet.

In the recent past, the Affiliate Marketing business has enjoyed extraordinary growth, and experts are foreseeing that the upward trend will continue. One of the best news about this trend is that about 81% of online sales have involved an affiliate marketer and according to a study by Forrester Consulting, by 2020, the industry's spending in the United States will exceed $6.8 billion.

The core concept of Affiliate Marketing is that it is performance-based, it has an element of independence, the partnership element, and universality. The core players involved in Affiliate Marketing include:

- The merchant/advertiser, brand, or retailer
- The consumer
- The affiliate marketer/publisher
- The affiliate networks
- The affiliate programs

In terms of payments, Affiliates need to think about the percentage of the total sales they will get, how the parties deal with reversals and the locking periods involved. Furthermore, the incentives available for the marketer, how many times an affiliate will expect to receive payment over a specified period and how much money an affiliate marketer should have to make before withdrawing his or her earnings are important.

An affiliate Marketer needs to capitalize on the advantages that are the result of search engine optimization, which he or she will need to learn how to use the right keywords, define the ideal length of the posts, and how to go about On-Page and off-page optimization. These days, it is impossible to make it without Mobile Optimization because the number of mobile Internet users is rising every day, and so is the size of the online mobile market.

Interested Affiliate Marketers need to know how to use Social Media to market their products, and the main strategies most successful marketers out there are using to continue to succeed. These Marketers must identify the main sources of traffic and the process of keeping people coming to their pages. Furthermore, so many marketers have made mistakes that future marketers do not need to repeat since it is possible to learn from their mistakes. One more thing a beginner Affiliate Marketer should take time to consider is the niche he or she will invest in and the Affiliate program ideal for his or her needs.

The next step is to implement all the instructions and suggestions in this book because the proper application of its contents will ensure success.

When you have read the complete book, you will develop a total grasp on the concept of affiliate marketing. By now, you should be all ready and geared up to start your own business. If you keep thinking and rethinking, you will never be able to start and now will always be the best time to start.

With affiliate marketing, you will oversee all the decisions as you will be working for yourself and not anyone else. The main effort is to set up your strategies and content. The phases that come later are mostly about reaping the benefits and some tweaks here and there. The key benefit of being an affiliate marketer is that you are not actually making any of the products, you are only selling them.

But even affiliate marketing is all about the audience and so you must do everything you can to keep your audience satisfied and provide some actual value through your content. If you create something that is already present on the internet, why will the audience come to you? The goal is to be unique and authentic. Your posts should have your personal touch that no one can replicate.

You can also try creating videos to make the content even more enticing and immersive. Who doesn't love the idea of making money while you are enjoying your vacation or sipping your coffee? With affiliate marketing, you can make that dream come true.

Lastly, I hope with all my heart that you have enjoyed this guide, and that it has been useful to you! And if you have come to this point of the book, thank you also for the time you have devoted to reading! I'm sure you've understood that it took a lot of effort to write it, and I'd be extremely grateful if you'd leave me with a 5-star!

I wish you every success with all my heart!

NETWORK MARKETING AND SOCIAL MEDIA 2020

HOW TO UNDERSTAND SOCIAL MEDIA TO HAVE MORE SUCCESS AND DEVELOP THE RIGHT MINDSET TO SCALE UP YOUR BUSINESS VERY QUICKLY

PAUL J. ABRAMAH

Introduction

We love network marketing. This profession has truly changed our lives. However, it wasn't always rain bowing and unicorns; we had to weather many storms, especially in the initial seasons of our business. When we were introduced to network marketing, we didn't have any business or leadership experience. We always joke with our mentor that we were a huge project, and we thank her and all the other people who poured so much of their wisdom into us. With their help along with God's blessings and provision, we were able to make our dreams come true in this profession.

We decided to write this book because we see a disconnect between the reality of network marketing and the way much of society views it. Many people believe network marketing is beneath them, but from our perspective, everything they want—uncapped income, leverage, time freedom, and little financial risk—is available as a package only in network marketing.

Network marketing professionals, or should we say unprofessional, are the reason behind this negative perspective. We include ourselves in this category because we have made these mistakes and have been "That Guy" many times. Really, we're not all bad people who lay our heads on our pillows at night with a maniacal laugh and scheme up ways to burn our friends.

Network marketing professionals are good people who make mistakes because we simply don't know not to make them. These mistakes may have been modeled by certain leaders and were then passed down through their teams like a bad generational iniquity. And again, we've done the same, so please don't think we're standing on a podium pointing fingers at everyone else. You will see throughout this book that in most of these mistakes, we are pointing the finger at ourselves!

Also, the mistakes we discuss may seem like common sense, but they're not. If they were, so many people out there wouldn't be making them repeatedly. That's what makes these mistakes so deadly: people don't think they need to watch out for them! They're like an insidious virus infecting the organization and crippling it from reaching its potential.

We want this book to be entertaining, and we want this book to be value-packed with tips that can truly transform your business and your team. At times, we may get passionate and you may feel a little butt kicking, but just know that we are writing it out of love. We've been there, and we'd rather you not go down the same path.

If you want your team to flourish but dread the awkward conversation about how they're unknowingly acting like "That Guy," we recommend taking a preemptive strike and getting this book into the hands of all your leaders, business partners, and every new person who joins your team. Let us have the awkward conversation for you, especially with those who have already been in the business. They may read these s and be able to see that they're making some of these mistakes. And here's the best news of all: they can do it privately and begin to make changes instantly without you having to intervene.

We are a husband-and-wife team, and we both passionately poured our experiences into this book. This is how the book will read: Michelle, who for some reason made more of these mistakes, writes a lot of the stories and examples of "That Guy." Adam, who is a master at coaching, provides the tips to implement in your business. We have equal parts in our contributions; Michelle loves telling stories and Adam thrives on giving meaty take-aways. We hope you enjoy reading this book—and that it transforms the way that people on your team represent network marketing.

Chapter 1 What Is Network Marketing?

Network marketing is also known as multi-level marketing or referral marketing. There are two revenue options with network marketing: sales and recruitment. Salespeople can recruit other people to sell products, when the recruited person joins, they are under the salesperson who recruited them. Salespeople recruiting others receive bonuses when someone begins to sell under them. This structure of earning money for recruitment is why some people consider network marketing "pyramid selling" and liken it to pyramid schemes.

It is also confused with affiliate marketing for the same reason. Affiliate marketing has a pyramid structure like network marketing, in that the people at the top of the pyramid started with the company earlier than those who joined recently. Those at the top of the company tend to earn more because their affiliations or networks are wider spread than those who just began. Affiliate marketing is where you sell a company's products online, using wholesalers and manufacturers. You essentially market their company with your own website, with an investment to pay for the website and the training. Think of affiliate marketing like it is a franchise that is online selling products.

Network marketing is product or service based, where you can sell online or in person. You have an inventory. Product sales are the best money-making revenue stream for network marketing. The definition of network marketing is direct selling, where salespeople sell products directly to consumers through referrals and word of mouth marketing. You may have some companies in mind that are true network marketing companies, after all, they have been around for decades. You may have attended a party for a bridal shower or hosted party, without understanding that it was a network marketing company behind the curtain. The term is one that has been around, but we often consider such companies as part of the door-to-door sales type.

Major Network Marketing Companies

- Avon

- Mary Kay Cosmetics

- Tupperware

- Pure Romance

- It Works

- Young Living

- Doterra

The misconceptions about network marketing have come about because of fraudulent pyramid schemes, but from this list you can see there are legitimate companies offering part-time, flexible work to people who need extra cash. It is only when network marketing firms offer more incentives for recruiting new members than for the sales of their products or services that rumors of fraud begin.

History of Network Marketing

The concept is not new because network marketing started in the 1920s. Nutrilite, formerly known as California Vitamin Company started in the 1930s. California Perfume Company also started in the 1930s and is better known as Avon.

It has evolved from door to door sales and house parties to online sales. Women mostly joined network marketing companies to work, without being out of the house the entire day. It gave women something to fill their time. It also gave them products to use, and ways to be social. Anything from cosmetics to kitchen items are sold through network marketing companies. Pampered Chef, for example, is one company that offers cooking utensils, pots, and pans.

Women could use their income from these sales to help the household or buy things they wanted. It still works like this, only now men are also beginning to join in network marketing. It went from a pastime for fun and entertainment, to a legitimate way to increase one's monthly income.

The internet brought new changes to the industry. Door to door sales and house parties still occur; however, most sales are done online. If you like a product, you may decide you want to establish a website, sell the product, and recruit new members to help you market those products.

How Internet Network Marketing Works versus Historical Network Marketing

1. A company offering network marketing will provide you with a website and products to sell, often asking you to have a certain amount of inventory on hand.

2. You buy the website, set it up with your details, and take orders.

3. If you have the stock, you fill the orders. If you need the stock, you order it and either have it shipped directly to the client or shipped to you and you can ship it or drop it off to the client.

4. You get to decide the time, effort, and marketing packages you use.

Before the internet and still today, the salesperson asks their friends if they would like to host a party. The salesperson brings their "kit" filled with samples of the products, a few products to sell during the party, and order forms. Snacks and drinks are available. Comradery occurs before the host introduces the salesperson. From there, about an hour is spent with the salesperson showing their products and discussing the product benefits. Everyone is invited to make purchases throughout the rest of the evening after the demonstration is over.

The slogan "Avon is calling" was popularized because Avon salespeople came to the door, knocked, and entered a home to share their products.

After building their client list, they would either be called with an order or asked to stop by when they were in the neighborhood. This method happens less now because of the internet, mobile phones, and other forms of communication.

What Network Marketing Does for You

The main goal of network marketing is to supply you with added income. It is a part-time job, for extra income versus a full-time job.

It also allows you to socialize with friends, family, and new people.

You have a portal to sell products or services you believe in, when you join a network marketing company.

Any career or secondary income pathway has its advantages and disadvantages. You need your eyes open when you choose a network marketing company to ensure you are gaining more advantages, then disadvantages.

Network marketing can only help you supplement your income, unless you are a dedicated salesperson. There are plenty of Mary Kay and Avon representatives who commit wholeheartedly to selling products for the companies and do not have another job. For most people, it is a secondary source of income that is done for fun and socialization. What you get out of network marketing is what you want to get out of it—the effort you put in equals the rewards you see.

Chapter 2 Choosing The Right Company

Now that you've decided on your niche., you want to decide which company to join. Not all companies are created equally.

Leadership

We talked before about how important leadership is when it comes to your upline. It is equally important that the executives of the company be equipped to successfully grow a company to become a billion-dollar company. On the company's website, there should be information about the executives. A simple Google search could prove to be very insightful.

When the company I was originally with started making a lot of changes that seemed to be detrimental to everyone's business, I decided to do a search to see if I could find anything on the CEO. The first page of search results was full of information from lawsuits the company was involved in, specifically naming the CEO.

There were court documents that included several different email chains between the CEO and two other individuals. One was fighting for the quality of products while the CEO was fighting for higher profits, while the third individual was trying to find a balance between the two. Then it showed an email between just the two other individuals without the

CEO included where it was that the CEO has no experience running a company and it was handed to him because of his mother.

Spicy! Who doesn't love a good soap opera? No one once they realize that soap opera is the reason, they have lost two-thirds of their income. If it were appropriate to use emojis in a book, I would absolutely use the face palm emoji right now.

There's no guarantee that things won't still happen after you join. You're never going to really know what you're getting into until you're in the thick of it. No one involved in a company is going to be forthcoming about issues they see when you're talking to them about possibly joining. They're focused on themselves, growing their team, and their paycheck.

At least you'll know that you did your best to ensure that you were getting involved with a company that has competent and experienced executives.

Another point I want to mention is not to be immediately concerned if an executive was once involved with another MLM. Do more research and see what you can find.

This should not be a rash decision. Make a pros and cons list for each company you're considering. Get the full picture before you decide. A company could have the best products, but if the company is not being managed by the right leadership, it won't make a difference.

Remember how I shared about the software changes that ended up causing all kinds of problems for customers and distributors? It became pretty clear that they did not vet the company they decided to go with very well. The company who created the software participated in the company sponsored trip and spoke to the distributors about everything they were doing and working on, what was coming, etc. None of it ever happened. There were even times when my friend would log in and a different network marketing company's name was listed. What a mess, right?

Then at the next company convention, the executives shared that they've hired an IT team to build out a brand-new software program for distributors to run their business. They introduced the head of the IT team to walk everyone through a demo of what they were working on. Six months later, another company announced that he had joined their team.

Talk about losing all faith in the executives of the company. Let's not even discuss all the problems that came with the second software program they implemented!

The next catastrophe was when they "revamped" their flagship product. The claim was that it was the same, only better. It was not. It wasn't even close. Many people said it had the opposite effect of the original.

The beauty of social media is that you have access to lots of personal s and opinions on various products with a simple search. There may be false information. There may be some people who are just bitter. But just like they say there's some truth behind every joke, there's likely some truth behind every post.

Wouldn't it be better to know these things before joining a company, rather than learning about them after you've already invested a lot of time and money?

Up & Coming

Every company is going to have someone who was their first consultant. That person is often the top earner in the company. Many people think, "If I had just gotten involved earlier, I would be more successful like all of these people." The pioneers. I can see how that thought process makes sense.

Here are some flaws with that theory though.

A brand-new company has very little credibility with the public unless they transitioned from a traditional business model to one of direct sales. If you're selling a consumable product, most people are going to want to hear about other people's experiences. They want to read s. They want to see progress after 30, 60, 90 plus days. I'm not saying you can't sell it. I'm only saying that you're going to have to overcome these objections from day one.

Look at how long the company has been in business and whether they have clinical studies or the like to substantiate their claims. The FDA does not regulate most of the products sold by MLM's. Many companies will spend the money to have third party testing done to be able to provide the public with data to support their claims.

Products that have been around for some time are established. If people had adverse reactions, it would be discovered by now. An established product immediately has more credibility. We live in a time when people are worried about the health risks that could come from using certain chemicals and such. They want to know that not only does the product work, but it's safe.

There's been chatter around a popular skincare line causing skin cancer. The EWG (Environmental Working Group) Skin Deep database rates the ingredients in skin care from 1, being least toxic, to 10, being most toxic. When looking up the most commonly used ingredients in this company's line of skincare, there were several that rated 7, 8 or even 9. They rave about how effective their products are at removing things like sunspots. Congratulations, we've bleached your face and now you have skin cancer.

Not exactly something you want to encourage your friends to start using! That brings me to the next topic.

Lawsuits

Let me start by saying that I am not a lawyer and the information provided throughout this entire book is just my opinion based on my experiences.

It's a good idea to see if there are any class action lawsuits against the company you're considering joining. If there is an active class action lawsuit, there's likely a lot of chatter on social media about it. Class action lawsuits usually lead to a lot of negative press. Particularly by competing companies that want to use it as an opportunity to tout that their company and products are better.

Your friends could hear about it before you ever share anything you love about the company. This will make it hard for you to have success starting out because your warm market could already be skeptical and apprehensive to try the products, let alone join you on this new adventure.

Another important question that a lot of people fail to ask is "What if someone tries to sue me personally because I recommended this product to them that caused them harm?"

You want to make sure that the contract (Policies) you're signing when you join the company contains an indemnification clause, which is essentially a contractual transfer of risk between two contractual parties. Basically, it means that the company is going to be held responsible of fault and not you personally. If you can't find the information up front, contact the compliance department for the company you want to join. They are responsible for enforcing the policies and should be able to provide you with an answer immediately.

Now, let's say that there has been a class action lawsuit brought against the company. What was the ruling? If the court ruled in favor of the company, you can breathe a sigh of relief because precedent is now on your side. If one court has already ruled against the claims brought by consumers, it will make it a lot less likely that another lawsuit will be brought. They would have to provide new evidence that is different from the evidence presented otherwise the court is likely going to see it as an attempt at a frivolous lawsuit.

If the court ruled in favor of the consumer, then you may need to do more research and see what effect that had on the company. Did they have to make changes to their product(s)? Were those changes made? Were they required to pay damages? This segues perfectly into my next topic.

Financial Stability

It's important to know whether the company is financially stable. There are several different reasons why this is important, but we'll start with the topic of lawsuits since we just covered that.

In 2015, Herbalife settled with some distributors for $15 million. Then in 2016, they agreed to settle a Federal Trade Commission suit for $200 million dollars, only to then be hit with a class action lawsuit in 2017 for $1 billion dollars. That's a lot of financial hits. Although the class action has not yet been decided, the company is still spending a great deal of money to fight it.

If a company is not financially stable, just a single lawsuit could bankrupt them depending on the outcome.

Also, in 2015, there was a lawsuit between Privet and their product developers, Forever Green. As part of the contract, there was a requirement that the company purchase a specific amount of liability insurance. They only took out half the amount in liability coverage and the developers sued them for breach of contract and requested a cease and desist order to prevent the company from selling any further product until the liability insurance amount was increased.

What's the first thing that comes to mind after reading that? For me, all I could think was "how harmful is this product if the developers are requiring such a large amount of liability insurance before they are comfortable putting that product out to the public?" They are clearly anticipating lawsuits. We all know by now that there are companies that think it's cheaper to settle lawsuits than it is to recall their product or revamp it. They are willing to take the risk for the financial reward.

The Lie

When I was involved with my initial company, the people who had reached the top ranks were notorious for making comments about how anyone who stays with a company for 5 years and is committed to their business will make it to the top. This was not based on facts or evidence.

I can tell you from personal experience that despite my daily efforts, I had little to no movement in my business after the second year. With the changes to the products and the system changes, I could not gain any momentum in my business. It's not about how long you stick it out. Sometimes, it's beyond your control.

Before moving onto the next, I want to make sure to remind you that there are no guarantees in life. No matter what you do, things may not turn out the way you hoped. You can do all the right things, and something that is beyond your control can take it all away.

Chapter 3 How to Find Prospect

They're everywhere. 80% of Americans are unhappy with their jobs. A survey by USA Today several years ago revealed that 96% of all Americans had thoughts at one time in their lives that they would like to own their own businesses. Almost everybody needs to make more money. And a lot of people don't have much job security. In short, this country is chock full of people who want the benefits of what we have to offer. They just don't know how to get them.

- **Almost Everybody You Meet Is a Prospect**

Get their interest. Then get their contact information and follow up as soon as possible. When you are following up on a stranger, do it quickly, before they forget who you are.

You can wear a button or badge.

One network marketing company that specialized in weight loss products gave their distributors buttons to wear that said, "LOSE WEIGHT NOW ASK ME HOW." Those buttons get a lot of attention in a nation of overweight people where almost everybody wants to lose weight, but nobody wants to change their eating habits.

What kind of button could you wear that presents you as a person they need to know in order to better their lives? It could either promote your product or your business opportunity.

In my area, a lot of Realtors® wear professional engraved name badges when they are out in public. The badges simply give their name, the title Realtor® and the name of their company. You can order these badges at an office supply store.

What if you wore a professional engraved badge that had your name and underneath your name said something like?

- Income Consultant

- Early Retirement Consultant

- Lifestyle Consultant

- Success Mentor

Enter the Room of Business

What if you could walk into a room full of successful businesspeople who were there to learn about you and your business? You can. It's your chamber of commerce. That's what the words chamber of commerce mean – room of business.

A chamber of commerce is not a government agency. It is a non-profit business organization that exists to promote local businesses and to foster a profitable business atmosphere in their area. Because they do a lot of good for their cities, some chambers get funding from their cities.

They are there for one reason – to promote business. They will promote your business if you're a member.

Most chambers of commerce have at least 2 networking events every month. These events are specifically designed to be places where businesspeople can go and share. Of course, to earn a hearing, you must listen to the other members tell about their businesses too.

- **How to Act in Chamber of Commerce Meetings**

Most of the people in chamber of commerce meetings are successful in their fields of endeavor. Don't be intimidated if they are all more successful than you are. Be friendly and confident and treat them like your peers. Don't look up to them, and of course, don't look down on them. They are just normal people, even if they are more successful than most.

Dress well. Here in Southern California, business casual works fine. In some other areas you might want to wear a business suit.

The Kinds of People You Will Meet in the Chamber of Commerce

For the most part, you will meet four kinds of people in the networking meetings:

1. You will meet local businesspeople.

They usually go because they have learned that it's good for business. They have learned that participation in the networking events helps them get new customers and maintain relationships with existing customers. Although they are looking for new customers, they are also opened to meeting new people who want their business, also. Most of these people will be more open to your product or service than to your business opportunity, so lead with the product when you are talking to them.

2. Representatives of local businesspeople

Sometimes local businesspeople do not go, but they send an employee to represent them. These employees do not own their own businesses, and they can be open to either your product or your business opportunity. Lead with the product publicly. Get their business cards and call them within 48 hours to see if they are open to another income opportunity. Always call their cell phones and not their office phones to help them avoid an awkward situation. Also, get their personal email address, not their email address from their company for the same reason.

3. Salespeople

These are the independent reps and the reps for other companies who are trying to sell to the local businesspeople. Many of these people do not own their own businesses, and very few of them have residual income. These can be some of your best prospects for recruiting. They are not afraid to talk to people, and many of them are very ambitious.

Again, it's normally not the best to speak about your opportunity in a chamber event, but to get their business cards and call them within 48 hours. Always call their cell phones and not their office phones.

4. Government officials

You may meet your city council people, your mayor, and representatives of your state and federal legislators. I have found that most of these people are not good prospects for anything, but they are good to know if you ever have an issue with the government.

Which one of those web designers do you think got the most attention?

When you go to an event like this, have your commercial scripted. Don't focus on yourself and your business. Focus your commercial on problems your hearers may be facing and how you can offer the solution. If you do that one thing, your commercial will be more effective than 95% of the others you hear. Your hearers will be more interested, and they will remember you longer.

- **Join a Networking Group**

Networking groups are clubs that meet once a week for breakfast or lunch. They allow only one person from each business category to join and participate. A networking club, for instance, may have 1 dentist, 1 lawyer, 1 plumber, 1 chiropractor, 1 insurance agent, 1 florist, 1 banker, etc. They may have more than 1 network marketer, if the network marketers are selling different products. Most networking clubs have about 20-30 members.

Networking group meetings are somewhat like chamber of commerce breakfasts or luncheons, with a few differences. They focus on getting leads for their members, and they expect you to bring leads for other members regularly.

You will have the opportunity to get up and give your 60-second commercial. During your commercial, you will tell your fellow members the types of people or businesses that are the best leads for you, in the hopes that the other members will know and refer them to you. Of course, you are obligated to share leads with the others also.

Members of these networking groups usually form a close bond with one another in a spirit of mutual friendship and help.

While there are a few national and international organizations that have local networking, there are also a lot of independent local networking groups.

The major networking groups are BNI, LeTip, Leads Club and TEAM Referral Network.

After you have experience in a networking group, you might want to start your own. It's a lot of work and a lot of responsibility, but it can generate a lot of leads.

- **Use Social Media**

Do you use Facebook? If not, create a Facebook account and learn to use it. Invite the people you know to be your friends on Facebook. Soon, some of their Facebook friends can become your Facebook friends too.

As you build your Facebook audience, you can build a fan page – a page that features your business. Your Facebook Profile is the page about you. Your Fan Page is the page to promote your business.

Also, get a Twitter account and learn to get your message out by "Tweeting." Follow others on Twitter, and others will follow you. The bigger your following, the more people you can potentially recruit.

- **Buy Leads**

There are several companies that advertise on the Internet and elsewhere to generate leads of people who are interested in having a home-based business. They then sell those leads to network marketers.

Some of the leads are very good; others are worthless. Whenever you buy leads from a company, buy a small quantity to start. That's enough to get a good feel for the quality of the leads.

One lead I got one time was a lawyer who was the mayor of a classy suburb of a large city. He was getting tired of the legal profession, and he was exploring his options.

Leads can cost as little as 5¢ each, or as much as $5.00 each. The nickel leads are usually not very good. The more expensive leads can be very good.

The best leads are called real time leads. When you purchase this type of lead, you will be notified immediately by email whenever a person fills out the form requesting more information. These are some of the best leads you can buy.

One time I got an email about a person who had just signed up for information. I called her immediately and shocked her. She was still looking at the web site when I called. She was so impressed; she listened intently to my presentation and joined my business.

- **Phone Surveyed Leads**

Some lead companies offer leads where they have surveyed a prospect on the phone. Since the person has already been surveyed on the phone, they are expecting a call. You will know some things about them before you call. These leads can be very good, but they're also expensive.

- **Exclusive and Non-Exclusive Leads**

Most of the leads you buy are not exclusive. They are sold to 2-4 different network marketers at the same time. When this is done, the lead companies are careful to not sell the same lead to more than one distributor from any one company. Non-exclusive leads, of course, are cheaper to buy. Most network marketers are not good presenters, so if you call your lead as soon as you get it, and if you make a good presentation, you will probably stand out from the others who call. Also, as crazy as it may seem, a surprising number of network marketers buy leads and never call them.

- **Long Form Leads**

Some of the web sites that capture leads require the people to fill out a long form, asking for phone number, address, age group, why they're interested in a home business, etc. Leads with this much information are better, and they're more expensive. Most people won't give that much information. Those who do will tend to be better prospects. Also, they're easier to talk to, since you already have a lot of information about them.

- **Short Form Leads**

These leads often give you just their name, email address and phone number. Since most people will only give this much information when asked for info, there are a lot more of these available, and they're cheaper. Most leads are short form leads.

Short form leads can be very good leads. Most of the leads my team and I have purchased are short form leads, and we've recruited a lot of people from them.

- **Aged Leads**

The newer the lead, the better it is. Some companies sell old leads very cheaply. Aged leads are generally 30-90 days old. That means 30-90 days have passed since the people asked for information online, and the leads have been sold 4 or more times to other network marketers before they are sold as aged leads. These leads are never as good as fresh leads, but they can still be good.

Chapter 4   The Art of Invitation

Starting conversations for Network Marketers is hard to do when you don't know where to begin. We are going to take baby steps.

Our first baby step will be to find people. Our second baby step will be connecting with people.

We are going to invite people. We are going to connect with people. We'll use a series of prefabricated messages for inviting people. We'll use prefabricated messages for connecting with people.

Starting conversations on Facebook is easy for building friends and relationships. Starting conversations on LinkedIn is harder.

Facebook makes it easy to build friends and relationships. Posting quotes, pictures or videos of your children's birthday parties is easy. They're great conversation starters.

LinkedIn is more about professionalism than about posting pictures and videos of family. LinkedIn is about building connections for business purposes.

So, we'll avoid posting cute pictures, quotes or videos. We will post things only for building business relationships.

Our conversations on LinkedIn will center around building business relationships.

What do we say to start? Our skills will help us with saying the right words.

Our first two baby steps?

- Step #1: Invitations.

- Step #2: Connections.

We will follow these two steps in sequence. It makes for a much smoother ride.

You're going, "Ugh! Ugh! That sounds too slow." Well, it is. Everything on LinkedIn moves slower than it does on Facebook. People do not spend hours a day on LinkedIn like they do on Facebook. They check messages about twice a week. They view posts sometimes three times a week.

Don't expect your invitations, messages or conversations to happen right away. They do not on LinkedIn. Sometimes you will wait days, and other times it will be weeks before you'll receive an answer.

But we can speed up the process. We will make things interesting. We will outthink the competition. We will grab the prospect's attention.

So, be patient. Your patience will pay off. So, let the conversations begin.

Finding People

We must find people before connecting with people.

To help us with finding people, we are going to need three tools.

First, head over to Evernote and download the app both for your cell phone and your desktop computer. It's a free app. Free is always better. You can sync your cell phone and desktop with this app.

Second, head over and grab a free online scheduler at Calendly. A more advanced online calendar for payment of a few dollars a month is at Schedule once If you have another calendar that you already use, it's okay too. Make sure people can click a link and setup a time for talking with you. If they cannot, you will need one of the two schedulers given here.

Third, we will need links to ten complimentary gifts. There will be more about the gifts later in this.

We'll start building connections with other Network Marketers. Starting conversations with them requires little convincing on how great Network Marketing is. They're already convinced.

We need to find people to connect with.

To find people on LinkedIn, you will need the following directions.

Go to the search engine in the upper left-hand corner of your home page.

- Click the search engine.
- A drop-down menu appears. Click "People" from the menu.
- The "People" page appears. Click on "All Filters."
- The "All People Filters" page appears.
- Under "Connections," you'll click 2nd and 3rd connections.
- Ignore "Connections Of."
- Under "Locations," you'll type the countries where your search will begin. Only type country names where you speak the language and your opportunity operates.
- Under "Profile Language," you'll click the language that you speak.
- Under "Current Companies," you'll type the name for a Network Marketing Company. For example, you'll type "Amway."
- A drop-down menu will appear where you'll find a listing of all Amway groups.
- Choose each Amway groups in the list for your search.
- Now, click the "Apply" button in the upper right-hand corner.

FYI: You can't find the 2nd or 3rd connections and your language?

- Instead of moving from step #3 to step #4, you'll stop after step #3.

- Type ""People" in the search engine after step #3 and click the "Enter" button.

- Then you'll continue with steps 4 through steps 13.

Some accounts have a flaw. 2nd and 3rd level connections and languages sometime do not show. The extra step corrects the flaw.

Some of you may be saying, "I don't know any Network Marketing companies, so I can't do a search." Yes, you can do a search. You have "Google Search" to thank. Type "Top Network Marketing Companies" in the Google Search Engine. There you'll find a list of Network Marketing companies for searching. If you want a search by country, you'll type "Top Network Marketing Companies + <the name of the country>.

Once your search is complete, the first page of connections will appear. Each page will list 25 connections. Some of them will be blank. Others will have "Message" buttons. The only connections that concern us are the ones saying "Connect."

You can scroll to the bottom of the page and click the page number for advancing to the next page.

The level of your LinkedIn account limits the number of connections for any one day. For the non-paid version, it is 25 to 35 connections a day. For the paid version, it is 300 connections a day. LinkedIn will notify you when your limit is reached.

Our goal for the non-paid version is sending at least 25 connections. Thirty-five connections are better.

For the paid version, our goal is 300 invitations a day. Yes, that means 7-day weeks.

Does it mean we'll start conversations seven days a week? Yes! The more conversations that you'll start, the more business that you'll generate.

FYI: If you decide for the paid version of LinkedIn, buy the "Business (Find Leads) Package." Do not buy the "Sales Package." Unless you have purchased the "Sales Package" for other purposes, it will not work for our purposes.

The Invitation to Connect

Once we find people, let's connect. We will start with an invitation. An "invitation to connect" is asking someone to connect with us. We'll invite people to connect using LinkedIn's powerful invitation program.

LinkedIn's invitation program allows 300 characters to send an invitation to connect.

After connecting, one single message on messenger can be no more than 2,000 characters. We'll never send a 2,000-character message. For our purposes, it is fruitless and not necessary.

This is going to be a copy and paste operation. Open your Evernote app and click "New Note." The New Note window opens. In the subject line you will type "Invitation to Connect."

In the body of Evernote, you will type this message for message #1.

I came across your profile on LinkedIn, and I see you're in_____. I thought it would be good to connect. Would love to connect if you are open to it.

Thanks,

Your First Name

Below that, you will type another message for message #2.

I see you are in Network Marketing. I'd love to connect.

Looking forward to it.

Thanks,

Your First Name

For message #1, you'll fill in the blank with the name for the Network Marketing company that you have searched.

For message #2, there is no need for a name of the Network Marketing company searched. You'll send the message as is.

Do not put any links in this message. Don't try to be cute. Putting links in the invitation to the connect message is unprofessional.

Sign only with your first name. Don't make it so formal with a first and last name.

What about the prospects first name? Ignore it. There's no need for putting the prospect's first name in our "Invitation to Connect."

Pretty simple, right?

Now that our "Invitation to Connect Message" is in Evernote, we can begin to connect.

We will copy and paste the "Invitation to Connect Message" into the LinkedIn "invitation" window.

Remember how we find people on LinkedIn? Find people on LinkedIn and then follow these steps to send an "Invitation to Connect."

- Click on the first "Connect" button and the "Invitation to Connect" window opens.
- Click the "Add Note" button, and a "Note" window will appear.
- From Evernote, copy and paste the "Invitation to Connect" message into the "Add Note" window.
- Click "Send Now."

Easy, right?

Follow the same procedure with all the people that have Connect buttons. Remember, ignore any Message buttons. For the non-paid version of LinkedIn, you will connect with no more than 35 connections. There are 25 connections on each page. So that amounts to 1-1/2 pages.

For the paid version, you'll send the "invitation to connect" message to 300 connections. That is 12 pages. With copy and paste, you'll find you can send 300 connections a day in about 20 minutes.

Chapter 5   Presenting and Prospect

The 7-Step Prospecting Presentation Plan

1) Always be prospecting. Always.

2) Be Prepared. Always.

a. Be very familiar with your products and company

b. Be familiar with the competition and how the products are different

c. If you were referred to this person, name drop early!

d. Have a success story ready to share

e. Be organized

3) Smile (and mean it)

a. It is nearly impossible to come off fearful and smile at the same time

b. If you are genuine, and you better be if you want to be a successful network marketer, you will build trust more quickly with a smile.

4) Stick to the script

a. If your company has provided you with scripts to use, memorize them and make them your own so you do not sound like a robot. But stick to them because obviously the scripts are tested and true! Don't reinvent the wheel thinking your way will be better because it probably will not be better.

b. In your presentation, you need to show that your company produces a high-quality product that will show results.

c. You need to get to the point quickly while presenting to prospects:

I. Build Interest

ii. Show that your product makes sense for their needs and goals

iii. Close the sale

d. If your company does not have scripts, ask why? This could be a red flag for an unorganized company. However, in some rare cases, there might be a good reason why scripts do not yet exist. Take the time to research and build your own scripts. Do not shoot from the hip or wing it, instead talk to your manager and others in your up line. Ask questions. Record them. Take notes. Their past success is how you will build your future success.

e. Practice the script in a mirror. You might feel a little silly but practicing in your mirror will reveal things about your verbal communication skills that you have never noticed. For instance, you might find you look way too serious and intense – stop that! Also, practicing in your mirror will get the marbles out of your mouth and get you well on your way to a smooth and genuine presentation.

5) Ask for the sale

a. If you can get through your presentation, get product on them or in them when appropriate, and learn about their needs and goals, you will usually sell a product. Once you get through your script, you should always ask for the sale when you have all your product information presented. If you do not ask for the sale, nothing will happen, and you will never know if you could have helped the prospect with a certain need or a goal. When you ask for the sale, you will get a YES, get a question or hear an objection that you will probably be able to overcome. Each of these situations brings you closer to another YES.

6) Stop Talking and LISTEN.

a. You must train yourself to become an active listener, if you are not one already.

b. This means listening more than you talk so you can better understand the needs and goals of your prospect.

c. Listening is also very important to hear the YES from the prospect. Often you might miss the sale because you have not actually heard the word YES come from the mouth of the prospect, but they are dropping other clues. Therefore, assume that every prospect is going to mean YES even if they do not say the word. After all, you have a great product that will help the prospect.

d. Listen to get to the root of an objection, which means understanding what a prospect is thinking and why they are hesitant.

e. Active listening is going to mean you must ask good questions.

Selling Largest to Smallest

Under no circumstance should you ever attempt to sell your product(s) to someone who doesn't need it, but if you chose the right company with outstanding products, this should never be an issue.

Because you are representing the most awesome of products for a very ethical company with fair price points and intelligent bundles, you will always want to be tactical about the order in which you offer your products to a prospect.

Usually, you should start from the high-dollar items and work your way down to the smaller, less expensive products. There are two main reasons why you want to do this:

1) All customers will generally receive more value for their money in the higher priced packages

2) You need to give them something to say NO to so they can then say YES

Letting Prospects Say No

A good rule of thumb in selling to prospects is always let them say no to something. It may sound a little odd to want to set yourself up to hear "no", but this practice can work to your benefit.

If the prospect passes on a premium product or package you are selling, keep stacking the value of meeting their long term goal and current need, that way if they already have a "no" on the table with you, they are usually psychologically prepared to say "yes" to something because they know you have their best interest in mind. You should make it a practice to always offer the top of the product line to purchase because this is the only way you will know for certain that you are not being self-limiting and underselling what the prospect might buy.

Upselling

Upselling is increasing the initial investment that the customer has agreed to spend. With a new customer, the starting point is usually the suggestion you made to help them fulfill a need or a goal with your product. With a returning customer, the starting point sale is probably just reordering the product they purchased from you last time.

Because your goal is to get to know the needs, goals and reason the customer is thinking about buying, the starting point sale should only be treated as the first product for the actual sale.

After you secure the minimum sale, you want to continue to conversation to gain a better understanding of the "Why" they purchased the product from you. Once you get to the why, you can better understand the actual need and the end goal. Certainly, you have other products that will help your customer get on track to their end goal and one product alone will probably not meet all their needs.

- Know as much as possible about what the initial interest in your product is for the customer

- Be able to make caring, well-informed suggestions relevant to the customer

- The key is making specific suggestions based on the knowledge you have about the customer and what the end goal is

Closing the Sale

Assuming you are representing the best company with the greatest products, you are going to have to ask for the sale and close the prospect. The process of converting the interest of a prospect to a closed sale is going to take work and skill. When you are in the "sales field" which is basically anywhere and everywhere you are, nothing is more gratifying then having a prospect buy product(s) from you to help them meet a specific personal need or goal. Closing is fun and rewarding! But contrary to what you might think, closing is not a natural skill for all. The vast majority of Network Marketers have had to learn to become great closers. Like anything else, developing your closing skills will require effort, time, and continual practice in your mirror, with your team and of course, with actual prospects. Your personal development in this area should be a goal over the remainder of in-office training, and, during your first 60 days of launching your network marketing career.

What is the worst that can happen if you DO NOT ask for the sale to close the deal? NOTHING. And that is exactly the issue. Nothing will happen. Your prospects will not typically volunteer to buy products from you. That is why you need to close sales.

While your company will certainly arm you with strategies to close sales, here are the top ten ways to ask for the sale. Some will become more comfortable and natural for you the more you practice and put some of these to work for you:

1) Silence.

2) Assume the sale and offer options. "Now which product would you like, Product A which does this or Product B which will do that."

3) Suggest a product. "I think you should go ahead and try Product a first because we already that it will help you with your goal."

4) Conclude and ask for the sale. "Do you have any more questions for me? (no) Great, Can I put you down for Product A?"

5) Suggest a product and share a success story. "Do you want to try the same product that Sally Smith took home? She had the same goal as you and had an amazing result in that she ..."

6) Use a "yes" to get a decision. "Are you wanting to get healthy and lose weight this year?"

7) Suggest a priority. "I think we should first focus on issue A and then we can focus on issue B."

8) Ask a question you have already to make the purchase common sense. "We have concluded that you definitely want to get rid of the brown spots on your skin. You have tried five over the counter products already and wasted a lot of your time and money. We have established that this product has worked for many of my current customers. So, do you want to start with the xx-ounce size or the xxx-ounce size?"

9) Have prospect make the choice. "So, we have three very specific needs and goals you have for yourself. Which of the three is most important to you to get started with?

10) Describe how the buying process works and how soon they will have product in hand to build excitement towards meeting their very specific need or goal.

Chapter 6 How to Promote Your Products and Events?

Advertisers have various attempted and tried strategies for creating effective new item showcasing technique, a considerable lot of which incorporate some sort of web-based life component. This implies another item promoting system is presently to a great extent dependent on the internet. Achievement consistently begins with a methodology, and for your new item, this is a need.

Web showcasing has become so immense that advertisers need various systems for promoting items through various online stage. A Pinterest system won't resemble a Facebook procedure; in this way, it is critical to figure out what sorts of internet advertising are generally suitable for your item. However, there are some broad practices that ought to consistently be applied.

Finding your demographic

When building up your new item showcasing procedure, start by ordering a rundown of the sorts of individuals who will be generally keen on your item. Be as explicit as would be prudent. It may be useful to take your portrayal of your objective market and distinguish genuine individuals on informal communities who speak to your objective client.

Produce a buzz

Offering complimentary gifts is additionally an incredible method to create a buzz about your item on the web. Request that individuals offer or retweet a photograph of your item for an opportunity to win one for nothing. Complimentary gifts and limited time offer can likewise light up your ordinary public statement to bloggers. Discover a blog that has a specialty that identifies with your item and offer them free examples in return for composing a survey of your item.

And when there are famous people or industry influencers that fit your objective market, offer them complimentary gifts. And when they like your item, odds are they'll send a "thank you" tweet or post that will drive heaps of online traffic to your item's web-based social networking records or site.

Use SEO

New item promoting technique ought to likewise incorporate search engine optimization (SEO). Dissect your intended interest group and make a rundown of watchwords they may use to look for comparative items. And when conceivable incorporate SEO in your item depiction or any public statements you submit on the web. Execute SEO through building up a blog as a piece of your item's site. Your blog's substance decides the accomplishment of your SEO procedure. Odds are contenders are utilizing similar words, so giving helpful substance to your objective market is significant.

Use blogging and different types of internet-based life to turn into a specialist in your item's industry. Use sites like meetup and Eventbrite to make incredible occasions encompassing your item and official statements to educate individuals concerning the occasions. Models incorporate display showings, tastings and design appears. Likewise, join or make LinkedIn bunches where you can share data about your item on dialog sheets. Sharing and connecting back to your site through these internet-based life outlets will likewise manufacture your SEO profile.

It is significant for organizations to have various strategies for advertising their items. The advertising techniques for a business are critical. The nature of the showcasing is can represent the moment of truth an organization's capacity to make deals and increase presentation. It is critical that an organization use a wide range of strategies to showcase their items. There are various manners by which an organization can showcase their administrations to the majority. For greatest outcomes it is educated that an assortment regarding distinctive showcasing strategies are utilized. Displayed beneath are various diverse item promoting techniques that people and organizations can use to expand their introduction and at last their income.

When formulating a showcasing plan, it is prescribed that organizations have more than one method for drawing in people to their items. Having an arrangement of promoting techniques guarantees that there is decent variety in the manners by which the organization introduces its items to buyers. This assortment additionally enables the organization to follow the presentation of the diverse advertising methods to figure out which one is generally beneficial to use in the long haul. While there might be an assortment of approaches to showcase an item or administration, not every one of them are viable for specific kinds of items. In this way, it is significant for people and organizations to manufacture a promoting plan which at first joins distinctive showcasing systems to figure out which techniques will create the best returns while introducing an item to customers.

As expressed above, there are various manners by which items are showcased. There are the customary print ads. These promotions are typically set in magazines or papers. There are likewise the regular postal mail promoting plans which essentially include mailing data about a specific theme to a mailing rundown of individuals. The mailing rundown can be an exceptionally focused on gathering of individuals that are probably going to be keen on the item that is being sent. There are additionally web advertising strategies that can be utilized to advance or sell an item. Such systems incorporate the utilization of full pages which are basically web promotions for an item or administration. These pages can incorporate anything about the item the business wants and, the page can be organized with the goal that it can acknowledge installments for the item that is being sold or advanced. Article showcasing has likewise become extremely famous and numerous organizations utilize this technique to sell their item as well as an approach to convey what their item is about and how it might be advantageous to them. With the expanding prevalence of internet-based life, there are numerous organizations that are utilizing such elements as myspace and Facebook and other web-based life outlets to advertise their items. With many individuals over the world that use an online networking every day this has become an exceptionally powerful route for organizations to build their introduction.

The most effective method to craft an effective product marketing strategy

Item advertising procedure alludes to a promoting creating plan which presents another specialized item. It tends to be an extremely energizing and testing part of item propelling and promoting for an item. Notwithstanding, it can likewise be easy, and yet extremely confounding just when we dismiss our goals. And when you are keen on seeing how to make an item promoting methodology, well this article will assist you with this undertaking.

Here are the basics you should incorporate inside your item promoting system:

•mission explanation: this incorporates the assembling targets, corporate mission statement, showcasing destinations and item improvement goals.

•customers: you should think about what number of clients you have? What they are purchasing? What viable and enthusiastic issues and issues would they say they are attempting to tackle? What size of your market? What is the client's value point? The stuff to be effective in a request? To what extent would it take to be fruitful with an item? How does a client utilize aggressive items? What is the present joy with contenders?

•market segmentation: you should incorporate set clients (needs appropriation, industry, and geology). What's more you should restricted and select the objectives, name the s, and think about the distinctions and likenesses.

•competitors: try to comprehend what your rivals are doing right now? Where and how regularly do they publicize? What might be the idea of the deal introduction? What is their evaluating? Dispersion techniques? The position they take. The response of the contenders towards dangers? How do lesser contenders' contrast from the fruitful? Promoting share standard? Correlation with your organization with dangers, qualities, and shortcomings.

•product position: it is vital for you to separate your administration and item. Keep in mind the open door is out there, it is dependent upon you to discover it, however. You should likewise portray your items and look for your client's advantages.

•understand your client's mental needs.

•market testing: that is, you should show your limited time ideas and item to clients.

•making key choices: wherein you choose better than ever income, benefits and development, new item advancement, valuing, appropriation, administration and deals power, client's mental elements (not advantages and includes), and on item advancement for every single new item.

•write an activity plan: which must remember a spunky diagram for item advancement, a schedule of arranged media, and a financial limit.

•implement your arrangement: you can hold day by day gatherings to audit deals progress and leads. It is basic that you give a lead following framework and return to your arrangement and update when important.

The last basics are suitable advertising procedures to help entrepreneurs when building up another item. It is extremely easy to pursue, anyway it is vital that you cautiously develop an item showcasing technique as per your specific item or administration. Keep in mind, this arrangement is the way into your item's prosperity, in this way, it is basic that you assemble satisfactory data to help successfully compose your item advertising methodology.

Chapter 7 Mindset to Became A Best Networker

Networking is all about interacting with the people around you to establish personal connections that will help establish and build your business. You sell your product by selling yourself with various social networking tactics, inspired by informational and honest conversation about your goods and services. You will never find a somber Avon representative or frowning Tupperware employee, because good salesmen know that a potential customer will not make a purchase from an unhappy representative who does not believe in their own company.

To become a truly experienced network marketer, you need more than just intellect to make a sale. Selling and buying products are mental and psychological exercises. Customers are emotional human beings, not robots who only focus on facts and logic. Therefore, expert salespeople are masters at controlling their emotions. Every great sales representative has a set of skills and personality traits that set them apart from the rest. They can use these elements to successfully direct and control conversations with customers and make huge sales.

Assertiveness

Being assertive does not mean acting like a desperate used car salesman who does not take 'no' for an answer. Unfortunately, this has become the universal image for network markers; but a representative who expresses this trait is often misunderstood. Assertiveness allows the marketer to push the sales situation forward while avoiding offending or angering the client. Keep in mind that assertiveness is not the same as aggressiveness; your job as a network marketer is not to annoy and badger your family and friends into making a pity purchase. Think of assertiveness as a trait located between belligerence and passivity. Here are three responses that demonstrate the difference between the three:

Aggressive: "If you do not purchase this item right now, then the offer is no longer on the table."

Assertive: "Can you give me a specific time when you will be able to make your final decision on this product?"

Passive: "You can just call me when you make a decision, there's no rush."

Passive responses will give the potential customer the power and puts the sale on hold indefinitely. You always want to be able to contact the client and feel comfortable doing so in order to make the sale. Definite answers will keep you from wasting your time and avoid making strained relationships. Aggressive responses, on the other hand, will put too much pressure on the customer and make them resent you to the point that they will avoid all future contact with you. This is how the misunderstood idea of the pushy salesman has come to be. An assertive approach will allow you to stay in control of the sale without forcing your customer to change their pace.

Self-Awareness

Your emotions play a crucial role in making sales and being a positive image in representing your company. To be a great salesperson, you must be able to identify your emotions, understand how they affect you, and learn to utilize them in order to strengthen customer relationships. You will never make a sale if you do not keep your emotions in check. Anger that has festered from a fight with your significant other, annoyance at the customer's lack of understanding, and worry about getting to the grocery store before dinner are just a few examples of how your emotions can get the better of you and end up ruining a sale. This four-step method of self- evaluation will help you gain a sense of self-awareness and prepare you for your next sales pitch:

1. Identify your emotions at that point in time. Recognizing how you are feeling is the first step to centering your mindset and overcoming your mental state. Is there anything that is bothering you? Are you worried, scared, angry, happy, relieved?

2. Based on past experiences, take a moment to predict how your current feelings will impact your sales effort. In the past, have your emotions gotten the better of you and hurt your sales pitch? Did they distract you from your sale effort? Or did they make you more appealing and relatable to the customer?

3. If you are experiencing negative emotions, compensate for them so they do not prevent you from making a sale. The best self-development gurus around the world insist that if you act a certain way, you will adopt that trait. For example, pretending to be happy or excited

will make you happy and excited. It is also a proven fact that making yourself smile and laugh will lighten your mood and make you feel better. So, whenever you are upset or emotionally unsettled before talking to a client, readjust your feelings and compensate for the bad with the good.

4.   Engage in your positive emotions that will make you the sale. It's true what they say: you will get back the energy that you put out into the universe. This means that if you put out positive, happy vibrations, that energy will come back to you. You will not receive a warm smile and welcoming conversation from a customer when you engage with them with a frown on your face. Whatever positive emotions you are feeling, expand them and use them to propel your sale.

If you find yourself unable to let go of any negative emotions, then take a break before engaging in a conversation with your customer. Try reciting positive affirmations, watching a funny video on YouTube, or calling a friend to vent about your day to get rid of any negativity that may be clouding your mental state.

Empathy

Sympathy is when you understand and pity someone else's situation or feelings. Empathy is when you put yourself in their shoes and imagine how they are really feeling based on your own similar experiences. To truly experience empathy, adapt your behavior to your client's emotions. Start by listening to the client and observing their actions. Ask how they are doing and empathize with what they say by feeling what the customer may be feeling – if relating to their feelings and adapting the conversation to their mood does not interfere with you making a sale or lead to misrepresenting your company.

Problem Solving

If you have ever worked in retail or sales before, then you know that the saying 'the customer is always right' is complete garbage. However, if there is a problem that you know you have the power to fix, then it is your job to solve that problem for your client. The customer is putting their faith and trust in you – that is the whole point of accessing your inner circle to excel in network marketing. This does not mean catering to whatever whim amuses them but meeting them halfway financially and emotionally to prove to the customer that you are reputable and reliable. Problem solving in network marketing needs to be done in a precise and professional manner through this four-step process:

1. Come to fully understand the problem before attempting to solve it. Let the customer finish explaining their issue and assess the situation before diving into it.

2. Do not attempt to solve the customer's problem before you fully understand it. See the circumstance as it really is, as some clients tend to exaggerate issues or there may be another side to the story.

3. If the problem at hand is not presenting a favorable outcome for your client, then help them visualize a more ideal situation. What do they really want out of the situation or offer? What were they expecting that did not occur? Once you understand their expectations, you can work to make them happen (within reason, of course).

4.   Once you have formulated a plan of action to satisfy the client, communicate that solution in a manner that helps your client come to a decision. Whether the customer wants to make a purchase or not, as a network marketer, you must help them come to that conclusion. You do not want a sales deal to become stagnant with indecisiveness. So, act and create a resolution.

While this process may seem relatively obvious, there are enough salesmen who practice the exact opposite tactics. They do not invest in their customer's experience and lose sales and clients because of it.

Optimism

If you do not believe that you will sell your product, then you will not make any sales. Tony Robbins once said that pessimists are realists while optimists are dreamers; but optimists also tend to reach higher and succeed with their goals, while pessimists will make less progress and settle. When things go bad during a sales pitch, or you just had a bad day in general, a sense of optimism will help you maintain emotional balance. A sense of optimism also keeps you from being thrown off if one sales effort goes awry. If your first sales call of the day goes wrong, then your performance with every other client has the potential to be affected. Keep your mind focused on the present and optimistic about the outcome of each sales effort, then your day will be filled with positive results and your attitude unhindered. Remember that every sales pitch is different; so, if the first one goes bad, then the next one will be much better. There are dozens of opportunities to make sales and become an even better salesman.

The Traits of a Great Salesman

- Caring about the client's interests
- Being Confident
- Always being on your game
- Being open and extroverted
- Listening to your client's needs
- Forming great multitasking skills
- Leading by example
- Engaging every situation with a positive attitude
- Remaining focused and in the present
- Staying organized
- Utilizing existing relationships to make sales
- Knowing your product
- Finding ways to go the extra mile
- Taking initiative
- Willing to learn from mentors and peers
- Staying passionate about your products and services
- Great time management skills
- Is relatable to clients

Practice Makes Perfect

1. Reciting positive affirmations

One of the worst ways to ruin a sales pitch is psyching yourself out before ever contacting a client. Your day should be filled with positive affirmations and self-assurance that you are more than capable of achieving your goals and making sales. Practice controlling your inner dialog by using affirmations that are phrased in the present, personal, and optimistic tense.

- I can do this!

- I feels great!

- I am a great salesman!

- I know I will make this sale!

- I may not have sold a product to this person, but I will make the next one!

We can control our emotions and the outcome of situations by keeping ourselves in a positive mindset. If you do not consciously try to keep yourself in a positive and optimistic state of mind, then your worry and anxiety will manifest into reality and your potential sales will suffer.

1. Using Positive Visualizations to Manifest Your Goals

One of the useful abilities is being able to visualize your goals as something that you have already achieved. Close your eyes and envision a clear and inspiring picture of your goal and ideal life to keep you motivated and working hard. Replay this image in your mind until you begin to see these goals manifest into your reality.

2.   Surround Yourself with Positive People

The people you spend the most time with affect who you are and the personality traits you develop. Your friends or family member's mood can influence yours in a negative way. Try watching YouTube videos and listening to podcasts by successful and motivational people: like Tony Robbins, Zig Ziglar, or Les Brown. These businessmen know what it takes to become a powerful force in the sales world, as well as the skills needed to influence people to believe in you and your product.

Chapter 8 Relationship Marketing

Relationship Marketing is a method of marketing a company's goods and services directly to consumers. Rather than spending millions upon millions of dollars trying to differentiate themselves from every other company and product in the marketplace an RM company works directly with distributors who are interested in their products. The RM business opportunity arises when distributors share the product and opportunity with those with whom they have or develop a relationship.

Monies the RM company would have directed to advertising, sales and distribution in the traditional system are instead channeled into supporting their expanding customer and distributor base.

A legitimate RM company understands that long-term relationships built with their current distributors and customers will lead to many more folks purchasing the company's products and joining the company for the RM opportunity. They do everything possible to support customers and distributors and to have maximum commissions and bonuses in order to attract other like-minded customers and distributors.

The Relationship Marketing business model is built on people's relationships and designed for an individual's success.

Relationship Marketing is an exciting business. It has the Power for anyone, regardless of current income, education, geographic location, ethnicity, gender, or limited financial resources, to provide long-term security for themselves and their family. Relationship Marketing is not a quick way to wealth. For those willing to work hard and assist others to build their dreams the rewards will far exceed any dream they may have imagined.

Comparison of Traditional Business to Relationship Marketing

Relationship Marketing provides a path to success that is very different than traditional business. For hundreds of millions of people traditional business no longer provides the security that it has in the past. The vast differences between Relationship Marketing and Traditional Business require explanation and understanding.

There are four huge differences between Traditional Business and Relationship Marketing.

1.) Cost of Entry. In a Traditional business merely to open the doors and before the first product is sold can require tens of thousands, hundreds of thousands, even millions or, tens of millions of dollars. In contrast, you may become a Distributor with a Relationship Marketing company for $500 or less.

2.) Profitability. In a Traditional Business ongoing and regardless of sales or general economic realities, payroll, taxes and other expenses must be paid each month. The company must survive long enough to become profitable. In your own Relationship Marketing business profitability can occur quickly as your cost of entry can be easily recouped and ongoing expenses are minimal and commensurate with your ongoing efforts.

3.) Owner's Income. Initially, the Traditional Business owner(s) may make little to no income as all monies are re-invested into the business. If the company succeeds ownership will often make ten to one hundred times or more the income of those the company employs. Ownership and key employees may also receive stock options and other benefits/perks that a typical employee will not receive. A Relationship Marketing distributor develops their business team and consequently can earn far more than is ever possible in a Traditional Business, even for the Owner.

4.) Personnel. In a Traditional Business the largest expenditures are often costs associated with personnel. Labor, employee benefits and taxes must be paid weekly/monthly. In your own Relationship Marketing business, you'll pay personal income tax on what you earn, but you have no employees.

Analyzing at a greater level of detail let's examine two critical business concepts, Residual Income and Time Duplication, and see how they operate within each business model.

1.) Residual Income. Monies paid for past accomplishments. Residual Income is a powerful method for earning significant income, yet most people will never experience its income potential.

A.) Traditional Business. Unless you are an Author, Composer, Actor, or, Inventor, you will likely never receive residual income. This most powerful income generator which those in the know strive for and demand that it be in their contracts, for you, is never even a possibility.

Yet even for those few who qualify, those obligated to contractually pay it attempt to restrict it as much as possible in that Residual Income is often paid instead of Immediate Income or at least is offset by a lower income. Legalese is employed to limit wherever possible the granting of Residual Income. Additionally, there may be a long wait for it to be received. Finally, there are often disputes as to how it is calculated and when it is to be paid. It can be an attorney's dream to sort it all out.

But why is it so hard to receive Residual Income when the contract so diligently negotiated delineates all the appropriate terms? The paying party knowing how lucrative this can become makes every attempt to limit its effect. Having already received your efforts which led to the song, book, movie, or invention – (whatever it is that you do), they have no more need of you. While they once saw residual income as an inducement to get you to provide your talents and expertise, once you provided your service, they no longer see you as a necessary expense. The "payers" thought process changes drastically. Why pay you afterward? Does the contract mean what it says or at least what you believed it to say? Maybe it does, maybe it doesn't. Why don't we just let an arbitrator or court sort it out? Often the receiving party must resort to a lawsuit to enforce the contract.

Thus, while both parties recognize the power of Residual Income their self-interest is at odds with each other. Having given of their efforts many find they must now go to arbitration or court to enforce the contract, hoping the arbitrator or justice system will see it their way. They are fighting a corporation with unlimited resources compared to their own simply to obtain that which they thought they had protected in an "ironclad" contract.

B.) Relationship Marketing. In stark contrast to the above scenario, Relationship Marketing is specifically designed to reward successful people for past accomplishments. Perhaps the most significant difference is that Residual Income is available to all, (after advancement to the specified levels), paid monthly and in addition to immediate income. The company has every incentive to pay Residual Income as quickly as possible for they need people to be successful and for it to be known publicly, to provide a successful example for others to follow.

This highly public recognition is critical in order that the company may prove they are an ethical, moral company which performs precisely as it says. This principled perception is essential to future growth. If an RM company did not honor its obligations and behaved in the manner outlined in the traditional business discussion it would not long be in business. Their duplicity would quickly become known. No leader would stay, and they would take their teams with them to another company.

Unlike a traditional business wherein each instance of developing a contract containing Residual Income is individually negotiated and thus hidden from sight, in a Relationship Marketing business qualifying requirement for achieving Residual Income are published for all to see. If modifications are made, they pertain to all.

THE UNIMPEACHABLE PRINCIPLES OF TIME

- No matter how hard you work only a finite amount of time is available
- Time passes no matter what you do
- Time can never be re-captured
- Time Freedom, the ability to do not what you MUST do but what you would LIKE to do is both rare and precious

2.) Time Duplication. Time Duplication through enlisting the efforts of others is utilized by and critical to the success of both Traditional Business and Relationship Marketing business models.

A.) Traditional Business. In a Traditional Business time duplication is limited to a multiplying factor of the number of employees and their available hours of labor and/or subcontractors.

To increase output a traditional business may hire sub-contractors, demand a higher work effort from employees, or, hire additional employees. Each alternative has associated costs. Benefits (profits) accrue directly to the Business Owners/Shareholders who since they took the financial risk take the resultant benefits.

As an employee, you are on your own. If you are unable to work, your income ceases. If you are laid off (the modern term is down-sized, now doesn't that sound better?) perhaps unemployment insurance will last until you find your next job. Hopefully this will be accomplished quickly as most people do not have a reservoir of savings upon which to rely. There isn't any guarantee that the next job will pay as well as the one you just left.

In either case whether unemployment is short-term or lasts years, drastic changes will need to be made to hold on to your house, car(s), feed your family or continue to pay for your children's higher education.

Disability and an economic downturn can affect anyone (to varying degrees). The rich stay rich or relatively so. The rest must scramble.

B.) Relationship Marketing. Time Duplication in Relationship Marketing occurs on an exponential basis. This corresponds directly to the wealth available for distribution. For those that choose to work hard, Relationship Marketing has a huge potential advantage, one that Traditional Business can never overcome.

In Relationship Marketing, Time Duplication occurs when you share your product and opportunity with others. Customers purchase directly from you and may refer others. Those you sponsor build their own organization by also sharing and selling product to customers and sponsoring others, thus earning income for themselves. The benefits (immediate and residual income) of building your organization (time duplication) accrue directly to you.

This Is A Pyramid!

Some people shy away from Relationship Marketing because they have been told it is a Pyramid.

If a traditional business is large enough there is a CEO, President, Executive Vice President, Senior Vice President, Vice President, mid-level Management and Employees. This corresponds directly in Relationship Marketing to yourself as the CEO, the top level of the pyramid and those in your downline filling your first line of Associates, those they sponsor filling your second line, third line, fourth line, etc. This can go many levels deep encompassing hundreds, thousands even tens of thousands of distributors all contributing to some degree to your success.

As in Traditional Business, Relationship Marketing has adopted the Pyramid.

In a Traditional Business you are highly unlikely to rise to the top. There are only so many management positions open. Favoritism or nepotism may mean more than ability in determining job position and compensation. Union contracts set production standards that you are not to exceed. Your compensation is often no higher than those who contribute minimal effort. Promotion and pay are determined by the success of the overall effort. You only have a small part in the overall picture and certainly cannot unless you are in sales (and often not even then), determine your pay. Raises when given are at annual intervals and often not adequate to your contribution. Recognition for a job well done is largely non-existent. You may be laid off or fired for reasons beyond your control. The job itself may be mind-numbingly repetitive.

Even if highly dissatisfied with your job you may be reluctant to change jobs. You have already learned that the grass is not necessarily greener at another company.

The traditional business model is not built for the individual's success. It is successful because it is the most efficient form in which to manage people. Goals are set at the top and everyone has their assigned job that contributes to the whole.

Think of a beehive – the ultimate in rational management practice. The Queen bee has a single purpose, to birth bees that contribute in many ways to the viability of the hive; construction, repair, exploration, gathering pollen, heat regulation (too hot or too cold and the hive dies), protection, raising the young and not the least of which is the care and feeding of the Queen herself. When a Queen dies the bee, colony selects another to fill this role.

Chapter 9   Mistakes New Networker Made

Any business venture you are interested in has pitfalls, disadvantages, and advantages. The key is to turn potential disadvantages into nothing and gain success. One way to find success in network marketing is to avoid the common mistakes people make. The information included here is a list of the most common mistakes people make when they begin their network marketing career.

Taking Advice from the Wrong People

There are various individuals you will want and need to talk to before you take the plunge into network marketing.

Your family and friends' group are people who will love to offer you advice and opinions. But, before you make decisions on what they have to say, consider what they know.

Has anyone in your family or friends circle owned a business? Has anyone tried network marketing? What are their opinions and how do those align with yours?

As an example, there was a college student who wanted to change schools. She was worried about income in the new location because she would not have a job right away. She was also going to live off campus. She thought signing up for Mary Kay might be the right thing to do to ensure some income would be coming her way.

After speaking with her family, she thought about the work involved. It would take an effort to build a client list in the new city. She would not have family or friends in the new city to help her. College students are on a tight budget, so income from that circle of people would not work. Furthermore, it was in a time before internet market was huge. Her effort would involve socializing, something that is difficult when taking 16 credits a semester. She is also an introvert, so socializing is not really her thing.

Weighing the time and effort required, the lack of support system, and her own personality—she knew network marketing would not work for her. Family helped point this out.

Your family and friends may also be able to help in this manner. Sometimes negative opinions about a situation can help you see the truth. It can also push you to succeed where others thought you could not.

However, do not shut down the advice, listen, consider it, and then decide if their opinion is worth following. People who do not know a lot about network marketing may have the wrong impression. They may think it is all fraud schemes. They may also warn against it because they have never had a business and do not like the sounds of the investment required.

Research and talking with the right people are the best way to avoid this mistake.

The right people to talk to are those who have been involved in network marketing. It is also best to talk with people in the company, not just the person trying to sign you up, but also other representatives. Yes, it can sound great when statistics are being bandied about. But, are the statistics only about the top sellers or are you given a clear picture of the possible income?

The more you research and speak with people in the network marketing industry, the more you will understand the details, the possibilities, and the effort needed to succeed.

Not Taking Your Choice Seriously

How do you currently make money? Have you ever sold products through cold calling or door-to-door? Network marketing is different from retail, restaurant, and other career options. You can get started immediately, with very little training. It is also freelance, with flexible hours.

It can give you a view that you do not have to be serious about the work and the effort you put into the marketing work. Nothing could be further from the truth. You need to expend more energy with network marketing, than in your typical career. You still need to be serious about your choice.

All your determination, time management, organization, and career skills are necessary to succeed. The minute you forget to take network marketing seriously—is the minute you make peanuts for the effort you put in.

To take network marketing seriously, you must commit to making sales through the various avenues open to you. These avenues include website management, social media marketing, content marketing, and word-of-mouth sales. Every avenue you must make a sale is one you need to utilize, even if it means chatting up a stranger in the supermarket when they ask you about your product bag.

In fact, you will be given a kit by the network marketing company, as well as incentives for reaching sales goals. Sometimes this means you get a purse, bag, pin, or other display item you can carry with you. Phone cases are even handed out through some network marketing companies. These items are conversation starters.

Choosing the Wrong Network Marketing Company

There are quite a few network marketing companies out there. Some have a long history like Avon, Mary Kay, and Doterra of delivering quality products. Other companies are not as transparent, and they do not have a long history to back up their reputation.

It does not mean all of them are bad. It does mean that some of them are not transparent and could be selling you on an idea that is not going to work out.

The amount of research you do is going to determine your success in network marketing. If you do not fully research the company, you could end up losing money instead of making it. Rather than put yourself in that position, here are some things to ask when viewing a company from a business aspect:

How long has the company been in business?

What is their marketing plan? How do you sell goods, what do you start with, and how much advertising do they do?

If there is an affiliate part to the network, i.e. recruiting members that are under your representation, what are the incentives? Do you earn bonuses if you make certain sales? Mary Kay used to provide a new car to their sales people if they reached a certain mark. The mark was both for selling products and recruiting new members.

Are there already representatives in your area? How many people work in the same location? Does the market warrant another person selling the same products?

Do you have a market you can sell to, even if there are too many representatives marketing the same products?

Are there any Better Business Bureau complaints? Any news articles against the company? Is the news mostly positive?

The answers to those questions are going to determine if your endeavor is successful. Companies that want to hide the truth or do not provide enough information at the beginning are usually not giving you the best opportunity.

If there are too many complaints about a company, there may be issues. No business is perfect, but you do not need to set yourself up for failure due to the wrong choices.

Beginning the Work with Improper Expectations

What are your expectations? What are your goals? It is reasonable to have goals. It is also important that you plan. However, there are certain expectations that can make you give up before you truly start.

Write out your goals. This will help you see what you want from your business endeavor. Do these goals align with the benefits mentioned in 2? If so, then you are on track, but you still need realistic expectations.

Benefits and goals are a good place to start and assess what the business can do for you. As you examine companies—ask yourself—does the company have the same goals as you? Do they provide a quality product you know you can sell? Are there any benefits or goals you cannot meet with the companies that are top on your list?

Companies are not going to provide you with every benefit. Sometimes they cannot, but if you can find a company that fits most of the benefits and goals you have, it is possible to be happy. It is like any job or career you choose, there are downsides. If you know what those downsides are, you can have realistic expectations.

The main area that many people fall short of when assessing a company and determining their goals is the income, they can generate with the network marketing company they have chosen.

A lot of companies try to bring you in by promising the top sales projections. But you must understand the effort and time it takes for you to reach those goals. It is not an easy process. It does not happen overnight. You may find that you cannot reach the top sales goals, and possibly there will not be enough income generated from the company for other reasons.

The internet breeds half-truths and incorrect information. Some companies also want you to be extremely excited, so you will sign up to be a network marketer. They share with you all the success stories of getting a brand-new car worth $20,000, their sales people making $50,000 per year, and neglect to tell you that is 1% of the marketers in the company. Most of their members never reaches the new car or more than $10,000 per year, if that much.

Only the effort you are willing to put into network marketing will determine how much you can make. If you host one party per month, with two of five people buying on a regular basis, you are not going to make more than a few hundred dollars.

Realistic expectations require you to commit to the career for more than a little income, if you have the desire to reach a decent, full-time income.

Choosing Business Partners Incorrectly

Network marketing does use a team. There are teams in each of the major cities who have been recruited by one main person. If you have business partners who are unwilling to sell or stop selling because they are not making enough, this will hurt your incentives; thus, your bottom line. You want to trust the company you work for and the people recruiting your or being recruited by you.

Giving Up without Proper Effort

Effort, it seems to always come back to the effort. But it is the truth, the more effort you put into your network marketing choices—the more you make. If you are not committed to putting in social effort to gain new clients, then you won't make a lot. Yes, it is nice to get discounts and a little income here and there, but if you really want to make money as a network marketer—you need to put in the effort.

Choose a company after careful research.

Pay the upfront costs for the kit and website, if there is one.

If you do not get a website, sign up for one and create your own. You can also use social media platforms for this instead of having a separate hosted site.

Begin following people on social media.

Let your family and friends know you are a company representative.

Start hosting events with the people in your life.

Let the word spread that you sell products via these events and social media.

Keep repeating the process and eventually you will gain stability.

It is when you fail to keep repeating the process of reminding friends, family, and coworkers that you have certain products that you will lose your customers.

Remember customer retention is about keeping your products in the minds of people. The more effort you put in, the more you will be rewarded.

Chapter 10   Develop Your Leadership

- Continually Practice Being a Better Leader

When you are building your business, you want to continually practice being a better leader. Always focus on your leadership abilities and look for opportunities to expand your success as a leader. You should remain dedicated to your own success, as well as the success of others. Take the time to acquire feedback from your team, complete leadership-oriented training seminars, and classes, and continue studying what successful leaders are doing in business. Remember, you can take leadership advice from people beyond the network marketing world. A powerful leader is a powerful leader, and they all have excellent advice and information for you to adapt for your own business. The more time you invest in becoming a powerful leader, the greater your business is going to grow.

- Take Part in the Existing Team as Well

If you built your business properly, you likely have a great team above you already. Your upline likely has a great team who are supportive and models many of the qualities that you want your own team to have. In the beginning, you can use this as an opportunity to provide massive support for your new recruits. You can add your new recruits to your own business group, as well as to any groups hosted by your upline.

Encourage them to become active in your group but remind them that your upline has a strong existing support team available as well.

Additionally, take part in the team that exists above you. Take the time to bond with other leaders, and other members who are at the same level as you are. This will give you the opportunity to expand your own team's resources, gain information about how you can succeed as a leader, and otherwise encourage the success of your business.

It is likely that your upline has spent a long-time generating success in their own business, so taking advantage of the support and culture that they have already built. This is a great way to network for your business and increase your ability to expand the success of your own team.

Take Advantage of New Marketing Opportunities

Over time, new marketing opportunities are rapidly becoming available. In the past, parties, word of mouth, and business cards were major marketing opportunities for people in network marketing companies. Nowadays, social media is where the bulk of the business is done. Over time, the strategies that are used to generate successful marketing campaigns evolve. Since you want to maintain a relevant and sustainable business, you want to take advantage of these new marketing opportunities as they arise.

While you don't need to spend every day invested in new marketing strategies, you should certainly revisit your marketing techniques every two to three months. This will allow you to notice the evolving trends in the online marketplace and get a good idea of what is sticking and what was a passing fad. The ones that stick are the ones that you want to invest in when it comes to your own business.

- Network, Network, Network!

You are running a network marketing company, after all! Networking is a major part of building your success in this business. You want to take the time to really learn how you can build genuine relationships with other people in your business and attract new people in. Learn what it takes to generate powerful relationships with your customers, your potentials, your team members, and anyone else associated with your business.

Networking gives you the opportunity to gain new ideas, share your business opportunity, and get your product in front of more people. The more you focus on networking, the more success you will have in your business. People are attracted to a charismatic leader who is social and who can make everyone feel comfortable and welcomed into the business. Whether you are already a natural at this or you need to build your networking skills, it is worth noting.

If you are unsure as to where you can start, a good idea is to join niche-specific groups and business-oriented groups with many like-minded people. You can communicate with other business owners and others who are passionate in your niche and start building relationships. This can be done through online groups, or through offline groups. Either way, be very intentional about where you commit your time and devote your time and attention to these areas. For example, if you join an online group make sure that you spend a few minutes each day communicating with the members inside of the group. This will ensure that they know who you are and can spark a curiosity in them to learn more about what you do and what your business is all about.

Networking is the backbone of your business, so you need to practice with it. You should also teach your team to do the same. The more successful you are with networking, the more success you are going to have overall.

- Make a Schedule and Stick to It

Having a business schedule can be very helpful when it comes to running your own business, especially one with a larger team. It can be easy to get overwhelmed with work or become uncertain about where you want to devote your time to each day. By making a schedule, you can ensure that you know what to do each day. Make your schedule realistic and easy to accomplish so that you can stay on top of it each day. Keep your tasks intentional, and make sure you focus on money-building and team-building tasks that are going to have a large impact on your business.

Some things you might want to include on your schedule include:

- Networking
- Team-building activities
- Training and live conference calls
- Live events
- New offers and opportunities

- New free offerings (unique to your personal business)

Every successful business runs on a schedule. You should also include your "opening" hours so that you know when your working hours are, and when they aren't. This means that you can focus on business-building activities during working hours and that you disconnect and focus on your personal life when it is not business hours.

Stay Focused on Morale

The morale of your brand and your team is important. The morale you boost on your team will have a heavy influence on your success in the business overall. Make sure that you are regularly promoting a positive, energetic, and success-oriented morale in your team. If you notice that your morale is falling low, that certain team members aren't getting along, or that you aren't having the type of impact you want to have, it is time to act and build success in your business.

As the leader, it is your job to take control of the morale being generated by the business and really make sure that everyone is feeling excited and energetic about their own businesses. The more you can encourage people to stay positive and focused, the more success you will have in your business overall.

- Build Leaders

When you are building your business, focus on building leaders as well. Take notice of the go-getter style members on your team and really encourage them to take a leadership role. These are the members who are most likely to be able to generate their own successful teams, and they are the ones who are going to be dedicated to the success of everyone overall.

Some ways you can build your leaders include through inviting them to host live training events for your team, giving them unique and personalized 1:1 training to help them excel as leaders, and helping them build their own teams. Unlike the other members who you are coaching to succeed as business owners, you want to coach these members to become business executives. These are the members that are more likely to grow massive teams, just as you are. The more successful they are at growing these teams, the more successful you will be. This is an important part of the business.

- Nurture Your Personal Life

One important way to remain successful in business is to maintain your personal life. Many people join network marketing companies because it affords them the freedom to be their own bosses and thus, to take the time in their day to enjoy it in any way that they like. People don't want to see that you are working harder in your network marketing business than you ever did at your regular job because then they are not going to be attracted to the network marketing lifestyle.

Instead, they want to see that you are having fun and living your life. They want to see that you are enjoying the freedom that they are seeking to experience in their own lives. Ultimately, they want to see you sharing the adventures you go on, the hours you spend relaxing, and the way you enjoy your time with family and friends. People are nosy, and they want to see directly into your life. They want to know that you are modeling the life they want to live because then they know that you will know exactly how to help them do the same. They want a leader who is actively leading the life they desire to have.

- Keep It Simple

Many people might feel convinced that they must go to extensive lengths to establish a business model that will help them succeed. They feel as though they must fulfill complex strategies and roles in order to have a network marketing company that will be effective and bring in both passive and linear income. The reality is, this is not true. In fact, the aim is to keep it simple. The simpler your business structures are, the more success you will be able to generate with them.

Remember: you want to be a leader, sell products, and grow your team. That is all. You want to take the time to invest in strategies that are going to help you succeed with these efforts and strategies. The more focused you are on these strategies, the more success you are going to have. You do not need to waste your time investing in complex and advanced strategies that are unlikely to acquire larger results than the easier strategies. These types of techniques will simply generate success and leave you feeling burnt out and confused about where to go in your business.

- Stay Motivated

As with any business, there are going to be periods in your network marketing company where things are "down" or not as productive as normal. In fact, many people experience a "down" period right out the gate. While you are building your structures, spreading your message, and becoming known for your business, it can be slow rolling. Some people come out of the gate hot, but not everyone does. In fact, most people find that it takes six to twelve months for them to add their first team member. This is not unusual, and it is not the reason for you to quit.

The more dedicated you remain and the more consistent you are at building your systems and structures and creating a successful business, the more sustainable your business will be. You always want to pay attention to the "tomorrow" in your business. Sometimes, the "today" may not look bright, and that is okay. Every business has ups and downs, and every business takes time to grow. The more you remain consistent and focused on your growth and success, the more you and your team will experience. Stay dedicated and do what you must in order to stay motivated.

Chapter 11 Absorb Best Strategies and Tricks from Top Network Marketers on The Market

We will use differentiation strategies to develop and market unique products for different customer segments. To differentiate ourselves from the competition, we will focus on the assets, creative ideas and competencies that we have that none of our competitors has.

The goal of our differentiation strategies is to be able to charge a premium price for our unique medical transportation products and services and/or to promote loyalty and assist in retaining our customers.

Differentiation in our medical transportation business will be achieved in the following types of ways, including:

- Product

- Complementary services

- Technology embodied in design

- Location

- Service innovations

- Superior service

- Creative advertising

- Better supplier relationships

Differentiating will mean defining who our perfect target market is and then catering to their needs, wants and interests better than everyone else. It will be about using surveys to determine what's most important to our targeted market and giving it to them consistently. It will not be about being "everything to everybody"; but rather, "the absolute best to our chosen targeted group".

In developing our differentiation strategy will we use the following form to help define our differences:

- Targeted customer segments

- Customer characteristics

- Customer demographics

- Customer behavior

- Geographic focus

- Ways of working

- Service delivery approach

- Customer problems/pain points

- Complexity of customers' problems

- Range of services

We will use the following approaches to differentiate our products and services from those of our competitors to standardized offerings:

- Advanced technological features
- Engineering design or styling
- Additional product features
- An image of prestige or status
- Specific Differentiators will include the following:
- Being a Specialist in one procedure
- Utilizing advanced/uncommon technology
- Possessing extensive experience
- Building an exceptional facility
- Consistently achieving superior results
- Having a caring and empathetic personality
- Giving customer's WOW experience, including a professional customer welcome package.
- Enabling convenience and 24/7 online accessibility
- Calling customers to express interest in their challenges.
- Keeping to the appointment schedule.
- Remembering customer names and details like they were family

- Assuring customer fears.

- Building a visible reputation and recognition around our community

- Acquiring special credentials or professional memberships

- Providing added value services, such as taxi service, longer hours, financing plans, and post-sale services.

Primary Differentiation Strategies:

1. We will supply information about "hidden" commercial charges, such as fuel surcharges, vehicle charges and rental equipment as part of our estimate so there are no unexpected surprises.

2. We will utilize software tracking systems to continuously monitor all transports, and provide online access to customer transaction history, preference profile and information about all the services of interest to that client.

3. We will enable the online and fax ordering of our services.

We will develop a referral program that turns our clients into referral agents.

5. We will use regular client satisfaction surveys to collect feedback, improvement ideas, referrals and testimonials.

6. We will promote our "green" practices, such as establishing a recycling program, purchasing recycled-content office goods, using bio-diesel fuels and responsibly handling hazardous wastes.

7. We will customize our offerings according to the language, cultural influences, customs, interests and preferences of our local market to create loyalty and increase sales.

8. We will develop the expertise to satisfy the needs of targeted market segments with customized and exceptional support services.

9. We will proudly feature our low (10%) driver turnover rate, Out of Service Rates well below the National Average, a zero Accident Frequency Rate and a Satisfactory Safety Rating.

10. We will promote our same day pick-up services.

11. We will install a software system that not only tracks our vehicles, but also projects where the vehicle will most likely be needed over the next few days.

Our online marketing strategy will employ the following distinct mechanisms:

1. Search Engine Submission

This will be most useful to people who are unfamiliar with (company name) but are looking for a local Medical Transportation Company. There will also be searches from customers who may know about us, but who are seeking additional information.

2. Website Address (URL) on Marketing Materials

Our URL will be printed on all marketing communications, business cards, letterheads, faxes, and invoices and product labels. This will encourage a visit to our website for additional information

3. Online Directories Listings

We will try to list our website on relevant, free and paid online directories and manufacturer website product locators.

The good online directories possess the following features:

- Free or paid listings that do not expire and do not require monthly renewal.

- Ample space to get your advertising message across.

- Navigation buttons that are easy for visitors to use.

- Optimization for top placement in the search engines based on keywords that people typically use to find medical transportation companies.

- Direct links to your website, if available.

- An ongoing directory promotion campaign to maintain high traffic volumes to the directory site. Ex: www.fleetdirectory

4. Strategic Business Partners

We will use a Business Partners page to cross-link to prominent (city) area web sites as well as the city Web sites and local recreational sites. We will also cross-link with brand name leasing companies and parts suppliers.

5. YouTube Posting

We will produce a video of testimonials from several of our satisfied clients and educate viewers as to the range of our medical transportation services. Our research indicates that the YouTube video will also serve to significantly improve ranking with the Google Search Engine.

6. Exchange of links with strategic marketing partners.

We will cross-link to non-profit businesses that accept our gift certificate and free Medical Transportation Services as donations for in-house run contest prize awards.

7. E-Newsletter

Use the newsletter sign-up as a reason to collect email addresses and limited profiles and use embedded links in the newsletter to return readers to website.

8. Create an account for your photos on Flickr

Use the name of your site on Flickr so you have the same keywords and your branded. To take full advantage of Flickr, we will use a JavaScript-enabled browser and install the latest version of the Macromedia Flash Player.

9. Geo Target Pay Per Click (PPC) Campaign

Available through Google AdWords program. Example keywords include interstate medical transportation, logistics services, transport services, long- distance medical transportation, local Medical Transportation Services, wheelchair transport and (city).

10. Post messages on Internet user groups and forums.

Get involved with medical transportation related discussion groups and forums and develop a descriptive signature paragraph.

11. Write up your own Myspace and Facebook bios.

Highlight your background and professional interests.

12. Facebook Brand-Building Applications:

As a Facebook member, we will create a specific Facebook page for our business through its "Facebook Pages" application. This page will be used to promote who we are and what we do. We will use this page to post alerts when we have new articles to distribute, news to announce, etc. Facebook members can then become fans of our page and receive these updates on their newsfeed as we post them.

We will create our business page by going to the "Advertising" link on the bottom of our personal Facebook page. We will choose the "Pages" tab at the top of that page, and then choose "Create a Page." We will upload our logo, enter our company profile details, and establish our settings. Once completed, we will click the "publish your site" button to go live. We will also promote our Page everywhere we can. We will add a Facebook link to our website, our email signatures, and email newsletters. We will also add Facebook to the marketing mix by deploying pay-per-click ads through their advertising application. With

Facebook advertising, we will target by specifying sex, age, relationship, location, education, as well as specific keywords. Once we specify our target criteria, the tool will tell us how many members in the network meet our target needs.

13. Blog to share our success stories and solicit comments

Blogging will be a great way for us to share information, expertise, and news, and start a conversation with our customers, the media, suppliers, and any other target audiences. Blogging will be a great online marketing strategy because it keeps our content fresh, engages our audience to leave comments on specific posts, improves search engine rankings and attracts links. In the blog we will share fun drink recipes and party tips. We will also provide a link to us

14. Other Embedded Links

We will use social networking, article directory postings and press release web sites as promotional tools and to provide good inbound link opportunities.

15. Issue Press Release

We will create online press releases to share news about our new website.

We plan to implement the following strategies to reduce our start-up business risk:

- Implement our business plan based on go, no-go stage criteria.

- Develop employee cross-training programs.

- Regularly back-up all computer files/Install ant-virus software.

- Arrange adequate insurance coverage with higher deductibles.

- Develop a limited number of prototype samples.

- Test market offerings to determine level of market demand and

- appropriate pricing strategy.

- Thoroughly investigate and benchmark to competitor offerings.

- Research similar franchised businesses for insights into

- successful prototype business/operations models.

- Reduce operation risks and costs by flowcharting all structured systems & standardized manual processes.

- Use market surveys to listen to customer needs and priorities.

- Purchase used equipment to reduce capital outlays.

- Use leasing to reduce financial risk.

- Outsource manufacturing to job shops to reduce capital at risk.

- Use subcontractors to limit fixed overhead salary expenses.

- Ask manufacturers about profit sharing arrangements.

- Pay advertisers with a percent of revenues generated.

- Develop contingency plans for identified risks.

- Set-up procedures to control employee theft.

- Do criminal background checks on potential employees.

- Take immediate action on delinquent accounts.

- Only extend credit to established account with D&B rating

- Get regular competitive bids from alternative suppliers.

- Check that operating costs as a percent of rising sales are lower as a result of productivity improvements.

- Request bulk rate pricing on fast medical transportation supplies.

- Don't tie up cash in slow medical transportation inventory to qualify for bigger discounts.

- Reduce financial risk by practicing cash flow policies.

- Reduce hazard risk by installing safety procedures.

- Use financial management ratios to monitor business vitals.

- Make business decisions after brainstorming sessions.

- Focus on the products with biggest return on investment.

- Where possible, purchase off-the-shelf components.

- Request manufacturer samples and assistance to build prototypes.

- Design production facilities to be flexible and easy to change.

- Develop a network of suppliers with outsourcing capabilities.

- Analyze and shorten every cycle time, including product development.

- Develop multiple sources for every important input.

- Treat the business plan as a living document and update it frequently.

- Conduct a SWOT analysis and use determined strengths to pursue opportunities.

- Conduct regular customer satisfaction surveys to evaluate performance.

Chapter 12 Exploding the Reach of Your Network

So far, we have setting up your profile correctly to have it be as attractive as possible for potential connections. We also talked about laying down the foundation and the groundwork for searching for the right kind of groups to join and finding the right kind of people to bring into your network.

Now let's talk about strategies you can incorporate to make the most of your searches.

There is absolutely a method to my madness regarding how I grew my connections from 500 to 25,600 in 30 months, how I get 20 to 40 conversations per week, and how I enroll anywhere between two and six people per month.

I'm going to show you exactly what you need to do daily to make all of this happen. I'll go through it slowly because there is a process, and I'm going to explain some tools that you need to make this work effectively for you.

So, first things first. Start from your home screen.

The methodology begins with sending anywhere between 25 to 50 connections every single day. This is imperative because if you don't reach out, people won't know who you are. You can't expect people to reach out to you first. I know that to some people 25-50 connections per day may sound like a lot, but, if you want to have more conversations you have to grow a big network. Now when I say reach out to 25 to 50 connections every day, that doesn't mean that all of them will accept your request. That's 25 to 50 people that you're looking to connect with who are the right fit for you that will enable you to grow a big network. With, I'm going to take you through my daily habit of what I do to connect with my network.

I'm a big believer in being genuine and authentic, and not having to pay for leads if it's not necessary. I also believe everyone is on LinkedIn to network for the right purpose, especially for a network marketing business. We are here to create real conversations with real people to grow a real network for your business.

The first thing to do when you wake up in the morning is to have a marker of where your most recent connections are. You'll need to click on "My Network". This is going to bring up a couple different things. It's going to bring in some people who are looking to connect with you. It's also going to bring up the "People You May Know", which I'm going to get into. But the most important thing is your connections, and what you're going to do is you're going to click on "See All". What this is going to do is going to bring up your connections and it is going to is show you "Most Recently Added".

Now, the idea is to keep track of your new connections and to find out who they are, because your new connections are your new leads. Now, for example purposes only, we're going to pretend that you went to "My

Network" and you clicked on "See All". Let's say that Rick Arthur was your most recent connection. So, what you're going to do is get out a piece of paper, and you're going to write on the top "Most Recent Connection" and add rows for Monday, Tuesday, Wednesday, etc., and then you're going to put Rick's name for whatever day you found him.

So, this is going to be your marker. You need to have a line in the sand to know exactly where you need to work up from. Your most recent connections are at the very top. Your older connections that you've connected with are below them. Now you have your marker.

Here's my connecting style. On Monday, Wednesday and Friday I do specific searches, the reason being with the free version of LinkedIn you are only allowed 12 to 15 searches per month. If you've been on LinkedIn and tried doing searches before, you will get messages that say that you're getting close to your commercial limit for your searches. Trust me, I went through that. I was searching way too much.

So, Monday, Wednesday, and Friday, you're going to do specific searches, and on Tuesday, Thursday, Saturday, Sunday, your 25 to 50 connections sent are going to come from the "My Network" area. These are the people you may know, and they represent your first connections, which is your network. With the free version of LinkedIn, you can tap into them right away.

Let's run through an example. If it's Tuesday, I'm going to look for 25 to 50 people that I can connect with that fit my description of the mirror image of me, whether it's personal trainer, someone that's in health and wellness, or even gym owners—and I'm very, very specific.

Another thing that you want to look at is the mutual connections. The more mutual connections you have with a person, the more likely they're already connected to someone with your opportunity. Therefore, you want to look for someone that has a very, very small amount of shared connections. For me, that's typically 50 and less. That's just me because I have so many connections already. Your threshold can be more or even less than that, it's your preference.

To, on Tuesday I go through my 25 to 50 connections first thing in the morning, then I define my marker, and I'm done for the day because I sent out my 25 to 50 connections. On Wednesday morning, I go to my home page and check my most recent connections again. Now, we're going to click on "My Network", then we're going to click on "See All", and we're going to look through the list and find Rick. But now Rick is not on top anymore, because we notice, for example, that we have five new people. They now represent your brand-new leads and are your brand-new connections.

You then directly message them, and in the next will discuss what you will say in more detail. Remember that once you identified your new leads, the only name that you really must write down is this first name at the top of the list because that's your new marker. Let's say the person's name is Nancy. The next time you receive new connections, Nancy is now your new marker and every new connection above her name is a new lead.

Since it's Wednesday, this is one of your search days, so you're going to do a specific search. If you're going to do a specific search, let's say that you are a bookkeeper, but you also are in a health wellness beauty network marketing opportunity. So, you're going to type in "bookkeeper, wellness" and you're going to search. Now again, you're going to filter out by "People" and by second connections. If you don't get many results, you can broaden your search

The broader your search is, the more results you're going to get. So, you do your search, you get your results, you send out your 25 to 50 connections.

You wake up Thursday, you go back to "My Network", you go back to "See All", and you see who has appeared above Nancy, who was the person from the day before. So, this is a way to start accumulating leads. So, the first thing you always do is to get your marker and send messages, then the next thing you do is to get those 25 to 50 connections out, and you're just going to windshield wiper back and forth between those activities.

This is the basis for what you're going to do. It's 25 to 50 connections every day. On Monday, Wednesday, Friday you do specific searches. On Tuesday, Thursday, Saturday, Sunday, you grow "My Network".

Every day, you're sending out those 25 to 50 connections. That's the activity that will build your pipeline consistently.

In five, we're going to go over messaging those brand-new people, what to expect with responses, and what kind of scripts you can use that are genuine, authentic, and what you can say to them to get started.

Key Takeaways:

- Commit to doing something every day to build your network. Do searches on Mondays, Wednesdays, and Fridays. On Tuesdays, Thursday, Saturdays, and Sundays, send your connection messages. Respond to incoming messages every day.

- Do specific searches to find people with your shared interest and look for people with few shared connections. This increases the possibility that these people have not heard about your opportunity yet.

- Have a marker so that you can keep track of your recent connections. This will help you not skip any new connections or accidentally send an opening message to the same person more than once.

Chapter 13 Opportunities or Scam

Another stigma that has affected network marketing recruiting is that the business is full of scams and people trying to take your money. The business can get sticky when a company is more focused on hiring new recruits than selling the actual product or service. In this case, the network marketing company in question would be considered an illegal pyramid scheme. However, there are dozens of network marketing opportunities out there; so how do you know if a company is legitimate? The reason there are so many fraudulent companies out there is because network marketing enterprises are normally exempt from business opportunity regulation, and therefore are not classified as franchises under federal and state franchise laws. There are several signs that may give hint as to whether you can trust a marketing company. The following indicators are tell-tale signals that a business is not worth you are investing your time and money.

Network marketing scams seem ideal on paper because they feature get-rich-quick self-employment opportunities that allow you to run your own business. But these are just eye-catching features designed to lure you into paying up-front fees and finding other new people to join. Here's how to avoid falling victim to such scams and finding real business opportunities:

1. Do not plan on making money by recruiting other sales representatives

An entire company based on how many members you can get to join is one of the biggest multi-level marketing scams you can find. When most of the income you earn is from finding new members and getting them to join the program, it is known as a pyramid scheme. What makes a pyramid scheme seem so appealing is that you could potentially make an endless amount of money, all you need to earn an income is a few new recruitments. However, pyramid schemes are illegal and should be avoided at all costs.

2. Do not pay to be a part of a business opportunity

Unfortunately, there is a common saying in the business world that is designed to convince you to invest in whatever business opportunity comes your way: "it takes money to make money." However, forming your own network marketing side-business should not take hundreds of dollars out of your pocket. Any business that requires you to pay a membership fee or purchase a significant amount of their inventory before starting your own branch of the company is a scam. Not only does this scam thrive on your bank account, but also the wallets of anyone else you get to join. A legitimate company will work to meet the needs of the customers and only ask that you pay marketing and operational costs. This could mean purchasing a sample kit of whatever goods you will be selling; in which case, it is more than fair that you pay for the products you will be using to make sales. Membership fees for the privilege of starting up your own business is not normal. If you are being asked to pay multiple unnecessary fees, then this great opportunity is probably a scam.

3. Ask Difficult Questions

The most dangerous scams are the ones that seem like they provide an explanation to the simplest questions, so that you do not end up asking the members anything that may expose their illegal activity. There are several questions that you can ask to identify a scam and keep your bank account safe.

- Did a member contact you to inform you about the actual value and need for his or her product, or for the opportunity to make money?

- Is the product likely to successfully sell based on its qualities? Or does the product or service have to go through a multi-level marketing distribution system?

- Does the network marketing company focus on quality products that add value to the customer's life, or does it use trends and good timing, or special or secret formulas to sell their products?

- As a sales representative, can you make a significant income based on the time you spend selling the goods and services without having to recruit a new person to join the company?

- Would other distributors who hold a higher position than you be compensated with a payout with each sale you make, regardless of whether they were involved in making the sale?

- Are the prices of the products or services still competitive with similar products and services available through other sources? Does the company offer products that are inexpensive enough to make sales, but respectable enough for you to make money by selling it?

- Has the person who is attempting to recruit you been devious or forward about his or her attempts in getting you to join the company?

- Will you be compensated with free training programs, videos, conferences, and classes to prepare you for work? Or are you expected to pay for your training yourself, so that the company can make even more money?

Even with these careful questions, it can still be difficult to decipher which network marketing opportunities are legitimate, and which ones are scams. These false business fronts have been around for decades and have evolved into carefully planned schemes that seem impossible to expose. As more companies pop up on the internet, and new ways of communication come into play, there are very few times when you can immediately tell that a business is really a scam. And with so many people looking for opportunities to work from home and become self-sufficient, most optimistic aspiring entrepreneurs will overlook many tell-tale signs that signal a bad business opportunity. If you cannot find the answers to the questions listed above or are still unsure if a network marketing company is right for you, use the following criteria to help confirm your suspicions.

1. The company focuses more on recruiting members than selling their product…

The most prominent feature of a pyramid scheme is when members are required to recruit a certain number of people to join in order to get paid. A red flag that will quickly indicate a pyramid scheme is if a member is trying to recruit you to join the team, rather than attempting to sell you their product. Does it seem like the company is more focused on "building the sales team" than marketing the actual product? If it seems like recruits are the company's target customers, then you are most likely being pursued by a pyramid scheme.

2. If the company does not take the time to train you properly…

Why would a company not put a significant amount of time and effort into making sure their business is represented by the most efficient, successful, and informed team members? Because the product is not what brings in the money: new recruits are. If a network marketing company is offering you a chance to work for them, ask about the training they provide and the support you receive. If the team members are avoiding directly answering your questions, then you may be falling victim to a multi-level marketing scam. Does the company offer free training seminars and an employee support office to help solve any future issues once you start working? If the training phase does not focus on teaching you how to sell the product or you are required to pay for training, then this may be a scam.

> 3. If the company is pressuring, you to pay more money after you have joined…

Are higher-up team members pressuring you to invest more money into purchasing more of their products? Are you being asked to join a "fast track" or "elite" employee system that will help you buy a greater amount of inventory all at once, rather than paying for whatever products you need as you go? A real network marketing company is focused more on successfully selling the stock you already have, rather than having an endless supply of goods that are going unused and risk being sent back to storage. Any pressure to "invest" in better sales training or basic supplies is a sign that you may be in trouble with a scam. This is especially crucial to keep in mind when the company offers to help you out by putting your costs on a credit card, rather than only taking cash. They may try to convince you by assuring you that this is a business investment that will pay off in the end.

4. The network marketing opportunity seems too good to be true…

Unfortunately, there are only a handful of businesses in the entire world that have pure intentions and honest opportunities. So, if you find yourself looking at a job ad for a network marketer, or in a conversation with an employee of such a company, then ask yourself "is this too good to be true?" Are the representatives of the company attempting to convince you to join by praising the opportunity and talking about the "amazing" program, without having proof or enough information to back up their claims? If it seems too good to be true, then it is almost definitely a scam.

Important Social Networks

Welcome to the world of social media. In the past ten years, the communication landscape has been completely transformed. Although the old media is still around and frankly as big as ever, the attention of people is now split between many different communications technologies. And this is very good news for small businesses. The days of three network television stations and a couple of radio stations, which required a massive advertising budget to get any airtime, are long gone. In their place is a dynamic and easily accessible landscape where you can get followers and new customers without spending any money, and if you do spend money, you can use targeted advertising without breaking the bank.

The power to do targeted advertising is one of the most important reasons why your business should be on social media. You can zoom in on any demographic, location, or interest that is related to your business and your ideal customer. If you don't yet know your ideal customer, advertising on networks like Facebook is a great way to find out who they are.

The problem for many people in small business is they don't really know which social networks they should be using to reach their prospective audience. Second, they aren't sure how to reach that audience, even if they have some idea which social networks are the most powerful. We hope to demystify these issues in this book. Let's get started by looking at the most important social networks that you should be using to focus your attention.

Chapter 14 Important Social Networks

Social media has become incredibly diverse and fractionated. However, the major stalwarts remain where the action is. In our experience, Facebook, Instagram, and YouTube are King. In fact, these social media networks are so important that you could devote all your time to using these networks, and you'd get all the results that you want for your business.

That said, there are many social networks that can also be leveraged to bring in new customers. But which ones are worth bothering with? The first thing is that it depends.

Knowing who your ideal customer is will be one of the central things that you need to keep in mind with your business. Of course, you already knew that because everyone in marketing knows how important that concept is. When you know who your ideal customer is, then you can target them more easily and effectively.

The first thing you want to think about is what gender are you marketing to. Is your customer base primarily female, male, or a good mix of the two? How old is your typical customer? Are they 25, or 65? These are important things that need to be taken into consideration when using social media as a part of your marketing plan, because people of different ages, on average, can be found in different places. Let's look at the demographic data of some of the social media sites and apps.

Pinterest

If you read a lot of books on social media marketing, many of them are going to hype up Pinterest. And with good reason. According to the web traffic sit Similar Web, last month, Pinterest had an astounding 848 million visits. The bounce rate, which tells you how many people only look at one page and then leave, is about 43%, which is a pretty decent value. So, it sounds like you should be on Pinterest!

The reality is that it depends on what your business is about and who you are trying to reach. Let's start with gender. According to the Omni core Agency, 70% of Pinterest users are female. The trend has become a little more balanced in recent years, with 40% of new signups being male users, but that still leaves men in the minority on the site. If you are marketing products that are of interest to men or to both genders, then Pinterest is not something you should be wasting your time on. On the other hand, if you are targeting young adult females, Pinterest might be exactly where you want to be.

Among active users, females are three times as likely to be an active user as compared to a male. And they trend young. Some 34% of Pinterest users are aged 18-29, and 28% are 30-49. Only 17% are 65+. So, if you are advertising hearing aids, trying to do it on Pinterest is probably not the ideal course of action. But if you are selling shoes for women made in hot colors – it might be exactly where you want to be.

Instagram

Interestingly, Instagram also trends female, although the demographics are far more balanced. Some 52% of users are female, so there is a slight imbalance. In the United States, it is estimated that 43% of adult females use Instagram, and about 31% of adult males use Instagram. Overall, 110 million Americans are on Instagram, and some 130 million users will tap on a shopping post to learn more about a product. A large fraction of American users, some 63%, look at Instagram at least once a day.

If you aren't on Instagram with your business, you're already late to the party (but don't worry about it, it's never too late). It's estimated that 25 million U.S. businesses have an Instagram account. The app is extremely popular with so-called influencers, with surveys showing that nearly three-fourths of them list Instagram as their preferred social media site. The total possible reach on Instagram is 800 million people worldwide.

One of the factors that has made Instagram such a success is the fact that it's a mobile application rather than a website. Now you can reach Instagram through a website, but most users access it through the app. Why is this important? Because an app is something you always have with you since people are glued to their smartphones. An app also makes it easier to check, rather than jumping on a desktop computer to find out what is going on with some website. People still use desktop and laptop computers, of course, but an app just makes it easier for them to access. An app is also good for advertisers. Instagram is a simple visual medium where you can post images with a message or short 15 second videos. This opens great marketing tools for small businesses.

Instagram opens a little more of an older audience than Pinterest does, but 72% of teens are on Instagram, and only 31% of those aged 18-24 use it. Not sure why there is such a large drop-off, people who are aged 18-24 were young when Instagram came online about 8-9 years ago, you would think they would be completely accustomed to it.

In any case, the numbers are quite large – meaning it's worth utilizing for many businesses. Wouldn't you like to have instant access to 31% of 18-24-year-olds?

Facebook

Facebook is the granddaddy of social media sites. Although it has lost some popularity with teens and young adults, it remains a major workhorse. The great news for marketers is that Facebook has a very balanced audience, with more equal numbers among males and females, and an even distribution among the different age groups. This may be in part because of the age of the site and its general focus. Facebook was around before smartphones, and the focus on linking family and friends is something that appeals to all age groups, including older folks. In fact, 62% of people aged 65+ who are online has a Facebook account.

The bottom line about Facebook is the audience is enormous, and everyone is on there to one degree or another. Facebook has 2.4 billion monthly active users, making it one of the most trafficked websites of all time. Although 1.5 billion people access Facebook periodically using desktop computers, the platform also has a mobile app, and nearly everyone accesses it at least some of the time via the mobile app – including seniors.

Facebook makes it easy to target large audiences. You can do this using organic methods or paid methods or some combination thereof. Facebook not only lets people "connect" and share videos and images; it is also home to many interest groups. People love to form online groups of like-minded people so they can discuss hobbies, sports, academic sites, or access support groups, and Facebook has made it very easy to do it. Rather than going through the hassle of starting your own website, you can leverage the Facebook website to create your own group, and millions upon millions of people do. You can also post messages to reach your customers, and the sharing capabilities of the site will help to automatically get your marketing exposed to larger numbers of people through people's various "friends."

As we will see later, advertising on Facebook is easy, quick, and cheap. You can also laser target advertising on Facebook in ways that have never been possible through the entire history of business.

In our view, no matter what you are marketing and who your target demographic is, you are going to want to be on Facebook.

YouTube

YouTube is nearly as big as Facebook, with some 2 billion monthly active users. It's estimated that some five billion videos are watched on the site every single day. About 73% of adults in the United States use YouTube, with about 60% of monthly active users being male. Nearly all U.S. adults use YouTube, and although there are more males than there are in the general population, it is easy to reach both genders on the site. It is also well distributed among all the age groups, and those aged 35-55 are the fastest-growing demo. YouTube is fast becoming the go-to source for how-to videos and tutorials, and it's also a place where you can find old music videos, news reports, and old tv shows, and funny cat videos are still quite popular.

The great thing about YouTube is that if you set up your videos the right way, you can get lots of organic views. And even if you can't get organic views, you can use advertising to reach people without spending hardly any money. YouTube is another site that is a must when you are going for social media.

Snapchat

If you are looking to target younger people, the app Snapchat may be of interest. Snapchat is a messaging app that allows people to share images and videos. In recent years, it has become more popular for influencer marketing. However, the app is a little bit awkward, in our opinion, as compared to Facebook, Instagram, and YouTube. Currently, we don't recommend Snapchat for marketing purposes, but it is something to keep in mind as a possibility for the future.

Twitter

Well, everyone knows Twitter. Of course, it probably goes without saying that the site has drawn a lot of attention in part because President Trump uses it – either to great effect if you are a fan or as a menace if you can't stand him. Either way, you must admit that he can draw a lot of attention using Twitter. Many celebrities are using Twitter to get their message out and to communicate with fans. It has its benefits, and it makes it easy for people to communicate and get short messages across. The site has become extremely political. Although the site is heavily trafficked, compared to some of its colleagues, it's on the smaller side. There are reported to be 330 million active users. The site tends heavily male, with some 66% of users being male. Only about 22% of US adults use Twitter, which is quite small compared to Facebook and YouTube. The number of users has declined, and in the 2016 election, and since it became highly politicized.

Chapter 15 The Tools You Really Need

You'd be amazed at how many people try to start a business without the necessary tools, the basics that can dramatically increase your effectiveness and efficiency.

Planner

You need a planner for your business and your life. You need somewhere to write down and keep track of all your appointments. Don't trust your memory! Write it down, write it down, write it down. Whether you use an electronic planner or a paper one doesn't matter - use what works best for you.

Nothing will cost you more than missing an important appointment. Make a commitment to get organized and never let that happen to you.

Phone

Having a cell phone will dramatically increase your productivity. How? Well, when you're stuck in an airport or somewhere else where your time would be spent in an unproductive way, you can make calls then. If you don't have a cell phone, get one. Always carry your memory jogger with you so that you can make calls when you have a spare moment here and there.

Notebook

You should keep notes on every call you make, every conversation you have, every customer you talk to, every prospect you talk to... You'll never know when your notes will come in handy. Keeping track also helps you see how much you are doing (or not doing).

Contacts List

I talked about it earlier - this is the heart blood of your business. Without a list of contacts, there is no market! Build your market, build your contacts, build your business, build the life you want.

How to Talk to People

I'm going to let you in on a little secret...

You have no idea how to talk to people effectively.

It's ok - very few people do. Professional network marketers do though. They've studied communication, language, and conversation. They understand, like Aristotle, the power of dialogue. Become a student of people. Learn to learn from others. Learn to listen. Learn to communicate more effectively.

If you haven't read, "How to Win Friends and Influence People" by Dale Carnegie - buy it now! It's one of the all-time greatest books on communication and relationships.

Here are some of the basics of talking to people you must master's in network marketing:

Starting Conversations

I learned a great way to start conversations with strangers. Want to know what it is?

Just say, "Hello."

Wow! When my mentor told me that, I thought "What an idiot! that's so simple..." But then I tried it and, guess what, it works! EVERY TIME (almost)!

Now, if you say hello to someone and they respond in a negative, quiet, or frustrated way, you might ask them something like, "How's your day going...?" They'll probably be happy to complain to you about how much their life sucks - and that's good. Maybe your product or your business could help them improve their life. You'll never know until you ask.

If they respond in a happy, cheerful, or enthusiastic way, TALK TO THEM! Ask them questions about them. These are the kind of people you want on your team - people. People who love helping others, who are excited about life, who have passion.

At the end of the day, who do you want on your team? People who are negative and mean or people who are enthusiastic, full of energy and fun to be around? Then focus on recruiting the people you WANT to work with – people you admire and enjoy being with.

Building Relationships and Rapport

Most people are oblivious to how others feel. Learn to listen to how others feel. Learn to show others that you understand them and care about them. Let people know you're on their side - you want to help them.

When someone knows that you have their best interest in mind, even if you just met them, that relationship will be as solid as a rock. If they doubt you, no matter how long you've known them, that relationship can crumble like sand any moment. If you want to build a rock-solid business, show others that you have their best interest in mind by your actions and your words.

Resolving Conflict

Conflict is a part of life. Often it happens when one person's expectations are not met. Then they may get upset. If someone is upset, angry, frustrated, or confused - ask them questions. Don't respond by getting upset. Ask them questions like,

"I'm curious why you feel that way, would you mind telling me...?"

Sharing and Being Generous

Your job as a distributor is to be a generous person who shares as much as possible. When you're sharing your product or business with someone new, don't look at it as selling. Yes, you're trying to make a sale – but 95% of network marketers are very uncomfortable selling. But everyone is comfortable with sharing!

Furthermore, your friends, family and prospects will respond better when they feel like you're sharing vs. selling them. Would you rather receive a phone call from someone trying to sell you or someone who's sharing something great with you?

What to Avoid

Don't be pushy!

Too many new distributors (and long-term distributors who just never seemed to learn) make the mistake of being too pushy. They just talk, talk, talk, talk, talk… and don't listen. They don't ask questions they just tell you what you should do. They give you a brochure, CD, DVD or business card before you can even get a word in sideways.

These people make you feel horrible – and you're likely to avoid their phone calls and if you see them in public, you'll probably walk the other way. Is being pushy a successful business strategy? Absolutely not!

Instead of being pushy, ask questions.

Instead of talking more, listen more.

Instead of trying to get a sale, try to make a friend.

This business is about creating long-term relationships. If you focus on the relationships, the sales will come. If you just focus on the sales, you won't build a long-term business.

Talking Too Much

This is the #1 mistake I see most distributors make. They talk way too much. Ask questions. Listen. Learn to REALLY listen to others - not just the words, but the emotions. Learn to listen to what's being said and what's NOT being said. Learn to live in other people's worlds.

They say, "People don't care how much you know until they know how much you care." It's true! Show people how much you care by listening to them. Only then will they truly listen to you. And that is what you want after all, isn't it?

Bad Breath

Practice good dental hygiene. If you have chronic bad breath, it's probably because you have a very poor diet. Get some books on nutrition, specifically on how to get more raw foods in your diet. Bad oral health can be a sign of periodontal disease, heart disease and inflammation.

If you have bad breath (go breath in someone's face whom you know and trust and ask them) then get it under control and do it NOW! Nothing will turn off people faster than bad breath.

Improper Attire

If you're a woman, don't dress like a bimbo. If you're a man, don't dress like you're homeless. You don't need to impress people with your clothing, just don't let it distract them from who you really are.

There's a great saying, "God looks at people from the inside, but people look at you from the outside." Make sure what's on the outside of you reflects who you are on the inside.

There are two modes of thought when it comes to professional network marketing clothing and attire. The first is that you should dress for success. Wear nice clothes and look like a business professional.

The other philosophy is that you should wear casual clothes. Just look, feel and act comfortable. Act like you work from home and don't need to dress up to impress others. This is my philosophy and I love it! I find people are attracted to me because they see I'm just a down-to-earth kind of person. I don't overdress them or try to impress them with flashy jewelry or fancy suits. Average people connect with me because I wear average clothing – but I talk like a professional and I have a huge business.

Who would you rather work with, someone like you or someone who shows off fancy clothes and jewelry?

Poor Eye Contact

Make it a habit to always look people in the eye. Don't stare but connect with them. Make it natural. People say the eyes are the window to the soul - let your soul shine and share it with others.

Studies have shown poor eye contact can cause others to distrust you. And trust is the heart of business, especially in network marketing. The speed at which your business will grow is directly proportional to the amount of trust developed between you and your team and between your team and its customers.

Persistence

Persistence is what separates the millionaires from the broke. It's what separates incredibly successful network marketers from those who never quite made it. Persistence is key in this business not just to grow your own direct sales and recruits but to inspire your team to persevere when the going gets tough.

If you give up when it gets hard, your team will emulate you. If you take two months off, your team will drop the ball on their business too. Your team will duplicate your activity – so make sure your activity is consistent and persistent!

Chapter 16 7 Steps to Effective Mentoring and Training

Mastering duplicable mentoring and training techniques will positively impact the long-term growth of your organization.

Here are 7 steps to developing an effective mentoring and training relationship with your team.

Step 1: Identify Their Statement of Purpose – Their WHY?

Duplication and process are critical to your success and the success of your entire team. If you were fortunate enough to receive proper mentoring and training you will have completed the important task of defining your personal and financial goals, including defining your WHY. Your WHY represents your unshakable reasons and motivations for joining the business opportunity.

Now it is time for you to pass it forward. Begin sharing your WHY with your team members. Take time to discuss their goals and why they need to develop a successful business. Make sure they write everything down and provide you with a copy. This document represents their "Statement of Purpose".

As you continue moving forward and working together, their Statement of Purpose will serve as a powerful reminder and motivator, particularly during the more challenging and stressful times.

Step 2: Identify and Respect Their Mandatory Obligations

Having personally mentored and trained thousands of network marketers in multiple countries I have learned they all share the challenge of leading very busy lives. Their days are consumed with personal and professional responsibilities. These responsibilities include working 8 to 10 hours a day at their full-time job. Also, they spend 2 to 3 hours per day on family obligations. This reality creates the perception of not having enough time to start and build a business.

The fact is, it's a perception and not a reality. This can be demonstrated by taking the time to fully understand their daily activities, identifying which activities are optional and which activities are necessary. Necessary activities include time spent at work, picking the kids up from school, attending recitals and soccer games, grocery shopping, preparing dinner, homework, working out at the gym, or enjoying quiet time with the spouse. These activities are mandatory because they represent the necessities of life and are the most important activities that truly define and add value to our lives.

A very important part of your role as a mentor and trainer includes identifying and respecting their mandatory obligations. More importantly, your role is to assist them in scheduling important business-building activities around those obligations. From time to time scheduling adjustments will be required to complete important business-building activities, however, always be careful to recognize and respect their mandatory obligations.

Step 3: Set Realistic Expectations

Network marketers should have clearly defined income goals and timeframes in which they'd like to achieve those goals. Whatever their financial goals, your role as mentor and trainer includes providing support and encouragement. However, your role also includes having an honest and straightforward conversation with them regarding what it will take to achieve their goals. This is especially true if they have mandatory obligations that limit the amount of time, they can put into building their business.

If their goal is to replace their current full-time income while spending less than 6 hours per week on their business, they should understand that realistically achieving their financial goals could take 2 years or more. On the other hand, if they are willing to do whatever it takes to devote 20 hours per week to their business, they might achieve their financial goals in 12 months or less.

Ultimately, it comes down to how much time they are willing to put into building their business and equally important, the level of focus and seriousness they apply to their network marketing activities.

Step 4: Discuss the Importance of Process and Duplication

Process and duplication are extremely important factors in achieving network marketing success. In fact, without them there is very little chance of achieving long-term success. Therefore, network marketers must have a clear understanding of the process and the importance of duplicating a proven system.

As a mentor and trainer this will be one of your more difficult challenges in working with team members. Especially when working with successful business professionals and individuals with advanced levels of education. Given their business success and advanced education these individuals can be resistant to adopting and duplicating a proven system. Instead, they may prefer relying on the skills and processes they have used to create past successes. Within the network marketing community this is commonly referred to as being "un-coachable".

If you're working with someone who is "coachable" that's great! Teach them the proven system that is already in place. Also, ensure they understand the importance of duplication and how it will maximize the long-term growth of their business and income.

On the other hand, if you are working with someone who is "un-coachable" a bit of tough love will be required. This can be accomplished by acknowledging their impressive accomplishments then quickly pivoting to the importance of duplicating the system and how it will positively impact the growth of their business and income.

Convey the message using your own words and voice, just make sure you strike the right balance of seriousness and authenticity. Chances are your message will be appreciated and well-received.

Step 5: Industry, Company, Product, and Compensation Plan

Network marketers must have a basic understanding of the industry, their company, and products, as well as the compensation plan. This information may have been during the recruiting process however, as their mentor and trainer it's your responsibility to this information with them. Do not simply rely on emails, company-sponsored training, and back-office resources. This exercise is critical to ensuring they develop the knowledge and confidence to effectively present the opportunity.

Step 6: Develop a 30-Day Activity Plan

Consider how Tiger Woods, one of the greatest golfers ever prepares to make a putt. He takes time to consider the distance between the ball and the cup, the subtle changes in the surface of the green, the wind speed and temperature, and even the type of grass itself. After careful analysis of everything that could influence the golf ball during its journey to its intended target, with his putter in hand he positions himself over the golf ball. As he stands over the golf ball his eyes continue surveying the entire path between the ball and the hole, over and over. He will not execute the put until he sees a clear path to success.

Now here is where things get interesting. Before striking the ball and sending it towards its intended target he begins focusing on the ball itself and the first 6 to 8 inches of its intended path. In fact, after striking the ball he doesn't look up until after the ball has rolled at least 8 inches. He does not look up because he's confident in his preparation and he understands seeing the entire path when striking the ball is not critical to his success. The critical part of the process is ensuring the ball starts on the right path, understanding the first 8 inches of the ball's journey will determine if the ball hits its intended target. That means after striking the ball and watching it roll perfectly through the first 8 inches of its intended path, he can be confident he will make the putt.

Many network marketing companies encourage team members to focus on recruiting immediately after getting started, even instructing them to begin making their prospect list within minutes of signing up. They offer fast-start cash bonuses to individuals that sponsor a minimum number of team members within their first 30 days. This approach is a bit short-sighted and prioritizes recruiting over learning and understanding the entire long-term process of developing residual income.

As a mentor and trainer try to help team members establish a healthy balance between recruiting and learning, especially within their first 30 days. Make sure they set aside at least one hour per day studying the industry, company, products, and compensation plan. Follow-up with them several times a week to discuss what they've learned and to confirm their understanding of the materials.

The first 30-days in network marketing are like the first 8 inches of a 30-foot putt. Your activities when getting started will determine your trajectory and how successful you will be in achieving your goals.

Step 7: Support, Encourage, Motivate

Building a home-based business can be overwhelming and stressful. Not to mention the daily stress of work and family responsibilities. When getting started daily support, encouragement and motivation are needed and appreciated.

This brings us back to the importance of duplication and process. As your team members begin recruiting and sponsoring new people, they will duplicate what you've taught them, assuming the role of mentor and trainer themselves. If they have received support, encouragement, and motivation, they will in turn provide the same for individuals they sponsor. Making sure these qualities are passed forward to each new team member will help to ensure your team continues to grow well into the future.

Chapter 17 The Three Business Building Phases of Network Marketing

As far as I can tell there are three normal stages that best networkers experience when fabricating their business. It is vital that you see every stage and never skirt any of them.

Stage 1: Creating Your Core Group

Stage 2: Launching Your Business Together - Your Initial List

Stage 3: Growing Your List

Before I broadly expound on each of these stages it is important that you comprehend where your underlying force will originate from.

Force starts with Phase 1 and 2. I've seen such a variety of individuals attempt to skip Phase 1 or 2 and attempt to begin working in Phase 3. This never works since they don't have that terrifically vital energy (Ill clarify why later). For the time being, comprehend that you should take after the regular grouping of eliminates laid in this keeping in mind the end goal to succeed in growing a major group.

Stage 1: Creating Your Core Group

Here's my most noteworthy suggestion for you when beginning your system advertising business: Don't go at only it!

Do you set off for college or University? Did you ever take one of those classes where your educator gave you a HUGE venture that made you feel wiped out to your stomach since you didn't think you could be that right?

I recall plainly what that resembled. It felt exceptionally overpowering and it gave me a bunch in the base of my stomach from the sheer nervousness of everything.

Be that as it may, I likewise recall the sentiment alleviation when my teacher declared, and this anticipate will be done in gatherings Whew! The majority of the sudden I realized that everything would be alright.

The force of a gathering!

Anything feels possible when you have other individuals working adjacent to you to achieve the assignment. It's astounding how a gathering can have all the effect on the planet.

In network showcasing some individuals allude to this as a driving force bunch. I truly don't care what you call it. You simply need to get no less than one other likeminded individual to construct your business with.

It could be your mate, sibling, sister, closest companion, colleague, and so on.

It could be more than one. For my situation, I began my business with my sibling and my father. If it hadn't been for them, I would be no place today. What a distinction my Core Group made in my prosperity!

So, who is your Core Group going to be? This is your initial step to achievement. Don't do whatever else until you choose whom you are going to take a shot at your business with. When you have your Core, Group built up you are prepared for the following stage.

Stage 2: Launching Your Business Together-Your Initial List

Ever heard the expression, the cash is in the rundown?

All things considered, in any case on the off chance that you have or not, it is reality. It doesn't matter what business you are in; the cash is in the rundown.

What is a rundown?

A rundown is a database of individuals you know, either specifically or by implication, which contains their contact data (i.e. telephone number and email).

When you first begin system promoting you are urged to work out the rundown

of individuals you know with their email and telephone numbers. This is the most basic stride in propelling your business.

You cannot manufacture a business without uncovering the item and chance to others; and the main way you can open it to others is by having a rundown of individuals to go to.

This implies it is totally crucial that you take a seat with your Core Group and assemble your rundown together. You can bail each other out by giving each different thought. Make it an opposition to see who can assemble the greatest rundown!

Here's a typical complaint I have heard consistently; I don't know anybody. By what means would I be able to do this simply utilizing the Internet?

Baloney!

On the off chance that you don't know anybody then you are in the wrong business my companion. This is system showcasing. If you don't have a current system, then you have a considerable measure of work to do.

The uplifting news is that everybody has a current system. As a rule, they're just excessively frightened, making it impossible to approach them. Keep in mind the segment on trepidation? It feels cumbersome and they get terrified.

Sound commonplace?

Oh, my goodness something. Your underlying energy will be made by your current system.

There's no chance to get around it. Face your trepidation and get over it. There are pioneers on your rundown sitting tight for the right open door - however if you don't take a seat and make it you won't ever discover them.

Is it accurate to say that all are records made equivalent?

No. The more trust you have with your rundown, the less demanding it is to open them to your chance and item. Have you ever pondered what makes somebody more powerful than another? They have impact since they have picked up the trust of numerous individuals.

That's why its exclusive common to accept that the BEST rundown is your current system. Their trust ought to as of now be high and they will listen to what you need to say.

If you are an exploitative individual and individuals don't like you well, you must change who you are first before you start assembling a business.

It's been set up that the cash is in the rundown. Its additionally a certainty that the more trust you have with your rundown the more responsive they will be to your offer.

This implies your essential employment is to assemble your rundown, keep it developing, and discover methods for expanding trust with the general population on it. Trust can't be purchased; it must be earned. It is just earned when you require significant investment to put resources into different people groups lives.

When you have made your underlying rundown from your current system and presented them to your chance and item, the following stage is to figure out how to keep your rundown developing.

To begin with, be that as it may, an expression of consolation: Some of your family and companions may scorn you for venturing fresh. They may even (deliberately or subliminally) need you to fall flat so they feel legitimized in not going out on a limb and doing things another way themselves.

They'll look for you to hit a knock, and spring up to say, I let you know so. Don't pay consideration on them. All things considered, you picked an alternate way to get distinctive results, isn't that so? Keep in mind, never quit accepting. Avoid individuals who make you question yourself!

Stage 3: Growing Your List

Its lone characteristic to accept that if the cash is in the rundown then the bigger your rundown is the more cash you'll make, correct?

It returns to trust. You can have a tremendous rundown assembled of everybody you've ever met, however if the trust isn't there you don't have anything. I've seen numerous individuals purchase a lead list with 10,000 names on it. Even though that is a major show, it is not exceptionally responsive at all and is extremely insufficient because of an absence of trust (the leads on the rundown have no clue who you are-there's no past relationship!)

Continuously take a gander at your rundown as your system. We've as of now talked about your current system; now it's opportunity to figure out how to develop your system. You need to perceive the significance of expanding your range of authority.

This is the place most system advertisers hit a detour. They begin their business off with a blast by setting off to their current system, however then things begin backing off on the grounds that they don't have any extension.

It's appalling that such a variety of system advertisers are not taught from the very first moment to keep their rundown developing and how to do it. Gives say you a chance to discover one okay pioneer from your current system that produces force in one leg. That's extraordinary, yet it won't pay you exceptionally well.

In most pay models you require no less than two legs. That is the thing that outings such many individuals up! You may have encountered it yourself - you appear to have the capacity to get some energy, yet you cannot appear to discover enough pioneers to keep it going.

As I would see it, you just need to buy and by patron three truly solid pioneers to get you to the top. That's it. That's how significant one great pioneer truly is! In any case, you MUST keep your rundown developing to locate those great pioneers.

This is the place the force of the Internet comes in!

Prior to the age of the Internet it was a somewhat monotonous procedure to keep your system developing. You needed to go out and meet individuals at business capacities, organizing occasions, classes, and so forth.

Presently you can without much of a stretch use online asset to keep your rundown developing and keep up an abnormal state of trust in the meantime. As your rundown develops your odds of finding another solid pioneer get ever more elevated.

Conclusion

Well, I feel like this is the end of a first date. You know, when you finally meet your dream guy or dream girl, and you have so much fun sharing experiences and insights over a nice bowl of chicken chow Mein. Before you know it, the check is coming out and the server wants you to leave so he can clean up your mess and go home. I feel like that right about now, because I truly want this relationship to continue. I know feels the same way, and maybe we're totally creeping you out right now.

What I mean is that we don't want this book to be our final contact with you. If you like what we had to share and you like our training style, I invite you to keep this relationship going by. We have a gift for you, and we aim to pump out weekly content that is entertaining and helpful for your business.

It is our hope that this book was entertaining, and value packed for you. We believe that network marketing can gain the respect that it deserves if we train people to operate with professionalism. Let's work together and eliminate the stigma so "That Guy" is a character of the past. This book is an invaluable tool that can teach your team network marketing etiquette, and the best news is you'll never need to have those awkward conversations.

We also love to train about these topics. For more details about bulk orders and booking us to speak at your upcoming events.

Thank you so much, and we look forward to coming alongside you to help you create your dream life in the amazing profession of network marketing.

I hope that you were able to learn all about how you can build a successful network marketing business. From choosing your company and establishing your brand to growing your sales and building a team, there are many activities that go into building your business successfully. It is important that you understand these activities and their importance so that you can have success in building your own network marketing business.

Remember, the industry is presently filled with a significant amount of advice that is ineffective and that may take your business in the opposite direction from where you want to go. It is important that you take the time to choose structures that are effective and that are going to help you create next-level success as quickly as possible. The sooner you ditch these ineffective strategies and take advantage of successful and proven strategies, the sooner you are going to experience massive success in your business.

The next step in creating success in your business is to start at the beginning of this book. If you have not already chosen your company or established a recognizable brand, then it is time to do so. You want to take the time to build this solid foundation so that your entire business can thrive with these basic structures in place. Having your brand easily identifiable and recognizable means that you will look even more professional in the eyes of your clients and team members, which is important if you want to generate next-level success in your business.

Once you have established your branding, you can go ahead and start practicing selling and building a team. Then, simply continue building your sales and nurturing your team. Over time, these strategies will help you grow beyond your wildest dreams. You will be able to take your business to the next level, and then the next level, and eventually the top level.

Lastly, if you enjoyed this book, I ask that you please take the time to it on Amazon Kindle. Your honest feedback would be greatly appreciated

Thank you, and best of luck in your network marketing business!

COPYWRITING 2020

THE ULTIMATE HANDBOOK TO LEARN THE ART OF COPYWRITING WITH A SIMPLE STEP BY STEP PROCESS FOR YOUR ONLINE BUSINESS

PAUL J. ABRAMAH

Introduction

The power of words can change a company's future. This might be a strong claim, but after reading this guide, you will understand the reason for this statement. It is the use of effective copywriting techniques that offer value to customers.

Based on experience, this writer asserts that having a love for words is crucial to copywriting. Continuing education and experience can play their part, but when it comes to copywriting, it would not be possible to satisfy a client without it.

Start right away by telling yourself that in order to create value with words, you need to use effective copywriting techniques. These are full of a talking and connected language in which, along with the application of an SEO strategy, you get carried away by the rhythm of the sentences, the light and non-resonant sounds, breathing between commas and periods, all capable of giving effect to a thought.

The skill of mixing all these elements together is not easy to acquire at all. Writing may be for everyone but doing it to achieve a goal is one of the most difficult aspects of the big and complex world of content marketing.

Many vital ingredients need to be present to achieve results through copywriting techniques:

- choose a strategy suited to the target
- evaluate the right tools to communicate
- organize useful resources for what is told
- consider the client as a person, and not as a public

To all these components, add the most important: the ability to tell by revealing one's own character. Only a company that offers its client something of himself can be appreciated. The customer wants to feel pampered and not deceived by the phrases made (what do you think when you read "industry leader"?). He wants to find out who is behind a brand, to feel part of something beautiful, because it is clean from logic oriented exclusively to the business. Further, the customer wants to bring stories home. It is not because he loves storytelling. Most often than not, he might not be even aware of what it is. He wants to know the stories because they transform a product or a service into something useful and indispensable.

Presenting a company with copywriting techniques

In order to make a company known, it is necessary to choose the right words – words that talk about the business not with the objective of selling but offering added value instead. To accomplish this effectively, copywriting techniques are a big help. These are the tricks that word professionals use to mix strategy and heart together.

How do you do it concretely?

Before the indispensable techniques to show the corporate soul of a brand will be explained, there is something you must do beforehand.

Approach the screen.

Do not worry, you will only be told to scan each syllable well.

Before writing about a company, listen to what the entrepreneur has to say.

Do not think about the right words. For now, lay aside the thought that you need to put into practice everything you have learned about SEO copywriting. Forget the company's strategies for a moment. Take some time to listen to what the brand wants to tell you.

Translate his message and read what is inside his entrepreneurial heart. Live with the entrepreneur the emotions, and the features that make what he sells unique.

Listen to it several times, take a long breath and put everything in your mind.

Here and now, you are ready to write using copywriting techniques. Now, you can choose the right words. Five essential techniques are suggested:

Define a tone of voice that will speak for the company.

Capture your attention with an appealing incipit that contains the main keyword of your SEO strategy.

It takes care of the simplification and the legibility of the text.

Create a link with the reader through words.

Share a true story.

The copywriting explained to the client is how important it is to tell oneself online. If you follow this path, it becomes the best way to empathize with the customer who does not need a showcase site that displays a list of products and services. He wants to know and satisfy all his consumer curiosity, to understand, and imagine with his mind. All these are possible, thanks to words.

Company and reader become two characters of a common journey, in which one esteems the other.

A company or an entrepreneur who is presenting and offering himself online should do so without fear and doubt. He must not be afraid of making mistakes. In the event this happens, he admits the mistake and prepares to make improvements. A company grows in small steps together with the words it publishes. It does not insist on being seen for what it is not. It does not self-criticize, nor does it promise the impossible. In addition, it listens to the advice of those who follow its adventures on the web, those who show themselves to be human. If all these can happen, between a web marketing strategy and an essential dose of empathy with the customer, words can create value and lead to a result. This is how the fate of a company will change.

Chapter 1 What's Is Copywriting?

What exactly is copywriting? Make a guess. Now, with your guess still fresh in your mind, let me give you a true glimpse of what copywriting is.

Copywriting is the aspect of writing copies for the sole purpose of marketing or advertising. The written copy is a piece of document meant to persuade a potential buyer or customer to buy the product or influence how they view the product in question differently.

In broadcasting, marketing, and advertising, someone who writes copies is called a copywriter or continuity (in broadcasting). The work of a copywriter is straightforward: create taglines, webpage content, and direct mail pieces. Copywriters who write web content prefer the name content writer to copywriters.

The scope of responsibilities a copywriter holds in his or her cap is not limited to the above list; it goes further than that. Copywriters also create newsletters, online ads, internet content, press releases, catalogs, brochures, and other marketing materials, TV and radio commercial scripts and many more.

Additionally, a copywriter also has some role to play in book publishing. In this field, the copywriter is responsible for writing the jacket flap and flap copy with a compelling summary of the book. As I have indicated, technology space has expanded tremendously. Today, copywriters are also very prevalent in social media, social networking, and blog posts.

Before the advent of technology, and the freelancing craze, copywriters were (and still are), employees within organizations such as public relation firms, advertising agencies, book publishers, creative agencies, and advertising departments within organizations. This has changed to a certain degree with the rise of the internet.

Many copywriters are choosing to become independent. They are choosing to freelance for different clients and specialized copywriting agencies. In this type of setting, the copywriter has more 'string' to his or her writing because they are able to perform tasks such as editing, message consulting, SEO consulting, proofreading, design and layout etc.

As a copywriter, you will have to be a team player because often, copywriters work within the confines of a creative team. For example, if you work for an advertising agency, the organization may pair you with an art director. However, your main role is to create a verbally and textually compelling content derived from the copy provided by the client. The responsibility of a copywriter is to tell a story; a story that resonates with the reader, viewer, or potential customer.

I find it necessary to point out that there is little difference between a copywriter and a technical writer. The only difference between the two is that the work of a technical writer is simply to inform and not persuade. Here is a good comparison of the two parts of writing even though the careers of either often overlap. A content writer's work is to write a car ad to persuade a potential customer, while the work of a technical writer is to write about the operations of the car from reading the manual.

If you are wondering why you should bother learning the skill of copywriting, here are a few reasons.

As a copywriter, you get a chance to influence the masses by creating an ad or creative piece that remains on the mind of the viewer.

You get to work in the exciting field of advertising for TV and radio. In addition, you get to interact with some interesting people in the field of broadcasting.

Content writing is a creative venture. Therefore, if you love writing, you get to enjoy yourself while making a ton of money (yes, copywriting is a very profitable business concept).

Now that you have a better understanding of what copywriting is, let us look at five things every copywriter should know.

Copywriting: origins

The term copywriting dates to the nineteenth century and is specifically related to the journalistic world.

In the editorial offices of the most authoritative newspapers, the figure of the copywriter dealt with drawing up announcements of all kinds.

Subsequently, the advertising media boom, first in print and then on radio and TV, totally changed the cards on the table.

In fact, copywriting work was increasingly associated with advertising.

Contributing as a protagonist to the creation of a successful advertising campaign, starting from the creation of slogans to promote the product, were the main work activities for the copywriter, before the advent of the web.

Then, the success of digital marketing has radically changed his duties. So much so that in addition to the professionals who still work in tandem with the art director, who specializes in graphics, there are more and more freelancers covering the multiple textual aspects of the content put online: think for example of the texts for social networks, to corporate blogs where product need to be structured for SEO, so that they are attractive to the various search engines, so that Internet users can find the relevant information.

In short, at present copywriting is an integral part of internet communication.

Knowing how to communicate the message of a corporate brand, using the right words, the appropriate vocabulary and the specific SEO oriented writing technique are requirements that only a few possess.

Therefore, companies are increasingly looking for highly specialized figures in the world of the business writer.

And perhaps this research should be based on even more selective criteria, given that unfortunately in an increasingly more competitive market like today, many companies tend to rely on those who ask for lower compensation.

This is a huge mistake. There are those who write and those who write well. And to those who write well, merit must also be paid to the economy.

Chapter 2 The Best Platforms Where to Learn From/Examples of Experts

Social media is one of the most powerful platforms to stay connected with the latest news online. Especially for niche-based topics, I think we can all agree on the fact that the general population now relies on social media for the latest news rather than using traditional methods like newspapers or news channels. This is not to say that newspapers or news channels are dead or useless, but most of the time social media delivers the news to us faster than any news channel or newspaper would.

So, it is a no-brainer for most of the bloggers to stay up to date with the news and latest trends utilizing social media as their tool. There are three leading social media websites that I would recommend you use. The first would be Facebook.

As we all are aware, Facebook is one of the biggest, most popular social media websites there is, so on anything even remotely related to your niche, Facebook will have news and updates for you. The second one would be Instagram. I would highly recommend using Instagram to stay up to date with any news or controversies regarding your niche.

Finally, the third social media platform I would recommend using would be Snapchat. Recently, Snapchat has started to use its platform to provide its users with news and updates on more niches than you could conceive. Quite frankly, the stories are often subpar at best for the most part, but sometimes they can really help to keep the creative mind flowing and send you in different directions to do more research on a specific topic. With that note, let us get into the specifics on how these three platforms can be used to your advantage.

Let's first discuss Facebook. By now, Facebook has around 2.27 billion active users, so it is safe to say that Facebook has more news and up-to-date trends than you could imagine. More specifically, if your goal is to learn more about your niche and its latest trends, then consider joining fan pages related to your niche. Facebook has a lot of fan pages in many different areas of interest. It is unlikely that you will be unable to find a fan page related to your niche. The reason for having a fan page on Facebook is to provide the fans with its latest news and updates regarding what is happening in that area of interest, so definitely start using this platform to your advantage!

Instagram is a platform everyone has heard about by now. Slowly but surely, Instagram is starting to take over Facebook and become the next most prominent social media platform. The reason is simple – it is both fun and easy to use. Like Facebook, there are a lot of fan pages with every single topic you can imagine. Use this tool to keep yourself updated with all the latest trends and topics related to your niche.

Thirdly, we will be covering the platform known as Snapchat. Some of you might know about this social media platform, but it is mainly used by many to share photos that they might have taken. Snapchat has a feature known as "the story". The main reason for having stories on the Snapchat page is relatively simple. It is to provide users with the latest news and updates. The only drawback is that the niche isn't as "filled up" as compared to Facebook. But as I said, it gets the mind flowing. The niches covered on Snapchat are very broad ones. Albeit, this is a relatively new feature, so we cannot expect it to compete yet with Facebook and Instagram.

The two most popular blogging platforms are WordPress and Blogger (owned by Google). A blogging platform is simply a software that allows you to create, edit, update, delete, or generally manage your blog and posts.

Which of the blogging platforms is better? This is a question that people ask all the time. Now, bloggers and web designers seem to have reached a consensus that WordPress is better than Blogger for so many reasons. This is not saying that Blogger is not equally good.

As mentioned earlier, Blogger is owned by Google, and it is an excellent platform for people who want to host a simple blog that they can update and edit easily. Once you have a Gmail account or Google account, you can create a Blogger account – it is one of Google's integrated services. One good thing about using the Blogger platform is that you don't need to spend money on website hosting anymore. The created blog is automatically hosted by Google, for free.

Furthermore, if you don't want to pay for a custom domain (which is highly not recommended), then you can use a free subdomain provided by Google. Let's assume that the name of your blog is Car Racing; if there is no other blog bearing the same on the Blogger platform, then could choose car racing. blogpost as your domain name. The extension ". blogpost" is automatically attached to your blog name selected by Google.

If you want to remove the ". blogpost" attachment from your URL, you will need to buy a domain name, then redirect your blog on the Blogger platform to your new domain name. If you do that successfully, your new domain name will become "car racing" Note: the blog will still be hosted on Google. So, you are only paying for a domain name.

Once you have sorted out your domain name or blog name, you can choose any of Blogger blog themes, customize it as you please and then proceed to upload your first blog post. A theme shows how the different of your blog will look when viewed on desktop and mobile. If you don't like any of the default Blogger themes, you can pay for a premium Blogger theme or download one of the many available free Blogger themes on the internet.

One thing that makes many bloggers shy away from Blogger is that it has only limited themes and plug-ins. A lot of bloggers don't use the platform – as a result, theme developers don't find it necessary to develop as many themes for the platform.

Plug-ins allow you to add several interesting features to the existing features of a software. Most software plug-ins are usually developed by a third party to improve the performance or add more functionalities to existing software. There are some plug-ins that, when you install them on your WordPress blog, will help you share your posts to your different social media pages. Some plug-ins help you maintain the security of your blog. Some plug-ins help you improve the search engine ranking of your blog.

When it comes to plug-ins, Blogger has a minimal number of options. The reason for that is – since most people are not using the Blogger platform, software developers who develop plug-ins concentrate their efforts on developing plug-ins for WordPress rather than Blogger.

With just a few available and boring themes, many bloggers ditch the Blogger platform for WordPress. Apart from the availability of a wide range of plug-ins and themes to choose from, there are several other reasons that make people prefer WordPress to Blogger. Let's take an in-depth look at WordPress and some of the features that make it great.

WordPress

WordPress is a content management system built using PHP (a programming language) and MySQL (a database management system). One thing that makes WordPress great is that you can install plug-ins for added functionalities. Also, you can make use of thousands of available templates or themes – all this makes it very simple to create or set up a blog using WordPress.

The simplicity of use of WordPress is such that anybody who can send a text message on their mobile phone can use it. All you need is to download and install the content management system on your website host. Proceed to download and install any of the available WordPress themes – download and install some essential plug-ins – customize the theme according to your taste and start uploading your blog posts.

Many bloggers and website designers also prefer WordPress because of its improved security architecture. If you need extra security, you can download and install plug-ins that will help you secure your site from hackers and cyber-attacks.

Also, there are available plug-ins that can help you improve the search engine ranking of your blog. This is another important reason why so many bloggers prefer WordPress. As a blogger, search engine optimization is vital to you because if you write the best blog posts in the world and people do not get to discover and read them, then you have just wasted your efforts. SEO plug-ins that can be installed on WordPress help increase the search engine ranking of your website such that when people are searching for content related to the one you have on your blog; your posts will show up in their search results.

With WordPress, you will always get support whenever you need it. For instance, if you are doing anything on your site and run into a problem or technical difficulty, you could easily search online and find your answers on any of the many available WordPress forums littering the cyberspace. You may also get direct support from the WordPress support team.

Now that you have made up your mind to go with WordPress – next, you need to purchase a domain name and hosting plan.

Chapter 3 Transforming the World's Worst Sentence into Incredibly Captivating Copy

Successful marketing or advertising is an interesting combination of creativity, science, and a fair understanding of the human psychology. It must be noted, however, that insofar as marketing or advertising is concerned, mere knowledge of theories and principles is not enough; one must know how to apply them and how to do so effectively.

What makes for effective copywriting?

In the age of social media and constant bombardment of information, copywriting has become an integral part of any marketing or advertising campaign. We are talking about numerous write-ups for social media posts, copies for websites, and even scripts and spiels for campaigns in other forms of media. This brings us to the question: how does one make an effective copy for advertising or marketing?

The most obvious answer, it seems, is to avail of the services of a great copywriter, preferably a natural-gifted writer. And while talent certainly has a lot to do with great copywriting, it is an acquired skill as much as it is an inborn one. Yes, you read that right. You can learn how to be a great copywriter; you just must know what you are doing.

The primary goal of copywriting is to install a mental movie or a mental visual into the mind of your prospect. In other words, what any copywriter seeks to do is to use words in such a way that stimulates the imagination of the target demographic. When you are copywriting, your goal is not merely to inform, but also to persuade and what better way to persuade your target consumer than by titillating their imagination.

It is worth noting that currently, each of us is constantly surrounded by images and stimuli, so it is easy to get distracted. This is the main challenge confounding marketers and advertisers in the digital age: grabbing people's attention and holding on to the same. So, what can you do to market or advertise a product or service effectively? How do you catch your target demographics attention and hold on to the same? How do you make the most out of copywriting?

The answer: learn how to transform a bland sentence into a visually stunning powerhouse.

How to Write a Visually Stunning Sentence

In this part, I will guide you through the process of writing effective copies to stimulate the imagination of your target audience. If you are ready, let us get right into it.

Step 1: Find your message.

To begin, let us take what is possibly the most basic sentence that any marketer or advertiser can use: "Get something."

Now, let us take a moment to examine that sentence. Grammatically speaking, there is nothing wrong with the sentence, "Get something." It is simple, grammatically correct, and in fact has complete thought. Unfortunately, your target audience is not your English teacher. They are not looking for a grammatically correct sentence. In fact, they may not even be looking for anything at all. After all, it is your job as a marketer or advertiser to sell them something, to make sure that they feel the need to make a purchase. Certainly, telling them to "get something" will not prompt them to do anything. At best, you will probably get a response along the lines of a half-meant, half-mumbled, "Okay…"

Step 2: Make your object clear.

Since we are going for statements that on their own can create visual images in the minds of your target consumers, it goes without saying that for purposes of copywriting, the devil really is in the details. And how do you know which details to include? Well, a good exercise is to put yourself in the shoes of your target demographic, ask the questions that come to your mind, and answer the questions.

So now, let us go back to the sentence, "Get something." If someone were to say that to you, the first question that will come to your mind is this: "What should I get?"

While the sentence "Get something" is a complete thought, it leaves too many questions. "Something" is too vague and, as such, it is unlikely to leave an impact or to be remembered. That said, it is important to make the object of your sentence as clear and as specific as possible.

Having said that, let us now revise our sample sentence. Instead of writing "Get something", you should write "Get a printer."

Step 3: Describe your object.

Now the object of your sentence is something clearer. However, "a printer" is too generic. It could be any printer. It does not create a mental image. If you were in the shoes of your target audience, you would probably ask: "What kind of printer?"

Again, details are very important. You want to be very specific so that your target audience knows exactly what you are talking about. Your goal is to get them to remember your pitch so clearly that even after reading your copy, they still remember what you just pitched and can look that up themselves later.

With that, let us revise our sentence again. "Get a portable Wi-Fi printer." Now that is much clearer, right? Slowly, you are creating a more visually stimulating sentence for your target audience. Not only do they know what you want them to get (a printer, in this case), but they also know what kind to get (a portable Wi-Fi enabled one).

Step 4: Replicate your object in the minds of your target audience.

The sentence in the step might be a lot more specific already, but it is still not that optimized. After all, the descriptions are still quite generic and could be interpreted in any number of ways. That said, you want to create in the minds of your audience a very specific and very clear image – that of the product you are selling.

This is where brand names and various specifications come in. Mention whatever it is that makes your product attractive, unique, or different. It is not enough that your target consumers know what you are talking about, they must know what product or service you are referring to.

So, let us work on our base sentence again. We can revise it to "Get a Brand X portable Wi-Fi printer that weighs no heavier than your book and fits right inside your bag."

See what we did there? Now your audience has a very clear picture in their minds. They know the brand, the specifications, and, more importantly, they can picture themselves using the product in question. In a sense, you are providing them with experience even before they get their hands on the product you are marketing.

Step 5: Relate the object to the target consumer's experiences.

This is the last step, and this is possibly the most crucial one, primarily because this relates back to the eight hard-wired human desires. The trick here is to choose at least one (you can incorporate several, as you see fit) hard-wired human desire and to integrate that into the sentence.

For purposes of our illustration, let us take the fifth hard-wired human desire: the desire to have a comfortable living situation. Since this is an innate desire which every individual experience and, as such, can relate to, it serves our purpose of relating the object to the target consumer. You want your target audience to feel a certain connection with the product. You do not want to tell them to buy something. Instead, you want to make them feel that they need something, that "something" being the object of the sentence here.

To illustrate, let us revise our base sentence once again. We can turn it into "If you are tired of having to shuffle back-and-forth between your house and your office every single time you need to print an important document, then you should definitely get a Brand X portable Wi-Fi printer that weighs no heavier than your book and fits right inside your bag." See the difference between this sentence and "Get something"? "Get something" evokes no emotion or imagery whatsoever, but our final sentence revision paints a very specific image in the minds of your target audience. Even better, your target audience can easily picture themselves in the scenario you just painted. Not only that, but since you have made the sentence very specific, they know exactly what to do to address the scenario you just painted.

Talent is certainly a factor when it comes to effective copywriting, but that does not mean that you cannot learn how to write effectively. If you follow these five-step process, you should have no difficulty in transforming bland sentences into visually stunning powerhouses. With some practice, you will certainly be able to master this craft in no time and be on your way in creating powerful statements that can evoke the emotions and modify the purchasing behavior of your target audience or demographic.

Chapter 4 SEO And How to Rank on Google

OPTIMISING FOR SEARCH ENGINES

The skill of search engine optimization has changed and expanded immensely in the last few years! But it is still important for writers to understand how SEO relates to content writing and how to format your content so search engines can easily find and read your content.

It used to be pretty much all about:

1. The number and relevance of links to your pages

2. Site structure and navigation

3. On page optimization of your content

Now search engine optimization is all about:

1. The number and relevance of links to your pages (even more important)

2. Site structure and navigation

3. On page optimization of your content

4. Bounce rate on website

5. Engagement & number of pages visitors view

6. Number of authority connections via social media or links (how many authority sites or personal profiles are pointing to the website)

7. Semantic search

What this means is that Google and other search engines use many more indicators to evaluate a website page's importance. They want to know if anyone /website with authority thinks the site is good and how well it satisfies its visitors. They determine this by working out who is linking to the site and by looking at visitors' behavior onsite through analytics.

What can you do to make your page more authoritative and search engine friendly?

Well, the longer your page is (generally), the better you are at offering steps, facts, charts, images with properly formatted alt text descriptions and clearly visible titles (H1, H2 etc.) tags, the higher it is likely to rank. Your page also needs to have both a meta and H1 title that contains your main keywords.

Adding keywords to your title may be obvious, but the text you add around your title and the relevance of any subtitles to your main title also help Google's' semantic algorithms to determine the context of the whole article.

Make it easy for search engines to determine that your article contains lots of useful content. If that content holds visitors on site for longer than other websites' pages and has lots of 'votes' of confidence (links, shares and Google+1's for example), it is more likely to rank well.

If your content is easy to read for search engine robots and not just humans, your chances of ranking higher increase.

So, make sure, when you add images and see the option add 'alt text', add keywords that are relevant to both the image and to the keywords in your titles. Google can see what many images are, so be honest about describing what your images are and you'll enhance the searchability of your images.

Use H1, H2, H3, H4 tags. Surround title and bold text with other relevant text that gives context to those titles. For example, let's say the title of your article was 'How to Repair Cells at Home'. Google only knows what type of cell you are referring to from the surrounding text on the page. Are you talking about human body cells? Are you talking about battery cells? Maybe you are talking about cell phone cells.

The only way search engines know what you are talking about is through semantic indexing of your pages. The algorithm references images, subtitles, and surrounding text to determine what the page is about. The relationship between different elements of content tells Google and other search engines how useful the content might be to searchers. So, the more clues you can give the search engine robots that crawl your page (yep, they are robots and can't see the page like we humans can), the higher the likelihood of your pages ranking somewhere decent.

Then link back to your page from content that is also highly relevant to your page. Use hashtags and descriptions that closely relate to your page. If you can encourage 'authorities' to connect to your page though any medium, whether it be links (best to aim for) or social media, you will help search engines identify your page as 'popular' amongst the people who are most relevant or authoritative.

If your page is seen as popular, holds visitors' attention, and satisfies them in some way, you have achieved your goal of optimizing your page.

The content writing cannot ignore the SEO, that set of activities of optimization of the textual contents of a website that contribute to improving the positioning in the results of the search engines. In the world of communication today, it is not enough to be online; it is essential to be found. Therefore, entrusting to a copywriter the writing of the contents of his company website and possibly of his social channels is a winning move to get good visibility, especially compared to relevant research.

SEO Content writing combines two peculiar things: SEO and Content writing. Even if you have a good team of writers, SEO is a very specific niche that requires a solid foundation. Not everyone knows it, and even people who do it don't always know how to do it right.

When done right, SEO Content writing services can do the following things for your brand:

Enhance4 your search rankings: A great SEO activity makes your content more visible and will help to claim more important points in the SERPs, which is important since these commercials claim the most clicks and attention.

Money savings: If you have relied on paid advertising or paid placements, SEO Content writing services can be real savings. The SEO Content writing is aimed at customers with whom you want to connect and offers your content a path to classify them organically.

Keep content up to date: Search engines are claiming an increasingly large market share, so having a more prominent view within them is a great idea. How well you simplify the process for customers to find your business, locate your content, and have meaningful interactions with your brand, the more sales your company will enjoy.

Help you stay competitive: If you're not working on SEO, but all your competitors are doing it, you can bet you'll stay behind. Everyone is doing it today, and you can't afford to be the last one.

Proper web copy can increase conversions, gain more customers, and even increase Google's ranking. This is too important to ignore.

A good search that increases the value of your content

- Brand Management

Content writing is not art only at the service of the final sale of the product. In the business environment, resorting to a professional in the sector means using a resource in managing the brand image and the company. The task of the copywriter is therefore also to identify and communicate company values, to clarify the idea that the public has of the company and the brand associated with it. In this way, a well-written textual content allows people to understand the belief system as the foundation of the company and eventually share it, thus generating stable relationships between seller and buyer.

Empathy

Before being an expert in content marketing and writing techniques, a copywriter is a person with a wealth of knowledge and experience, usually with a marked sensitivity and excellent empathic abilities. In the study phase of the brand, the product and the consumers that precede the preparation of the textual contents, the copywriter can understand the meeting point between the brand identity, the benefits of the product, and the needs that the target manifests. In this way, it is able to make this information converge in a text in which the company can recognize the principles that inspire its work and the public, in turn, a company in which to place its trust, certain that the shopping experience will be satisfactory.

- Excellent Copy Becomes Fuel for Marketing

A good copy can become an essential tool for a company's marketing, a startup, or a freelancer for personal branding. According to Steve Blank's theories, referring to a startup or innovative company, it is important to consider marketing as well as product development and consequently content writing.

- If Everyone Looked the Same, We Are All Going to Get Tired of Looking at One Another

The best copies are those that differ from others. The first time we read them, they don't remind us of that old advertisement a few years ago, but they positively amaze us for the novelty. Returning to Apple, or rather to Steve Jobs and his Think Different, proved to be a more than winning weapon for his return to Cupertino, completely detaching Apple from all other competitors.

- Quality Text

In the age of the semantic web, when it comes to creating a website, the activity of SEO Content writing has become fundamental for positioning an internet site among the first results of search engines.

The latest changes to the Google algorithm, as well as substantial changes in the local positioning of the websites, have further highlighted the strategic importance of creating quality content to meet the standards of over 200 factors and positioning of the search engine and including information texts, original, well-structured and, above all, useful for the end user.

A clear, complete, easily readable text that can be consulted by any reference public generates an important positioning phenomenon: sharing, to create organic link building, which consists of increasing the incoming links to increase the popularity of the site in question. If the user finds the published content useful, there are concrete possibilities for sharing it via links on other websites: social networks, personal or corporate blogs, other sites. When Google finds these inbound links, the value of that page to the eyes of the crawler (the software that scans the contents of the network) increases, contributing to improving the overall reputation of the entire website, its positioning, and consequently the number of potential new visitors.

Writing copy for the web requires an approach for a brochure, a book or on any paper support, and in some ways even more complex pieces. The details to be taken into consideration before drafting a copy for the web are many: choosing the right keywords based on search traffic and competitiveness, analyzing the positioning and strategies of competitors, studying the density and prominence of the keywords calculating the relationship between text and HTML code of the entire site structure, monitoring the results and making periodic changes in the event of updates to the algorithm or improvements in the SEO strategy by competitors and, above all, writing for people, for their interests, their research and their needs. Content writing written solely for search engines - and therefore difficult to read for the user - means the balance for SEO content writing is fundamental.

Without going into the complex and necessary technicalities underlying a correct optimization (not easy to understand and explain for non-workers), a text written with the rules of SEO Content writing foresees a series of technical and creative devices to generate a satisfactory result that requires the intervention of professionals and different skills able to understand the best strategy to balance the need for information users are looking for when browsing and the specifications required by the search engine.

Above all, it must be known that Google's goal is to offer Internet users adequate results in relation to their research. When your visitor types keywords into the Google search box for your services, Google scans the millions of referral websites to show you the results that are most relevant to your search. Google will scan the pages of your site to check if its content is in line with the search, but also to determine what position your site can be proposed.

For example, if your site is less relevant than another, it may end up in the second, fifth, and so on. Google's algorithm considers various parameters, some of which we know: H tags, alt, keywords, relevance, site quality, incoming and outgoing links, and more.

Chapter 5 Best Niches to Copywriting for Profit

Figuring out where to start can be more than a little overwhelming when there are so many potential markets out there to explore. Finding the right niche or niches for you is an adventure that starts with a bit of personal discovery. The best place to begin is by taking a few minutes to look inward at your own interests and hobbies.

What are you into? What subjects are your most excited to talk to your friends about? Is there anything new you want to learn more about? Are you so well-versed in a favorite subject that you already know it inside and out? Is there a topic you've always loved and have dreamed of finding a way to make a living by doing some related to it? These are all great questions to consider before you go niche hunting.

Everyone is passionate about something. For most people, it doesn't take a lot of handwringing to generate a short list of dream topics that interest them. Here's a super quick exercise. Complete the following sentence with the first thing that comes to mind.

Chances are you didn't hesitate more than a second or two, if at all, to fill in the blank. If that's the case, Bingo! You've got item number one for your brainstorming list. But don't stop there! There's no reason to stick with just one item. In fact, you want to make as massive a list as possible.

The power of brainstorming

Knowing up-front what subjects, you want to write about the most can be invaluable when you set out to start researching potential niche markets. While you might immediately feel inclined to home in on one dream market, it's also a good idea to brainstorm a bigger and broader list to work off from. Until you dig into the research phase of this process, it's hard to get a good bead on how well your top subject picks will line-up with existing niche markets. You want to have plenty of backup options at the ready, too.

There's another reason why brainstorming a big list of your interests is important. Not only is it useful for helping to identify potential niches you can approach when you start your research, it also can easily spawn ideas for lots of sub-niches to purse, and make it easier to come up with ideas for specific articles to pitch within a given subject area. Mega brainstorming can open the flood gates for cool ideas to pursue in your writing, and I'm a firm believer in the usefulness of spilling the contents of your brain out onto the page in the form of lists.

When I'm doing any kind of research – whether it's for a new market I want to break into, a new book I hope to write, or a new article I'm interested in pitching – I spin up my mental Gatling gun, take the safety off, and pump as many hot idea bullets into the blank canvas as possible before I run out of brain ammo.

Some ideas that get spat out in the process will be definite misses, but the rawer thought content I can get on the page, the more I must work with when it comes to picking things over and whittle it down. I also find that many of the better ideas that survive the chopping block spawn other cool ideas and additional rabbit holes to dive into, which is why I find this process works so well.

Action Step #1: Brainstorm potential niches

It's time to act! You can either stop reading this book right now for a few minutes to complete this short exercise or come back to it later during a second pass.

Get brainstorming! I'd like you to brainstorm your own freelance niche list. Grab a piece of paper and something to write with or cozy up with your favorite computer device. For the next ten to 15 minutes, I want you to dump everything in your brain onto the page. Make a big messy list of any and every topic you've always wanted to write about, and you can even start blocking out ideas that might make for good articles to pitch, too. Consider both big picture subjects and sub-niches within a topic. Get it all out onto the page, and when you're done with that, let's move on to the next.

Once you've generated a large list of possible niches and corresponding sub-angles to investigate, pick your top three favorites to focus on for now. Set the rest aside in a safe spot, since you never know when they'll come in handy as fodder for your freelance engine. I like to post ideas on a corkboard nearby desk, for those moments where I need inspiration.

With that sorted out, it's time to dive into a little good old-fashioned research. To stave off information overload, it's best to focus your more in-depth research on one market at a time, but you do want to keep your other top niches in mind as you begin poking around. Always be on the lookout for other opportunities that might prove interesting.

Research (it's what's for dinner)

Spending hours doing web searches, pouring over the pages of physical and online publications, and tracking down intel on niche markets certainly isn't the sexiest aspect of this process, but it's critical. Taking the time to do proper research before you start slinging pitches is important on so many levels, because it lets you:

1) Gauge the size of a niche market

You want to scope out the lay of the land in each market to get a feel for what kind of potential it holds. The more outlets you can find devoted to covering topics within a niche, the more opportunities you'll likely uncover when you start pitching editors. An abundance of high-end looking publications is a great sign, but don't discount the smaller blogs and medium sites too. You never know where you might get a solid "in" that could lead to a sweet gig and propel you upwards within a market.

2) Find potential publications worth pitching within a given niche

There might be plenty of publications out there that run coverage within a niche, but how many of them are open to freelancers? That's something to think about and look for when you're researching. Some outlets post writers guidelines and contact information, while others expect you to do a bit more detective work. Look at the mastheads and staff pages for each outlet, too. If you see some of the same names popping up on the bylines for different outlets, that's a good sign of a freelance-friendly publication.

3) Find other writers and editors within a niche to network with

Making nice with other writers and editorial folks already entrenched deep within a specific market can be a great way to gather intel. Networking is huge. It helps you gain important connections and contacts that can be beneficial down the line, plus getting to know new writer pals is great. Social media is a great tool for this. Follow other writers and editors on Twitter, check out their websites, and make connections in other ways. You won't regret it.

4) Get specific ideas to pitch

One of things I like the most about researching outlets and niches is that it often gives me a ton of different ideas for potential pitches to play around with. Yes, I've already divulged my list-making obsession to you. Indeed, research throws gasoline on that fire. Seeing the kinds of pieces each outlet runs is a good way to inform your own pitches, and it also helps you get up-to-speed on what's happening within a giving coverage beat.

5) Identify sub-niches to specialize in

Every market can easily be broken down into sub-niches. Research can be a great way to get unique ideas on how to stand out from the pack by carving out a very distinct specialty within your niche of choice.

It's important to document your research journey as thoroughly as possible. Keep excellent notes, whether you're scribbling on paper scraps or typing things up in a spreadsheet or Word document. Copy-paste the names and URLs of publication and websites. Track helpful contacts and other resources you stumble upon. Compile as much info as you can on every niche, you're thinking of breaking into. All this great intel you amass will be needed for quick reference as you take your first action steps towards getting a foothold.

Trust me, fail to keep track of all this stuff as it comes up the first time, and you'll be kicking yourself later when you start working up pitches. Nothing stinks more than having to go back and spend hours re-researching stuff you're already uncovered but forgotten. Efficiency is a great thing.

Chapter 6 Copywriting for Social Media Ads

Copywriting for Facebook Marketing

In the copywriting industry itself, there are niches that you can also specialize in. One copywriting niche where demand for experts is increasing is the social media.

Facebook is the undisputed champion of all social networking website. Many websites have risen from obscurity by using Facebook alone as a marketing tool. Websites that struggled to gain traction when using search engine marketing are turning to Facebook marketing as an alternative solution.

Facebook Copywriting

Facebook is successful because of its ability to keep people's attention. The features in a user's profile page and timeline are so engaging that many people tend to spend hours in these pages without being aware of it. Companies and smaller businesses take advantage of these features by making sure that their posts show in these pages.

To be an excellent Facebook copywriter, you should first be familiar of the common objectives of companies and business that are using this social network as a marketing tool. Here are the common goals of companies that market on Facebook:

- Product/company introduction
- Awareness
- Popularity
- Event promotion

- Increase online and offline sales

Before you can start marketing on Facebook, you should first identify the need of your clients in their marketing campaign. If they are not aware of their marketing goals yet, then help them establish their goals by interviewing them and analyzing their motives.

Helping reach their goals through Copywriting

When copywriting for Facebook, you have your own tasks to help the clients achieve their marketing goals. First, you need to get the user's attention. Then, you need keep their engagement. In other words, you need to keep them reading. Lastly, you need to make them act.

In Facebook, a user can only do a few actions that can benefit your client; these are liking, sharing, and clicking on links. If your copy has made the target users take favorable actions, then you have done your part as a copywriter.

Liking

A "like" is Facebook's version of an up vote. It has two purposes. First, it increases the reach of a post. As people like your post, it may also be shown to their friends' newsfeeds. The posts that were liked by friends will show in the ticker in the upper right side of the newsfeed page.

The second function of a like is as a subscribe button for pages. The posts on a liked page will appear in the person's newsfeed. This will increase the probability that future posts will have better engagement because more people will see them.

Sharing

Sharing, on the other hand, is the feature that will make your posts become viral. When people share your content, it will appear in their timeline as well as in their friends' newsfeeds.

Clicking on links

If you promise your clients that you can make a lot of users click on their post links on Facebook, then you will have a considerable edge against your copywriting competitors. This task, however, is not easy to do because people don't easily click on links.

Copywriting on Facebook: How to Get Clicks, Likes and Shares

There are generally two ways to get clicks, likes and shares: through organic Facebook marketing and paid advertisements. Your role as a copywriter is to increase the likelihood that people will like and share content in organic or paid marketing.

You can do this by following these tips:

Appeal to people's emotions

People in Facebook are there to have a good time. They spend so much time in Facebook because posts remind them of people and things that they met and experienced in the past. That is why posts like "throwback Thursday" persist until now. To make them like or share a post of a page, you should use emotional topics in your copies.

Use your target user's language and way of speaking

When posting, you could appeal better to a specific market if you talk the way they do. If you are targeting engineers, for example, then you should also use jargons and technical terms that only they will know. If you are targeting a specific nationality, you may become more successful if you post status updates and links that speak their language.

Use words popular in the internet

Some words are more magnetic to people in the internet than others. For instance, the word awesome is a great word to use regularly if you are targeting users in their teens and early adulthood. Other magnetic words are: "Wow", "Never", "Inspiring", "Die or Dead", "Definitely", "Feel", "Terrified", and "Amazing."

In the past, words like "Free", "Now", and "You" are eye-catchers, but many internet users have now associated them to annoying ads and pop-ups. You should expect the same phenomenon to happen with any attention-grabbing words in Facebook. People will eventually learn to ignore them when they become too popular.

Use the "post description" to catch attention

The post or ad description is the first thing that users read after your page name. If that part is not interesting, then they will move on to the next item on their newsfeed. You should use this part to gain attention and create curiosity by adding more powerful words. For instance, popular pages use "this", "that" and similar pronouns often. Here are some examples:

"This man can't believe what he was seeing"

"That's not right. This shouldn't be legal."

Adding a picture that matches the description will also increase the likelihood of a like, a share and a click.

Use the power of the red arrow in photos

One of the most effective combinations when making people click on links is by using the powerful pronouns suggested above and adding a photo that has a red arrow to refer to the thing or person being represented by the pronoun. For instance, if your headline goes something like this:

"This is why you should not drink and drive"

You should also add a photo of a person driving while texting and an arrow pointing at the driver. This will not only grab the attention of the users but also make them curious of what will happen to the driver.

Copywriting for Twitter Marketing

You shouldn't consider Twitter as the second-best social network next to Facebook. From a marketing standpoint, Twitter is a completely different sport. One of the most important factors that make Twitter unique is its users. People who go to Twitter are there because they like to learn, be entertained and converse. Just like in the real world, no one will listen to you, laugh with you and talk with you if all you talk about are products and company promotions. Copywriting in Twitter should follow the unwritten rules that Twitter users observe.

Twitter etiquette

There are two important points that you should remember when copywriting tweets. Hashtags should not be in the beginning of the post. Hashtags are special codes that categorize your tweets. People who search the hashtags you use will be able to see your tweets.

The other rule that you need to follow is to put your links in the middle of the message and the hashtag. You must add a short message with everything that you share. When you are clear with these rules, you can now start copywriting tweets.

Establish your goal

Just like in any marketing campaign, you should first establish your goals for Twitter marketing. You should let the client know, however, that there are limitations when it comes to using Twitter. The obvious limitation is the limited number of characters that you can use per message. You can use photos and links to compensate for that.

The other limitation is with the reach of your tweets. Generally, the only people you will be able to reach are your followers. That means that if you have a new Twitter account for business, you cannot set ambitious goals like increasing sales.

Write in a conversational manner

After identifying your marketing goals, the next step is to establish the speaker's voice. People will use a generic voice when reading your tweets. You can include pictures of a company representative with your tweet to establish the voice in the readers' mind.

After that, you can start creating tweets that are conversational in nature. Refer to your reader in the second person and include words that are frequently part of retweets.

Use frequently retweeted words

Just like in Facebook, there are also words in Twitter that are more popular than the others. When including a link, use the verb "check out". When giving tips, use the phrase "How to" and use the hashtag #tips. Some popular headline tricks like "Top 10", "Exclusive" and "Free" are still popular in Twitter.

Identify the hashtags used by your target users

It is also important to identify the hashtags that will best help your client's marketing goal. If you are trying to make a Christmas promotion reach more people, you could use the hashtags #Christmas promo or #Christmas Sale.

Never shorten important words

One big mistake of people who try to cram too many information in one tweet is to shorten important words. People sometimes use the search feature to look for tweets that are relevant to them. If you shortened some of your words by deleting vowels or replacing multiple consonants, you will not be included in the search results of those words.

Manage the number of characters that you use

Make sure to tweet only one message at a time. If you have a long message, then Twitter is not the best place to deliver it. If your goal is to promote retweets of a post, you should make sure that that post has enough space for people to add their own input. For longer posts, put the text in an image and tweet the image instead.

Chapter 7 Copywriting for Email Marketing

Among the many online activities, newsletters are still of some importance today. Email marketing is a digital marketing activity that still works, especially if integrated into a structured communication campaign. It differs in newsletters, DEM (Direct email marketing), and transactional. According to a study, 12.4 billion emails were sent via the platform in 2017, with an opening rate of + 35.7% compared to the year. In the United States of America, over 240 million advertisements are received via email: around 7.7 for each user. 61% of these are discounts and promotions, yet I find that the most interesting information in the report concerns the reasons Americans decide to subscribe to a company newsletter:

- need for information and insights with respect to a given topic (35% of respondents)
- a reminder that is a sort of let's stay in touch (20.4%)
- interest in the proposed contents (18.4%).

But how to write a newsletter effectively? Here are useful tips:

Use an Object That Can Intrigue: A statement is often weaker than a question. In just a few words, you must push the recipient not only to open the mail but also lose a few minutes of his life to understand what we are talking about.

Be clear: Transparency always rewards, but confusing periods or attempts at click baiting will lead the user to abandon or, worse still, get angry.

Customize Those Who Register: Customize those who register often and leave the name, and there is software that can retrieve it to insert it in the text, even in the object. The more personal the message is, the more the user will be willing to open the email.

Work at Smart Call to Action: Always give a reason to act; it is not enough to say Buy, so to speak. The user wants to participate in the purchase process, does not like orders.

Remember the Visuals: The graphics are important. Make sure that the messages are well-integrated with the images.

Propose Exclusive Content: Doing Content Marketing does not mean obsessing over the reader with content represented to exhaustion on multiple channels. A good newsletter must offer exclusive content and always give the idea that by writing you can access an exclusive type of offer. You will get extensive ideas in other of this book.

Most people go into copywriting in order to make money, not do the work for free in their spare time. As a freelance copywriter, you need to be careful about the clients that you are looking at to make sure that you find the ones that will really work well with you and will pay you when everything is done.

There are many fantastic clients out there. They will answer your questions in a timely manner, pay you by milestones, and will fall in love with the ideas that you present to them. They pay you on time and make it easy for you to enjoy your job. Unfortunately, while there are quite a few great clients that you will be able to work with, there are also a lot of bad clients who will make you want to pull out your hair and quit copywriting right away. These are the clients that procrastinate all the time, who are difficult to get ahold of, and will neglect to pay for you and just disappear when the work is done.

As a beginner, you are going to run into more of these clients than you would probably like to admit. There are always shady clients who are going to look at you and think they can take advantage of you. But there are a few things that you can do to watch out for those bad clients including:

- The price is too high—if you are looking at a job posting and notice that the price is high for the work, higher than what is considered normal for the work that is requested, you should run away. These clients are usually just trying to attract beginners to do the work. The issue is that they will promise all this money but won't sign a contract and often take the work without ever offering a payment. Always be careful if the rate doesn't seem to fit in line with what is usual in the industry.

- The price is too low—most clients will list out how much they are willing to pay for the work. If you notice that the price is low, it is probably not worth your time. The client will expect to get high quality work for a price that is well below market value, and you will probably waste your time. Make sure to charge a rate that you are comfortable with and stick to that.

- Won't do a contract ahead of time—it is always a good idea to get started with a new client by writing a contract. This is going to be a good way to protect you and the client. This contract is going to list all the things that will happen while you are working together, including the work to be completed, the cost, and the deadlines. If a client won't fill out the agreement, there is probably something that is going wrong, and you need to be careful.

- Clues inside the posting—sometimes you will be able to see that there are issues with the client within their posting. If the wording keeps changing, there are issues with the grammar, or something else seems off with the posting, you should proceed with caution and look for another client to work with.

- The workload changes—when you read through the job posting, you will look to see what the workload is about and then fill out your application. Sometimes though, you will spend time talking to a client, and they will try to change the scope of the work or add on a lot more and still want to pay the same price. These clients often prove to be difficult to work with and will keep changing the scope or adding on more work without paying you extra. Set out the terms right away and only do the work that was agreed to.

- Client is hard to get ahold of—if you are having trouble getting your client to answer your emails or calls and the job hasn't even been awarded yet, you may need to worry. Times get busy, but if your client goes days without talking to you and then suddenly shows up again, you are probably dealing with a difficult client. Give them some time to respond, but if it seems to take too long, it may be best to pick someone else to work with.

Learning when to spot a bad client is one of the best things that you can do for your career. There are a ton of clients who are excellent, pay well, and are a joy to work with, and you will find plenty of these along your journey. But you will find that one bad client can ruin it all for you. So, make sure you are looking for some of these signs each time that you apply for a new job and find out which clients are the best for you.

Post comments on other related board pins, especially bigger sites with 1000 plus followers.

Remember to include the most important points for your audience and topic and to be helpful and knowledgeable at the same time.

Facebook Checklist

Purpose

To build social reach and attract new likes/followers from other sources. Use Facebook to find existing and new customers to share experiences with using media to give a multi-dimensional snapshot of what you offer.

Policy

Create interactive content that engages new clients through multimedia with use of popular #hashtags.

Procedure

Research popular trending travel related #hashtag topics, find other websites using these and like, contribute to, and comment on their pages. Offer content to big sites who want quality images and content to post. Comment on their content.

Look for topics your clients are interested in and create connective content between your site and theirs. Contribute to these pages with positive comments, interacting with potential client audiences.

Include #tags in content on your pages and other sites for your travel niches and on external Facebook pages.

These should be used EXTENSIVELY on bigger Facebook pages you have liked.

Consider adding Facebook or blog comments to blogs.

Add:

- Images – good quality pictures and videos
- Add # hashtags
- Add URL where appropriate

- Comment on other posts
- Contribute to other peoples' pages with helpful, relevant content

Use statements including phrases like:

- How to
- Why people
- You could
- If you
- Ways to
- Top reasons to
- Tops reasons why
- Why it's
- Things to consider
- Important things to remember

LinkedIn Checklist

Purpose

To create a visible presence on LinkedIn

Policy

Stay

Procedure

Follow topics that are being and leading personalities in the field you are writing content about. Engage with content and people.

Add:

- Images – good quality pictures and videos
- Create and contribute to discussions that are relevant to your audience
- Add URL where appropriate
- Comment on other posts/discussions and add useful ideas and contributions
- Endorse and invite other members

Use statements including phrases like:

- How to
- Why people
- You could
- If you
- Ways to
- Top reasons to
- Tops reasons why
- Why it's
- Things to consider
- Important things to remember

With all social media, remember to include the most important points for your audience and topic and to be helpful and knowledgeable.

There are two important starting points to remember when implementing your Google+ strategy:

First, use keyword and intent based combinations of phrases in your Titles and...

Second, use very specific and correct formatting of your posts' content. If linking to a page, use an enough word to make the post highly relevant to the page your post points to. If not linking to a page and creating an image post, make sure the description is a decent length to make it more searchable in Google+ and generic search engines.

Google+ Checklist

There are four steps you need to walk through when implementing any Google plus strategy:

1. Keyword and target page research and layout

2. Acquiring RELEVANT Followers

3. Participating in communities and commenting on posts (building relationships)

4. Posting sequence and formatting for Google search to make it easy for your audience to find your posts/page

Ensure that your Google+ posts:

- Are extremely targeted to the right audience (use keywords from your main website page titles)

- Are engaging and encourage curiosity (talk about the reader and what they want, then tie the features and benefits of your products and services into your post copy)

- Contain the right blend and number of #hashtags (4 to 5 maximums per post)

- Contain the right number of keywords (300 words - fewer is better)

- Link to the page I want to teach Google to have high relevance to my audience (to improve my overall website authority and relevance)

- Motivate readers to take a desired action or learn more by inserting copy that builds interest and trust (ask them to do something other than buying, e.g., read more about [insert what they are interested in in the form of a feature or benefit]

- Position you as an authority in your niche to both Google and visitors

- Help Google serve up your content as often as possible

- Lead visitors to a landing page that delivers what you promise in your content. This is the first step in your sales funnel (yes, your offsite content IS part of your sales funnel). Using templates dramatically reduces the time needed to post awesome posts both Google+ and your audience will love.

Chapter 8 Making Decision to Write

There are a million make-money-online schemes that abound out there, so, why should anyone ditch many of those and pitch their tent with blogging? This is a question that any logical person would want to ask. While the other numerous make money online schemes have great potential to make you money, blogging is unique for so many reasons, and we are going to talk about these unique benefits of blogging shortly.

1. Blogging can make you rich

While blogging is not a get rich quick scheme, it does have the potential to make you rich. One good thing about the income you earn from blogging is its passive nature. This means that you only must do the work once and watch your income keep flowing in even on the days you decide not to work. With such a passive income model, you can have all the time in the world to bond with your family, take vacations, and do other things that matter to you.

Another thing that makes blogging an excellent money-making business is that there are thousands of ways through which you can make money with your blog. You can sell ad space to advertisers – this is one of the most popular methods of making money with your blog. When it comes to selling ad space – you have many choices. You can let ad networks like Google, Bing, etc. place ads on your blog and pay you on a commission basis or you can develop your own unique pricing model, negotiate with companies directly, have them pay you money to place their advertisements on your blog.

Additionally, you can accept sponsored posts where businesses pay you money to place marketing content on your blog. This is how it works – a company writes a marketing post which they could use to drive traffic to their own website. Then, they pay you money to publish the post on your blog and link it to their website. You can accept as many guest posts as possible in a month, and you earn according to the number of such posts you publish on your blog. Also, how much you can earn through this income model solely lies in your hands. So, the better your negotiation skills, the more money you earn.

You can also promote affiliate offers on your blog and earn a commission when a sale happens through the link you promoted. Affiliate marketing is a highly profitable way of making money on the internet. With affiliate marketing, you do not need to develop a product – you promote the products already developed by other companies to your blog visitors. If a sale happens through your promotions, then the company that has the product pays you an affiliate commission.

Affiliate marketing is always a win-win for both you, the company that owns the product you are promoting and the customer. It is a win for you because you get to earn for promoting other people's products. It is a win for the company that developed the affiliate product because other people help them to promote their goods and services. And it is a win for the customer because you are helping them have access to products that can help them solve their problems.

There are thousands of affiliate marketing networks you can partner with and earn money when you promote their products on your blog. Click bank is a popular affiliate marketing network where you can find millions of products that you can promote to your audience and earn money. You can also consider joining the Amazon affiliate program where you promote Amazon products on your blog so that when people buy those products or even other products through your efforts, Amazon pays you money.

Most of the internet service providers you will be using their service as a blogger have affiliate programs which you can join and earn money by promoting some tools to your audience. For instance, you need a hosting service to host your blog; you also need a domain name provider

– the chances are that these providers will have affiliate programs. Now, when you promote their affiliate offers, and people get to buy hosting service through your affiliate links, you earn money.

There are also hundreds of other tools you need as a blogger and most of them have affiliate programs as well. For instance, you need an autoresponder for email marketing purposes, and most autoresponders have affiliate offers you can promote. Apart from the tools you make use of, you can promote a ton of affiliate software tools or products that you think your audience needs.

Another great way through which you can earn money with your blog is by selling digital and physical products. In fact, digital products are best because you don't need to keep inventory – you simply develop a single copy of the product and sell to millions of customers. The difference between a physical and digital product is that you can touch a physical product while you cannot do the same for a digital product. Digital products are held intangibly on offline and online storage mediums. Typical examples of digital products include eBooks, software programs, and digital games. Examples of physical products include wristwatches, shirts, hoverboards, etc.

Now, you don't need to be the developer of either the physical or digital products before you can sell them on your blog. If you want to start selling eBooks on your blog, for instance, you could hire a writer, provide them with an outline and have them create a good eBook which you can host and sell on your blog. As for physical products, you can enter into a partnership with major brands so you can drop ship their products on your blog. Once you have grown your blog's audience, selling products to them will not be a problem, and the return can be quite impressive.

Your blog can make you money through gated content – how this works is – you create some special high quality and high in demand content on your blog, then make it available on a subscription basis to only those readers who pay. You can create a members-only and hide away the more valuable content there – then when a member pays a stipulated subscription fee, you give them access to the gated member's only.

While the above is not so popular, there are still some bloggers who earn money through it. However, before you try incorporating such a model into your blog, you need to have grown the blog to a certain level. Obviously, you cannot adopt this model when you are just starting out, and you must have shown that you know your onions as well. If you want to make the model work for you, your free content must be compelling enough and packed with value to make the reader want to pay for more. If your general content is not good enough, no reader would want to pay you money to read more of your content.

The methods described above are some of the most popular means of earning through your blog. There are obviously more ways through which you can make money with your blog; we have just the popular ones. Depending on your audience, you can research and creatively come up with more ways of monetizing your content. In a subsequent of this book, we shall do an in-depth analysis of each of these blog income models. For now, let's continue to look at the other benefits of running a blog.

2. Blogging will help you improve your writing and technical skills

Blogging gives you a chance to learn and perfect some critical skills, such as writing and other technical skills. Even if you aren't writing your blog posts yourself, you will still be working with some technical tools, and the more you work with these tools, the more you learn and improve. If you are the one writing your posts, blogging will help you to improve your writing skills.

As a blogger, you will be using a lot of plugins and templates – you may also need to learn basic web design so you can always modify your blog without seeking the help of a professional that might be costly. The more you work with these online tools, the more you develop your technical skills.

3. Blogging will help you develop healthier habits

In addition to helping you develop some valuable technical skills, blogging also helps you to learn the art of commitment and discipline. Healthy habits like time management, dedication, etc. which you can learn while blogging can come in handy when you are dealing with other aspects of your personal and professional life. So, blogging does not just put money in your pocket alone; it helps you to develop some critical skills and learn healthy habits.

4. Blogging helps you build a network

When people face a challenge, the first thing they do is that they turn to the internet to seek a solution. By owning a blog and posting useful content, you can attract people who will see you as their hero – these people will consume your content, post their own thoughts in the form of comments, and some will even send your personal messages.

5. Blogging enables you to increase your knowledge of things in your niche and beyond

There is a hidden researcher in you, and blogging helps to bring him out. As a blogger, you must research, collate, sort information, and present it authoritatively to your audience. Remember, your readers are visiting your blog because they see you as an authority in your niche. So, you must do the proper research to ensure that you post only quality content. In your bid to put up new well-researched content regularly, your effort will lead you to the discovery of new things in your field and beyond.

6. Blogging gives you the perfect outlet to express yourself

Your blog, no matter the type of content you share with it is still your personal space – so, even if your blog is a niche one, you can still intersperse your opinions in your posts and get your voice heard. You can use your blog to air your opinions on trending issues while still maintaining a defined niche. A blog is a perfect outlet for self-expression.

7. Blogging exposes you to new opportunities and ideas

As a blogger, you will literally live on the internet – this means you will always get exposed to numerous opportunities and ideas that abound on the internet. It could be ideas on ways of making money or improved ways of living a healthier life – blogging just makes you more exposed than the average Joe on the streets. The more you get exposed, your approach to life will change for the better. The people you will get to meet will also influence your life positively, and the fact that you have people who see you as a hero will make you want to be of good behavior.

8. You can make a difference in people's lives

Millions of people around the world are facing one issue or the other, and they usually turn to the internet to seek a solution. These people are just looking for a little glimmer of hope or something to give them assistance during their despair and gloom. Even without your knowing it, your blog could be the tonic that someone needs to get their life back.

The above are just some of the few benefits of blogging of this guide, we shall talk about different blogging niches and how to choose the one that is best for you.

Chapter 9 Selling the Concept Not the Product

Copywriters write in order to sell. If your written works don't advertise products and/or services, you are not a copywriter. Newbies might consider this as a weird notion. If you are skilled in other forms of writing (e.g. fiction or news articles), you can express your ideas clearly. You can use words to amuse or educate people. As a copywriter, however, you need to overcome a new type of obstacle. You need to use words in convincing people to buy the product you are promoting.

This task can be quite challenging. It requires you to make various decisions. Additionally, the decision-making process requires knowledge regarding sales and marketing. If you're not familiar with the said topics, you have difficult problems ahead of you.

This will arm you with the basics of selling. It will teach you how to promote products using written words. By reading this material, you'll become an effective copywriter in no time.

Features vs Benefits

Copywriters need to focus on benefits. They must not talk about a product's features while writing copy.

Features are descriptions of a product/service. These are the characteristics or elements of a market offering. Benefits, on the other hand, define what the offering does. They explain what a customer will get while or after using the feature/s of a service or product.

For instance, you are writing an article about a watch. One of the watch's features is its ability to move its "hands" with absolute precision. These hands travel slowly and move inside a small circle with numbers and small symbols. The benefit of the watch is that it allows the user to know the time without using an hourglass or other primitive method.

According to recent surveys, a salesperson usually fails in making a sale because he/she doesn't explain the benefits of the product/service well. Keep in mind that people don't buy products and/or services. They buy the great things they can get after paying for a product or service. Unfortunately, many salespeople focus on the features of a market offering. They assume that customers already know the benefits offered by the product. A salesperson must convert features into actual benefits and present the information using customer-friendly language.

That rule also applies to copywriters. In most cases, newbies write about the features (e.g. facts or figures) of the product or service they're promoting. Experts, on the other hand, convert those features into benefits. They explain why readers should purchase the product/service being offered.

Here's a technique that you can use to identify the benefits of a product or service: list down the features of the product/service you're writing about. You can get this information by reading the background material provided by the client, by using the product/service, or by talking to people who are familiar with the product (e.g. salespeople, customers, retailers, etc.). Then, analyze each feature and figure out what it can do for a customer. Why should the customer pay for that product/service instead of the alternatives available in the market?

Important Note: It would be best if you'll divide your work into two columns. Write the features on the first column. Then, list down the benefits on the other column.

The Selling Sequence

These days, copywriters use various formulas while doing their craft. A formula called AIDA helps you write effective ads and other marketing paraphernalia. Using AIDA, you can grab the ATTENTION of your readers, explain the product/service to INTEREST them, convert the product/service interest into DESIRE, and ask the readers to act (i.e. by paying for the product/service being offered).

This part of the book, however, will focus on a formula called "Selling Sequence." You can use this five-step sequence in writing great copy. Here's the formula:

1. Get the customers' attention – Your headline and your visuals take care of this step. The headline must concentrate on the most powerful benefit offered by the product/service you're writing about. Many copywriters create headlines using puns and wordplay, then state the greatest benefit of the product/service at the last part of the material. This is a huge mistake. If your headline doesn't state the primary reason why the reader should read your work, he/she won't read the rest of your copy.

2. Identify a need – Every market offering either satisfies a need or solves a problem. Cars, for example, solve transportation-related problems. Toothpaste, meanwhile, satisfies your need for teeth protection. Unfortunately, the needs a product/service satisfies are not always obvious. That means you need to inform your readers that a need exists.

3. Position the product/service as a great solution – After convincing the readers regarding the existence of a need, you should explain how the product/service you're promoting can satisfy that need.

4. Support your claim – Saying that your product/service satisfies a need is insufficient. You need to prove that your product can do what it's supposed to do. You want people to part with their money and get the product/service you are promoting. You want them to hire you or buy from you. Thus, you need to prove your superiority over other alternatives.

You should also get the trust of your readers. Here are some techniques that you can use:

- Discuss the benefits offered by your product/service.
- Provide testimonials from current and/or customers.
- Perform product/service comparisons.
- Demonstrate the reliability of your company. Discuss your company's growth rate, annual sales, network size, etc.

5. Call for action – You'll work on this step at the end of your copy. Before the end of your article, ask your readers to perform an action. If your product is available online, ask your readers to launch their favorite web browser and access the company's website. Do everything you can to help readers in taking that desired action. For example, you should include the company's name, URL, and contact information while writing copy.

The USP of a Product/Service

There are countless products and services in the market. As a copywriter, you need to tell your readers that the product and/or service you are promoting is one of the best (if not THE BEST) offerings available in the market. You can accomplish this using a USP (i.e. unique selling proposition).

A USP is a unique benefit offered by your product. USP helps you in separating your product/service from the innumerable stuff found in the market today. Your product/service must have a unique benefit; otherwise, people won't prefer it to other products/services available to them. Here are the things you need to do:

- Make sure that all your ads have a proposition. These ads should state, "Get this product/service, and enjoy this particular benefit." Your copy's headline should always have at least one benefit.

- Make sure that the proposition is something that is not offered by similar products/services – Great benefits aren't enough, especially if they can be acquired from any product. That means you need a specific attribute to differentiate your market offering from its competitors.

- Make sure that the proposition is compelling – You can't use a negligible benefit. If you want to encourage readers to pay for the product/service you're writing about, your chosen proposition must make an important difference.

Chapter 10 How Much Copy Should You Write?

If you have impressive writing skills, then this is a good way to earn some more money. Even if you don't, you can take a writing course for as small a sum as $100. Even if you have a daytime job, you do not have to put that job on hold because of this.

Being able to write and building a good number of people who would want to pay to read what you write, can give you more money.

Writing and publishing an eBook can be excellent for anyone good at writing.

I'll explain something. You know what big publishing houses with editors, writers, and administrative staff do to get their books to sell all over the country and the world at large; how they work with printing presses and distribution centers to achieve that?

You can do all of that from your house, in your comfort zone, and on your computer or any other electronic device that has internet access. That's a lucrative business opportunity for writers, editors, and publishers.

You can publish an eBook on Kindle. People go to Kindle regularly to check for useful and recommended books. Writing and Publishing on it is a great way to earn passive income. You can write your eBooks yourself (or even pay writers to do that for you). But you must ensure you write what your target audience would consider knowledgeable, entertaining, or educational. You can write how-to manuals, recipe manuals, travel information, technology, self-improvement, and, of course, fiction.

Once you finish writing, you do not have to wait for any publisher, editor or printing press to facilitate your book sales, you can simply upload it to the website for download. So, once the book starts selling, you do not have to pay the publisher, editors, or printing presses anything. You keep all the profit for yourself. I've heard of people who have left the writing business, but still make money from the eBooks they already have on Kindle.

Even so, writing does not come easily for everyone. You need to identify niches that you know would profit you financially. You also need to use strategic keywords and social media marketing tools to promote your books and get them to sell.

This online money-making method is great for people who have deep knowledge of certain topics, or for people who love to do research and share their knowledge with others.

What to Consider When Starting a Kindle Publishing Business

- Your Descriptive Book Cover

The truth is there are lots of books available to readers on Kindle, and sometimes readers can be faced with a huge task of choosing from the pile of options available. Therefore, you should make sure your descriptive book cover is engaging and attractive. The bestselling author, Tucker Max, acknowledged this when he warned that the title you choose for your book is a key marketing decision.

It is also said that while a good title is not all your book needs to do well, a bad title might be all it needs to fail. Some people give little thought to the title phase of their books, but that is not the way to go. You should make time to brainstorm both the main title, and the subtitle. They must be able to resonate with your audience, while hinting at the book's main concepts.

Procedure for Publishing on Kindle

The first thing is to have your book ready. You then get an account on Amazon Kindle Direct Publishing. After that, you can follow the procedures below to publish your book.

On your Kindle dashboard, click on "CREATE A NEW TITLE," then hit the "+ KINDLE EBOOK" button. Space will be provided for you to add the title of your book. Next, you will enter the basic information of your book, such as the title, the language of publication, and other details that will be requested.

Then you will briefly describe your book by entering a description for it on the provided space. Next, you will select the keywords that will be associated with your book. Choose the category where your book belongs. Upload the manuscript of your book alongside the cover. Enter your desired pricing. Publish.

For this business, your expenses will very likely be on courses or books that will teach you to be a better writer. Once you have a computer and a smartphone, you can buy Udemy writing courses such as "Writing with Flair." You can also read Kindle how-to publish books on Kindle itself, such as the book by Tom Corson-Knowles: "How to Become a Bestselling Author on Amazon Kindle."

Blogging started in the early 2000s when several blogs on politics emerged. Later, blogs with instruction manuals on how to do various activities surfaced.

Blogging is the many skills a person needs to run a blog (otherwise known as 'weblog'). A blog ('weblog') is simply an online journal that displays its content in reverse chronological order. A blog is an online platform where a writer (blogger), or a group of writers, share their views and opinions on one or more subjects. The more frequent your blog posts are, the higher your chances of reaching out to your target audience and creating traffic on your site.

Blogging is also another way of building a brand, and, with time, you can monetize your blog!

It is simple to start a blog, and there are ways to monetize it. To start a blog for free, you can use WordPress or Blogger, and monetize your blog through their respective ad networks. Another popular way to monetize your blog is to display ads on your blog using Google AdSense. Google AdSense gives you a code which you place on your blog, and the ads will automatically appear. The good thing about Google is that it gives you ads that are related to your blog.

The ads work as pay-per-click. So, every time an ad is clicked, you earn more money. The amount might not be huge, but it all adds up over time.

The good thing about blogging is that you can use it to start and market other online businesses you want to develop in the future.

What to Consider When Starting a Blog

Blogging can be a lot of fun, and a lucrative way to make money without having to invest any capital yourself, but there are a few things to consider when starting.

I.   Blogging is so much more than just writing. Aside from writing your opinions on an individual subject, you can also post videos, photos, links to other sites, news, and other articles that relate to your niche.

II.   Original content and frequent updates. If I must read the same content in every blog I open, I would quickly get bored with it. Also, if I find a blog whose posts, I have interest in, but the content on it is not regularly updated, I would lose interest, and I'm sure I would not be the only one. Blogs need original content and frequent updates to increase your traffic and draw your target audience's attention.

III.   What kind of content should be provided? You can start and run a blog with anything that is engaging to your target audience. They can be how-to topics, top-10-20-50-100 lists, comments on what is trending in your niche, and tips and tricks on various topics. There is never a shortage of ideas to use for your blog. But it's advisable to use a niche that you are well informed about, and one that would draw your target audience.

What Do You Need to Start Blogging?

Let's look at the monetary requirement for the blogging business.

The only things you can spend money on are web hosting, domain name registration, SEO, and getting a WordPress theme. It is assumed you have a laptop and a mobile phone already, but even if you don't, you can get them, and still not exceed our $1000 budget.

WordPress Themes: For the WordPress theme, there are free ones you can get on the WordPress Theme Directory. They can do the basic options for you, but I will advise you to go for the paid ones because they are more responsive, have more customer support features, and allow for customizations to suit your taste. For the paid ones, you can get good ones on Theme Forest for as low as $39. But very good ones go for $69 - 79$.

Domain Name Registration: After getting your WordPress theme, proceed to get your domain registration. The domain name is the URL people will use to visit your site. A domain is the cheapest of your requirements. For as low as $10, you can get it for a whole year. Domain name registration services include GoDaddy and Namecheap.

Web Hosting: While WordPress will give you a theme that you can customize for your site, it is web hosting that makes this site accessible on the internet. You can choose from the common web hosting companies such as Bluehost, GoDaddy, and 1&1. They have hosting services ranging from $3 - $500 per month.

SEO: To be sure your blog is optimized for search engines, you need SEO. Thankfully, WordPress has simplified the process. All you need is to add a suitable SEO app as a plugin in your WordPress. I recommend you use Yoast SEO.

Chapter 11 Art of Personal Communication

Writing good copy is a little bit art and a little bit science; it takes a creative mind to find the perfect balance between the two. Copywriting also takes a certain amount of aptitude and knowledge. The artistic edge helps you create content that is geared for marketing and has just the right touch of persuasion while maintaining practicality. But there is no good copy if proper preparations are not taken. There are a lot of things that must be done before you ever put the pen to the paper, or the fingertips to the keyboard. The good copywriter understands how much work goes into the process prior to producing and publishing good copy. Here are some tips on how to prepare yourself to write not only good copy, but great copy.

Product Research

Every good copy starts with research. If you are going to write about a product in a convincing way, you are going to have to be much more familiar with the product details than the average consumer. You'll need to know how the product is going to benefit the end user. Compare it to other similar products that are currently on the market and determine how it is superior to the other products. Look at how the product is manufactured; how it is used and even how it is distributed. Find out what beta users have been saying about the product and how well it meets the user's goals and expectations. You may also want to determine if the product is based on a brand-new idea or an improvement on a prior one. Basically, you are going to want to know literally everything about the product so you can pass it on to consumers through your copy.

Market Research

The serious copywriter will also have to spend adequate time researching the market. You want to determine the market level of need and what other similar products are selling well. Find out precisely who the target audience is and if there are any obvious trends occurring. The copywriter is required to know a lot more about the market than anyone else. There are several ways to research the market. You may look at surveys, buying trends or marketing reports. You can also participate or just keep an eye on some of the more popular forums in order to discover important information about the target market.

Competition Research

Another important area to know about before starting to write copy is how the competition is faring. Even if it seems unnecessary, you really want to know exactly how the competition is doing. Find out what is selling and moving products for them. Take the time to check out their market media and find out what types of messages are bringing them their profits. By finding out where they are spending their marketing dollars and how effective it is for them, you can learn a lot about effective marketing. There are many online tools that can be used to sort of "spy" on your competition to see how they are faring. This type of information can be very useful when you get ready to begin writing your own copy.

Assessing Your Target Audience

Across all writing genres it is important to know about the audience you intend to address, and copywriting is no different. The more you can find out about your target audience, the better. What they think is what really counts when it comes down to selling a product or convincing them that they need it. You should be able to readily identify the target customers and what the typical customer might look like. Determine what is most important to this audience and what goals are they trying to achieve? You will even have to think about what they fear most in this area. Consider other similar products or companies that may have failed the consumer. Think about what the audience stands to gain from the product. Perhaps it is to look better, feel better about themselves or to stand out among their peers. There are certain influencers when it comes to what the consumer chooses to purchase. Do they read magazines? Does the target audience search the web for information; or look at other types of media? By finding out what they are looking at and why, you'll find out a lot more about the audience as well as the specific niche.

Consider the Type and Style of Copy to Write

Once you know your audience, you can determine which style of copy is going to be most effective at reaching them with your information. It's important to know copy style to use before you start planning out your writing. Below are several styles: -

For instance, do you want to address the audience with a storytelling copy as earlier? This style of copy will have a great storyline full of a setup, conflict, dialogue and resolution (solved by the product of course).

Conversational copy will present the information as if there is a conversation going on between the prospective buyer and the copywriter. It'll be as casual as if you were having lunch together.

Another example is the CEO approach where the "top dog" speaks directly to the consumer. It can be presented as a simple letter from the CEO that bears the facts of the matter and the benefits, they are offering the consumer.

Superlative copy will make extraordinary claims and make use of superlatives. There is an art to writing this style of copy as you do need to keep it from sounding like it is super hyped up.

Imaginative copy is a style in which you may ask the audience to imagine ways to painlessly lose weight, or how it would feel to be a successful entrepreneur. Imaginative copy usually starts with words such as "pretend for a minute," or "imagine." Basically, the copywriter is painting a vivid picture of achieving the perfect life using the product.

Finding the right style is important for the copywriter and it will depend largely on the target audience. It's essential to do all your research before you start writing the actual copy.

Chapter 12 Copy

You might be starting from scratch with your blog.

You might already have content.

Either way, I advise you to follow this path:

STEP #1: CREATE YOUR PRE-FRAME SALES SEQUENCE

Start by creating your sales sequence.

Forget traffic for now.

Why?

Because by starting here, you'll now be able to make sales with your content, even to a small audience.

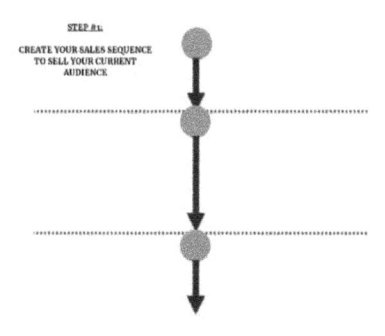

```
STEP #1:
CREATE YOUR SALES SEQUENCE
TO SELL YOUR CURRENT
AUDIENCE
```

Next?

You work your way upwards from the bottom of the funnel to the top...

STEP #2: CREATE 'SALES' SUPPORTING CONTENT

That's right, we start at the bottom first.

Why?

Well there are certain pieces of content that will help you sell.

They provide proof, create trust, and help remove any niggling questions or worries.

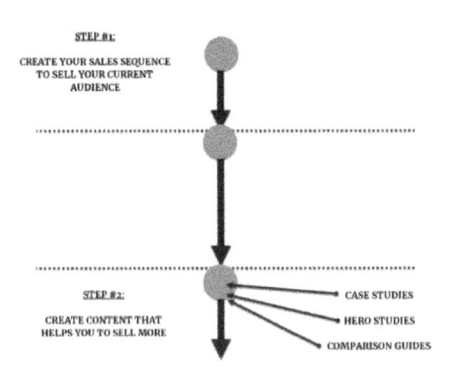

```
STEP #1:
CREATE YOUR SALES SEQUENCE
TO SELL YOUR CURRENT
AUDIENCE

STEP #2:                    → CASE STUDIES
CREATE CONTENT THAT         → HERO STUDIES
HELPS YOU TO SELL MORE      → COMPARISON GUIDES
```

Why care?

Because by creating this content, you'll now make even more sales from that same low traffic.

You're basically making your content sell for you and then making it do its job better.

Make sense?

Only once you've improved your conversions, you then move further up the funnel...

STEP #3: MOVE UP A LEVEL

At this point in your sales sequence, you're building authority and expertise.

Your customer is aware of their problem and looking for answers,

looking for people to trust, who can help them solve their issue.

So, you help them trust you more.

What content goes well here?

- Niche How To guides, and
- Branded solutions

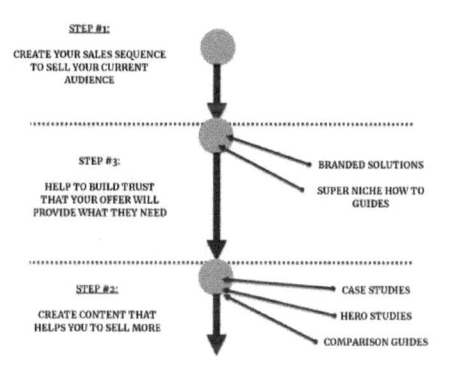

STEP #1:
CREATE YOUR SALES SEQUENCE TO SELL YOUR CURRENT AUDIENCE

STEP #3:
HELP TO BUILD TRUST THAT YOUR OFFER WILL PROVIDE WHAT THEY NEED
- BRANDED SOLUTIONS
- SUPER NICHE HOW TO GUIDES

STEP #2:
CREATE CONTENT THAT HELPS YOU TO SELL MORE
- CASE STUDIES
- HERO STUDIES
- COMPARISON GUIDES

By 'niche how to', I mean how to guides that cover 'later' questions your audience might have.

Rather than

"What is a Facebook advert?" it might be an in-depth guide to design adverts or getting more clicks.

Basically, content that helps, but it's not until they are deeper in their journey, they would ever search for this.

This content then helps add value and trust and helps you stand out even further against your competitors.

Better still?

Your audience will start to see you and your offer as the ideal solution, while pulling more of them to your offer.

STEP #4: THE TOP OF THE FUNNEL

Now that you have the content in place to support your sales sequence, it's time to add content that attracts and helps your audience:

- How To guides

- Ultimate Guides

- Data Backed Research

- Ego Gathering List Posts

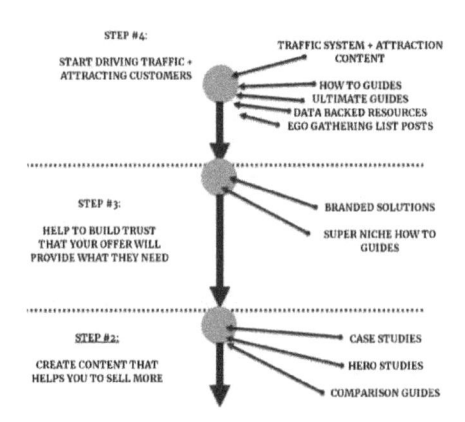

STEP #4:
START DRIVING TRAFFIC + ATTRACTING CUSTOMERS
→ TRAFFIC SYSTEM + ATTRACTION CONTENT
→ HOW TO GUIDES
→ ULTIMATE GUIDES
→ DATA BACKED RESOURCES
→ EGO GATHERING LIST POSTS

STEP #3:
HELP TO BUILD TRUST THAT YOUR OFFER WILL PROVIDE WHAT THEY NEED
→ BRANDED SOLUTIONS
→ SUPER NICHE HOW TO GUIDES

STEP #2:
CREATE CONTENT THAT HELPS YOU TO SELL MORE
→ CASE STUDIES
→ HERO STUDIES
→ COMPARISON GUIDES

Again, we'll cover all these soon...

Some of them tie into your traffic system content; others are designed to help answer questions and build trust etc.

I recommend these last simply due to priority.

Why?

Well, they generally take longer to create OR take longer to see an ROI from.

Whereas the content further down will help convert even a small audience.

Even better?

This means that, as you now start to scale and attract more people, all that new traffic will be far more effective!

Does that all make sense?

If you follow that process, you'll start to see more conversions and sales first, and then growth after.

Because that's we create content, right?

To help attract and sell.

So, you simply focus on what moves the needle the most first and then go from there.

All you need to do now.

Simply plan your topics then create them!

Talking of planning though, there is one more thing to keep in mind...

HOW TO COME UP WITH IDEAS

Posting content is going to be the most important part. I suggest posting at least three core pieces of content per week. If that seems too overwhelming for you and all you can do is post one per week, then one per week is better than none per week. You must recognize that it's going to take you much longer than you'd like to get the results you're looking for. If you're only going to post once per week, you can try a trick to keep the content day. For example, on Monday, you can post a topic and Tuesday a different topic and so on. That way, you make sure that you're creating pieces of content for each one of those days and you're rotating through your pillars and topics. So, if you plan to post five times per week, then create five different components. This way, you're talking about something relevant to your audience, but it's a different pillar piece of content each day, so you're evenly rotating through things and you're not just talking about one topic for five or six days in a row (and boring your audience to tears).

Once you've decided how many times per week you're going to post, it's time to plan your content; this is where keywords and titles come into play. I highly recommend that you plan at least a month in advance, and you do all your keyword research and all your title research and title writing in one sitting. That way, during the month, while you're going through and creating your content, there's a lot less friction in terms of anxiety. You're going to be able to be very strategic with the different topics, and you'll be able to space out your content and see everything that you're doing in a month. And then you can just put your head in the sand and make content and then come up for air at the end of the month.

When it's time to do your content calendar again, the next step is syndication. At this point, you know what your core medium is, what your content pillars are going to be, and you've organized your posting days of the week based on those content pillars. Syndication makes it easier for you to use single content types at various platforms. For example, videos can be posted to YouTube, Instagram, Facebook, and more. Then on LinkedIn, we can create a pulse post, and on Facebook, we post the thumbnail and the link occasionally. This is just an example of how you can take one piece of content and chop it up into little pieces and spread it out to other platforms. Now, of course, it's vital that it makes sense to chop it up and spread it out to other platforms. So, if you're doing the content writing, you could then have someone record the content and turn it into a podcast, or you can read through it and turn it into a podcast yourself. If you don't want to be featured in front of a camera, you can take that audio and put it on YouTube and put up some slides and have that be the entire video. Podcasts work successfully for quite a few businesses, so you can create a lot of content from all the initial work you did on just one of your core pieces of content.

You'll need to go through your content calendar again and decide on which days you'll post on those syndication platforms. This works well if you're looking at only posting three times per week on your main platform. Maybe you will want to investigate posting on those off days that you have on some other platforms that aren't going to require as much work. After all, you're just sending what you already put together.

Chapter 13 Editing Process

Editing your book before publication is one of the, if not the, most important part of this process to self-publishing.

This book will show how well you know your subject, how well the plot of a novel flows, how well you are in remembering your grammar lessons from 5th grade. In other words, when you pour out your soul into words in a word processing program (I recommend the most updated version of Microsoft Word), self-publishers are exhibiting their own professionalism as well. This will be like an inner photograph of you for the world to see. You do not want a pimple showing on your metaphorical nose. It not only lacks professionalism as a writer but could lose credibility going forward to future sales and other books.

Now, that is ok if you are a writer by profession. Even professional writers, however, have been known to misspell words, accidentally attribute political quotes to cartoon characters, and create a character so real that it turned out to be their third nephew on their wife's brother's-in-law cousin who does not like the way he is portrayed in your book. It is a lot of pressure on any one person to make sure everything is absolutely in line.

There are sources online and can be found at local libraries and universities who would be willing to do this grammar editing for you ... for a price.

These types of editors usually do a good job on grammar but fail to do well on plot flow, accuracy in facts, acknowledgments, and more. The more that you have them do, the higher the price. They have no ownership in your project except for the job for which you are paying them. When you have a publisher, their editors have more ownership in the work because they work for the publisher and want you to succeed.

Besides, be doubly careful of submitting your credit card to anything online or paying upfront for services not yet rendered.

So, if you are the self-publisher of your own book, you have double more ownership in the project. You not only want your work to be read, you want your work to succeed and guarantee sales!

There are, of course, some free programs online that can help you with editing portions of your piece for free. One of the ones I have used several times has been the Hemingway Editor (Hemmingway). Do not try to follow all the suggestions of any app editor because you do not want to lose your own voice, but these will help you when you are stuck with a grammatical concern and well, …. it is free now!

Formatting is another area where a self-publisher needs to be knowledgeable. Remember, you need the look of professionalism.

What has been helpful to me is something that is obvious. Look at professionally published books.

Examine them closely to see where the page numbers go on the pages; see what is on top of every page. Is there a dedication page and, if so, where does it fall in the front pages? Before or after the acknowledgement page? Do not choose just one book for examples, look at several because some are different from others. Do you want to have an author biography? Where do you want to place this? Does the book have the name of the author on the top? Do your research, check out areas on the web where it advises what to do but do not choose just one source.

These are all items that will make a difference between your book looking very amateurish or as close to a professional publisher as possible. You may be a self-publisher, but you do not want to look like one.

Examine Copyright pages and what information is required and in what order. (We will discuss Copyright more later). Check for Bibliography on how to cite a source. There are several web sites that offer free citing assistance. Check several in order to ensure your source is correctly arranged.

For formatting your book, Microsoft Word is a helpful tool for self-publishers. It has all the gizmos and more you could use. Here are a few of them you will want to pursue and learn further about no matter what word processing tool you choose.

- Page numbers (when to start your page numbers and what number to start with)

- Headers/Footers (title and author information and placed just right)

- Mirrored Margins (you will need to this so spacing is right for book binding)

- Font and font size (Garamond or Times New Roman, usually 11 size is the best)

- Tabs (make sure all the tabs are auto programmed; this will help in future when developing your book for online readers)

After you have finished editing your book, formatting your book, tweaking your book, set it aside for at least a month! Even if you hired a professional editor, still set it aside. Don't touch it, don't look at it, don't even think about it …. if you can.

Once the month is over, then gently, slowly reread your entire manuscript. I guarantee you will find areas to change and be glad you have done this. Remember, you want to look as professional as you can. You might even consider setting it aside for another smoldering period and check it again.

Beware asking a "friend" to read your manuscript unless that friend has writing experience. Besides, beware using any suggested edits from any friend or foe. One change can alter in your book elsewhere.

Although there are many self-publishing companies online, the one I use is Kindle Direct Publishing. They have many self-explanatory videos on how best to format your book.

Chapter 14 The Psychological Triggers

The term "sales and marketing psychology" may sound very technical and quite intimidating but is easy to understand once you get the hang of it. After all, sales and marketing psychology ultimately boils down to human nature. The trick, thus, is to use your knowledge and understanding of how people think, feel, and make decisions in pitching sales to your target buyers.

Having said that, in this, we will be talking about how you could get inside the heard of your target buyer to convince them to buy whatever product or service you are offering. To do this successfully – and effortlessly, to boot – it is important for you to master the foundations of sales and marketing psychology. Here, we will talk about the 11 psychological sales triggers, the very foundation of sales and marketing psychology, to enable you to convince practically anyone to buy whatever you are selling.

If you are already feeling intimidated, trust me, there is no reason to be. After all, the concepts we will be discussing in this are concepts and phenomena that we see in the real world practically daily. You might not be aware of what these concepts are called, or the rationale behind such concepts, but these are all things which you have surely encountered already. That said, if you are ready, let us go ahead and discuss these 11 psychological sales triggers.

Psychological Trigger #1: Fear.

Fear is one of the most basic and most innate emotions – and this holds true not only for humans but for all members of the animal kingdom. Since human beings are sentient, we feel this emotion particularly strongly. The universality, as well as the instinctive nature of fear, makes it a very powerful motivator. We see the power of fear almost every day, from electoral campaigns to health advisories. One common example of how fear is often used as a motivating factor is in the case of anti-smoking ad campaigns. In certain places, cigarette manufacturers are mandated to include a graphic warning as to the negative health effects of cigarette smoking. Anti-smoking advocates also employ a similar strategy, with anti-smoking ads showing graphic images of how long-term cigarette smoking can affect the human body. By capitalizing on fear, one can move the target audience into action.

That said, you must be careful when using fear and must only use it in the right way. One way of using fear when marketing a product or service is by amplifying a negative effect. For example, soap commercials would often place emphasis on bacteria, virus, and disease transmission. In the same vein, those selling locks would often talk about criminality and the possibility of burglary. By playing up on your target buyers' fear, you can sell your product or service in a way that would make it seem like the only viable solution.

Psychological Trigger #2: Transfer.

This concept might sound new to you, but chances are you are quite familiar with this already. This concept is not used that often in TV commercials, but it is a common strategy in print ads and promotional pages of websites.

In a nutshell, the concept of transfer is hinged on social proof or transitive trust, which really is just fancy and technical speak for brand connection. To illustrate this concept better, let us say that Brand Y is a new and unheard-of product. Since it is new, people will be hesitant to try it, especially since there is no guarantee as to its quality. To overcome this hurdle, the marketers of Brand Y can namedrop familiar brands which it has collaborated with, in this case, let us say Company A and Company B. Since people know Company A and Company B, and they know that these are reputable companies, they will also associate such good reputation with Brand Y. That said, this strategy is most fitting for newer brands which can best be marketed through familiarity with other brands, seeing as consumers are more likely to patronize a product or service which is connected to something they already know or trust.

Psychological Trigger #3: Bandwagon effect.

This is among the most popular and most understood psychological sales triggers. The bandwagon effect is a phenomenon wherein people do things (or in the case of sales and marketing psychology, make purchases) because other people are doing the same. This behavior is rooted in people's psychological need to belong. Essentially, all human beings, in one way or another, desire to be a part of something regardless of whether they might realize it or not.

I am sure that you have seen how this phenomenon plays out among entrepreneurs. Whenever something becomes popular – be it a movie, a product, or even a person – you will notice a meteoric rise in related merchandise and people who sell such merchandise. Since people generally want to belong, they tend to be willing to spend on products or services which are popular among their peers. The great thing about this strategy is that it requires minimal effort on the part of the seller or marketer. Basically, people will naturally gravitate towards products or services which they view as "in" or "trendy".

Psychological Trigger #4: Comparison.

Related to the concept is comparison. Human beings have an innate fear of standing out or missing out. Basically, we inevitably compare ourselves to our peers whether we may notice that we are making such comparison. This operates in two ways: first, we do not want to be the only one doing something in a way and second, we do not want to be the only one not doing something in a way. Hence, we are more likely to try something new if we see that everybody else is doing it already.

In terms of purchasing behavior, this means that consumers are more likely to try new products and services when they notice that their peers are already using these new products and services. Unlike the bandwagon effect however, which requires that the consumers themselves observe the existence of the trend in question, comparison is something that can be completely manufactured to suit the purposes of the seller or marketer. You can appeal to your target buyers by mentioning that everyone else is buying or using whatever products or services you are selling. Essentially, you want your target buyers to feel that they are missing out on a lot if they do not make a purchase.

Psychological Trigger #5: Liking.

This is another psychological sales trigger that I am sure you are aware of. The concept behind liking is quite basic, really: if you like someone, you are more likely to do what they say. This is where the power of celebrities come in. Brands pay good money for celebrity endorsements for one simple reason: well-liked celebrities who have a large and loyal fanbase can easily drive up sales. After all, people are more likely to heed the advice of their favorite celebrities. This means that not only are fans more likely to make the same purchases as their celebrities, their means permitting, but they are also more likely to purchase products which their favorite celebrities endorse.

Hence, another infallible sales tactic is enlisting the services of a prominent individual to endorse a product or service. Of course, not all companies can afford to do this, in which case sponsoring a celebrity (letting a celebrity try out a new product or service for free in exchange for social media exposure) is a viable alternative. The mere association can do wonders for the product or service in question.

Psychological Trigger #6: Authority.

This concept is somewhat like the one, liking. Whereas liking works because individuals are more likely to do what someone they like says or does, authority works because people are more likely to heed the advice of someone they respect. In a sense, authority functions as social proof, an attestation as to the credibility or effectivity of a product or service. That said, when a person of authority says or prescribes something, people are more likely to take an interest and to act.

How the concept of authority plays out in sales and marketing psychology is interesting. After all, actual authority is not always necessary as the mere semblance of it typically works already. Case in point would be commercials on antibacterial soap, toothpaste, or even shampoo which features actors wearing lab gowns talking about the merits of the products being endorsed. These individuals are not really doctor or scientists, but because they are being presented in a way that is akin to authority, the target buyers become keener to listen to them and, hence, more likely to buy whatever product they are advertising.

Psychological Trigger #7: Reciprocity.

Another powerful concept which sellers and marketers can make use of in improving their sales is reciprocity. The concept of reciprocity is quite simple. It sends to the potential buyers this message: if I gave you something for free, then now it is your turn to buy something. Therefore, whenever new food products or items are being introduced, the sellers would typically provide free samples. This is not only to convince their target buyers that their product is of high standards, but also to get them to feel compelled to make a purchase.

The concept of reciprocity is no longer only applicable to in-person sales. Quite the contrary, it works just as well for online websites, particularly those offering services. For example, fitness websites that earn money by selling and making workout and meal plans often provide subscribers with a free program sample. Websites which provides online seminars, meanwhile, would often give out materials absolutely for free. Even creative websites which offer a host of products such as desktop or mobile phone wallpapers will often provide some of their products to the general public for free. Giving out such samples certainly help target consumers to get an inkling as to whether they will enjoy the product or service in question. But even more importantly, by providing samples absolutely for free, no strings attached, sellers or marketers can create a connection between the product or service they are providing, and their target consumers. In a sense, target consumers feel somehow obligated to make a purchase, especially if they enjoyed the sample to begin with. Think about it: this strategy works perfectly fine with app and streaming services free trial, right?

Psychological Trigger #8: Commitment and consistency.

This concept can best be summarized as conditioning people to say yes but using it effectively can be a little trickier than the other concepts we have earlier. Basically, your goal as a seller or marketer is to try to get people to say yes – and say yes consistently. To do this, you must remain not only committed, but also consistent. Hence, if you take a stand on an issue, then you must stick with that stand all throughout your marketing spiel. Doing so will not only lend credence to whatever product or service you are pitching but will also help your target buyers to formulate their own expectations and act in accordance to such expectations.

This brings us to the crucial question: how do you condition people to say yes? The answer is a lot easier than you might think. The technique is to ask seemingly innocent questions which you know your audience will always say yes to. Thus, the trick is to not ask individual-specific questions, the answer to which will vary depending on the personal tastes and circumstances of the individual. Instead, ask questions which appeal to the human experience in general.

Chapter 15 How Much Money Can You Make Copywriting?

The rate card for a copywriter should be a document that is able to solve the great anguish of those who work in the field of writing, which is: how much do I have to ask for my work? Defining the price is a real issue and an obstacle that needs to be overcome by those who start operating in this sector.

Just as it is very difficult to put a price tag on creative work, there is likewise no clear parameter to delineate a copywriter's rate card. For many, this is dramatic news. Everything would be easier with, perhaps, an hourly regulation to give your pen a way to follow. Some of the most common questions asked are: Do I ask too much or too little? Will I look like an amateur if I keep my rates low? Or an inflated balloon if too high? Coming up with standard rates would be a great thing, but the simple truth is that it is impossible to draw up such a table. This is due to several reasons.

The rate card is a powerful document because it solves doubts and exonerates you from reflecting and revolutionizing your needs every day. You do not have to customize each quote. You only must look at the price list and give the price of your work. Therefore, the fee for a copy could be a resource.

All these become even more difficult when you work in ghostwriting, which involves working in the background, so you do not have a clear comparison with the world around you. The personal branding experts, though, have this clear advice: work for free or ask a lot. Do not compromise. Never be satisfied with crumbs. However, when you do not have the tools to define a starting point, look for the security, the scheme, and the stability of a rate card. The only problem is that the rate card does not actually exist. Do you know why? And do you know how much a freelance copywriter earns?

According to the Antitrust Authority, the rate card is illegal.

This is the primary reason why it is extremely difficult to have a single and common copywriting card. This writer was unaware of this detail until James Fitch, an important copywriter, shared a document that enshrined such passage.

Technically, creating a shared copywriter rate card is not a legal transaction, since it can be classified as an agreement restrictive of competition (a behavior that falls within the illicit). Since advertising is not an ordinary profession, there is the possibility of enjoying minimum rates.

In 2009, the defunct TP Association published jointly with the ACPI, a guide that had exactly the purpose of providing references, albeit in the form of indicative price ranges, about the rates to be formulated in the estimate. The initiative was promptly challenged and blocked by the Antitrust Authority, which, in 2012, condemned the two associations to a symbolic fine, distrusting them from reiterating the initiative. It should be noted that the boundaries of the question are particularly labile. On a purely theoretical level, even discussing informally among colleagues within a Facebook group of professionals sharing their own tariff references could configure a behavior aimed at limiting free competition, since it would lay the foundations for a potential agreement between more professionals among their competitors.

As you can well understand from the above words, there is no legal possibility to create an official copywriter rate card. But this is only the first reason that closes the doors to this need.

Creativity has no hourly rate

This is the second point that makes it impossible to create a rate card. Creative work cannot be summarized, nor can it be enclosed in an hourly rate for copywriters who must write 1,000 words per hour to earn the minimum wage. It does not work this way.

A copywriter cannot be paid for several beats or based on the time needed to attend to a customer. The reason is simple. There are jobs that require a few words and can be closed in a short time but highlight your creativity and experience.

A good illustration would be the creation of a slogan and subsequently evaluating it. This can be done in 30 minutes or 2 days. What parameters will then be used as the basis for payment? For a few words, will the price be only 50 cents? The work is too varied to create a good estimate.

Different valuations of work

Another reason to close the door to a shared copywriter rate card is the value given to work. Such value is not linear, and you cannot expect everyone to align with your way of seeing the world.

For instance, you see an item as worth 40 dollars and ask for this price. Another may think that it is worth more and will give a different value. The same goes for a product or brand names, a landing page, or an email object. Everyone can give the value they prefer to their work. This is a free market, and this is the life that the freelance copywriter must contend with.

How to create a private rate card

While it may not be possible to create an hourly rate for copywriters, it is also true that a professional must start in some way. Therefore, it is suggested that you create your own personal scheme with a list of services. Take a paper and a pen, and using a mind map or some other tool, start defining all the activities you do like naming, making slogans, creating headlines, writing blog posts and press releases, etc.

Give a corresponding minimum price to these items. It is you who must decide this. Others cannot choose the worth of the work you do. Remember, however, that experience has value and must be paid. You cannot define the price based on time or number of measures. There are some elements, though, that can determine a higher price for the estimate.

For example:

- Fast delivery.
- Particularly complex topics.
- SEO copywriting work for testing a blog/site.
- Editing and writing on paper.

Your price calculations must consider the taxes related to the VAT number and the expenses of your business. If you have an agency, for example, you must include rent, telephone, company electricity consumption, and the cost of an employee. In short, the right price is the highest price you can propose. Therefore, personal branding becomes essential. This enables you to communicate your value to customers.

How much does a copywriter earn?

How much does an advertising copywriter earn? You can be a copywriter with a high salary. On the other hand, you can also work freelance and obtain an important quote. The real scenario in America, however, is that the work of a copywriter is not the highest paid. Rather, you must have an important brand to raise prices.

Being a copywriter and earning more money is not child's play. Monetizing in this field means making a name for yourself. In the beginning, you must agree to work for a few dollars, but as soon as you can create a good portfolio, you have a few more possibilities. This is especially true if you can combine the needs of creative writing with SEO copywriting.

An important concept that is worth reiterating is that it is not possible to create a rate card for a copywriter for different reasons. The first concerns a legal question, the second is related to the practice of price, and the third is due to differences in personal parameters. Creative work is difficult to schematize in a price list.

What you can do is simply define a list of activities that you perform and indicate a starting point. You can then progressively update the prices based on your circumstances.

Chapter 16 What Does It Take to Become A Copywriter?

At the heart of copywriting is advertising. But far from the blatant hard sell you might encounter from an aggressive salesperson, a copywriter presents all the important details in an informative and an enjoyable format – this is what encourages readers to become potential customers.

You have what it takes to be a copywriter if the following qualities describe you:

1. Passionately Curious. A copywriter has an innate need to always know why. This characteristic is what allows him to enlighten himself on many different subjects. It gives him a chance to educate others as well.

This goes hand in hand with having the passion to write about everything under the sun. Passion is what makes a copywriter believe that every little thing is an interesting subject waiting to be written about.

2. Practices Self-motivation. Given that a copywriter must work on many different tasks at the same time, he should have the drive to work as efficiently as possible. This is easy to accomplish if he can motivate himself. He knows that he cannot expect his clients or employers to inspire him to write.

3. Shows Flexibility. Working as a copywriter requires the ability to easily handle multiple assignments that may or may not belong to the same category. Accomplishing them lets a copywriter's writing skills shine and gives him an opportunity to hone them as well.

4. Master of Conciseness. It takes knowing how to use plain English words to be a good copywriter. He doesn't have to resort to using

highfalutin words – a great copywriter does not want to sound pompous and turn off his readers.

It also helps when a copywriter has mastered the art of keeping things as short as possible. A great copywriter can inform and entertain his readers even when he goes straight to the point.

5. Great Storyteller. A copywriter may write to sell things, but this does not mean that he will produce an article that has "commercial" stamped all over it. He always strives to put an enjoyable narrative spin on his works.

6. Writer at Heart. A copywriter truly loves what he does for a living and does not mind putting in extra hours, if that is what it takes for him to deliver a well-written article. He also knows that his efforts are not wasted on projects that might have been rejected. Instead, he treats them as opportunities to improve on his writing skills.

7. Focused in Multitasking. Copywriters do not have the luxury of time and therefore it would help them to stay in the moment and set their minds on the writing projects at hand. This is especially important in a job where multitasking is a necessity.

A copywriter who is just starting out cannot avoid multitasking. He can't afford to turn down writing jobs outright, even if it means having to do several projects simultaneously. A great copywriter sees multitasking as a chance to showcase his writing abilities to his employer.

8. Open to Criticisms. On one hand, a great copywriter is confident enough to justify his work if he feels that he is not getting the right feedback for it. On the other hand, he also understands that his job involves having his share of criticisms from clients and editors.

A good copywriter knows it is to his advantage when clients and editors call his attention to mistakes, more so if they give him pointers on how to correct them. This means they want to continue working with him, which is why they are giving him the chance to redeem himself.

9. Enthusiastic Reader. A great copywriter reads as much as he can, knowing that reading is his tool for sharpening his writing skills. He understands that he should not limit himself to topics of interest alone. But then the mere fact that a copywriter enjoys reading allows him to become an expert in writing on a wide range of subjects.

10. Grammar Savvy. A copywriter learns that having the passion to write will not be enough to sustain him in his job. He understands that constantly working to improve his grammar skills is a key to his success in copywriting.

Still, the grammar savvy copywriter knows that perfection is impossible. He will readily acknowledge having committed some grammar lapses from time to time.

Moreover, he knows that it does not pay to be complacent about his job. Honing his grammar skills will give him an edge over other copywriters!

Which Type of Copywriter Are You? – Information in a Snap

A lot of different types of products and services are being launched in the market every day. This is the primary reason why copywriters are in great demand. There are various specializations of copywriters as well. Look at the following and see which type you are best suited for:

Technical Copywriter

User manuals and FAQs are the works of art of the technical writer.

Good Grasp

A technical copywriter has a thorough knowledge on a field of expertise. It would be difficult for other types of writers, or copywriters for that matter, to write an article on genetic engineering without studying the subject thoroughly. A technical copywriter, on the other hand, can do the job effortlessly.

Piece of Cake

This is the reason why a lot of technical writers do not count as professional writers. Instead, they are professionals in their own fields. A chemist would be able to write an article about The Importance of Chemistry without much difficulty. In the same vein, an engineer would have no qualms about composing an essay on The Best Architectural Designs within minutes.

A Shot at Creativity

Don't worry – this does not mean you don't stand a chance of becoming a technical copywriter based on your lack of professional training in these fields. You have an edge over these experts when your mind is not saturated with technicalities that can hamper creativity in writing.

For example, you could write about Why Chemistry Rocks or Home Designs to Blow Your Mind, which sound much better than the chemist's and the engineer's articles.

A Chance at Rubbing Elbows

On that note, becoming a technical copywriter means you get to work with the technical professionals themselves. You'll find yourself gathering ideas from lawyers, engineers, and computer programmers to use in creating useful articles that will attract your target audience.

You also have the advantage of charging a higher amount for your articles due to the amount of research and concerted effort poured into it.

Content Copywriter

Product scripts are the specialties of the content copywriter.

Good Command

A content copywriter knows how to maneuver his way around words to make his how-to articles sound serious and engaging at the same time. This is an important skill to have if you desire to go into copywriting that involves the presentation of facts about a product in a logical manner. The copy, nonetheless, should be easy and interesting to read.

Target Sighted

A content copywriter strives to write on a single topic and turn out articles with different angles. The articles he produces will then be used in different websites that are targeted toward different types of customers.

Lure Them In

Content copywriting aims to update a website on a regular basis by providing the information that answers the concerns of a visitor of that website. But, the job of the copywriter does not end there. He must make the viewer interested enough to keep reading until he soon becomes a potential customer of the product or service endorsed by that site.

Step by Step

How to use a certain product is the main thrust of content copywriting. The steps are provided in a manner that is easy to understand and that can be followed by the customers without much effort. Therefore, it is important to engage the reader so that he does not lose interest and move on to other websites instead.

Get Inside Their Heads

The importance of providing useful information in content copywriting cannot be stressed enough. You must know who will read your articles, how they might react to your content, and why they respond in a certain manner to the ideas you have given to them.

SEO Copywriter

Blog posts and articles are what make up an SEO copywriter's arsenal.

High Visibility

The SEO copywriter is a master in the art of turning out blog posts that are tailored to rank high in internet searches.

Whether the purpose of these articles is to inform or to make an endorsement, the important thing is to write them in a surefire way that lands them a top spot in any search engine result's first page. This ensures that a website will get the exposure it needs to promote its products and services.

Wide Reach

Your value as an SEO copywriter also lies in your ability to draw in a huge number of potential customers to a website. Your articles enable a product to get noticed by people from all walks of life and on a global scale.

Highly Reputed

Being an SEO copywriter means you provide your client a great way to advertise its product without having to invest a huge capital. You are giving your client an opportunity to build a great reputation around the internet without spending that much because of your high-ranking articles.

Exclusive Service

Undeniably, your greatest contribution as an SEO copywriter is giving your client a means of having an advertising venue that works for him every minute of the day. Your articles give him a big advantage in enticing potential customers to buy his products and services.

Chapter 17 The Basics of Copywriting

Writing good copy is a little bit art and a little bit science; it takes a creative mind to find the perfect balance between the two. Copywriting also takes a certain amount of aptitude and knowledge. The artistic edge helps you create content that is geared for marketing and has just the right touch of persuasion while maintaining practicality. But there is no good copy if proper preparations are not taken. There are a lot of things that must be done before you ever put the pen to the paper, or the fingertips to the keyboard. The good copywriter understands how much work goes into the process prior to producing and publishing good copy. Here are some tips on how to prepare yourself to write not only good copy, but great copy.

Product Research

Every good copy starts with research. If you are going to write about a product in a convincing way, you are going to have to be much more familiar with the product details than the average consumer. You'll need to know how the product is going to benefit the end user. Compare it to other similar products that are currently on the market and determine how it is superior to the other products. Look at how the product is manufactured; how it is used and even how it is distributed. Find out what beta users have been saying about the product and how well it meets the user's goals and expectations. You may also want to determine if the product is based on a brand-new idea or an improvement on a prior one. Basically, you are going to want to know literally everything about the product so you can pass it on to consumers through your copy.

Market Research

The serious copywriter will also have to spend adequate time researching the market. You want to determine the market level of need and what other similar products are selling well. Find out precisely who the target audience is and if there are any obvious trends occurring. The copywriter is required to know a lot more about the market than anyone else. There are several ways to research the market. You may look at surveys, buying trends or marketing reports. You can also participate or just keep an eye on some of the more popular forums in order to discover important information about the target market.

Competition Research

Another important area to know about before starting to write copy is how the competition is faring. Even if it seems unnecessary, you really want to know exactly how the competition is doing. Find out what is selling and moving products for them. Take the time to check out their market media and find out what types of messages are bringing them their profits. By finding out where they are spending their marketing dollars and how effective it is for them, you can learn a lot about effective marketing. There are many online tools that can be used to sort of "spy" on your competition to see how they are faring. This type of information can be very useful when you get ready to begin writing your own copy.

Assessing Your Target Audience

Across all writing genres it is important to know about the audience you intend to address, and copywriting is no different. The more you can find out about your target audience, the better. What they think is what really counts when it comes down to selling a product or convincing them that they need it. You should be able to readily identify the target customers and what the typical customer might look like. Determine what is most important to this audience and what goals are they trying to achieve? You will even have to think about what they fear most in this area. Consider other similar products or companies that may have failed the consumer. Think about what the audience stands to gain from the product. Perhaps it is to look better, feel better about themselves or to stand out among their peers. There are certain influencers when it comes to what the consumer chooses to purchase. Do they read magazines? Does the target audience search the web for information; or look at other types of media? By finding out what they are looking at and why, you'll find out a lot more about the audience as well as the specific niche.

Consider the Type and Style of Copy to Write

Once you know your audience, you can determine which style of copy is going to be most effective at reaching them with your information. It's important to know copy style to use before you start planning out your writing. Below are several styles: -

For instance, do you want to address the audience with a storytelling copy as earlier? This style of copy will have a great storyline full of a setup, conflict, dialogue and resolution (solved by the product of course).

Conversational copy will present the information as if there is a conversation going on between the prospective buyer and the copywriter. It'll be as casual as if you were having lunch together.

Another example is the CEO approach where the "top dog" speaks directly to the consumer. It can be presented as a simple letter from the CEO that bears the facts of the matter and the benefits, they are offering the consumer.

Superlative copy will make extraordinary claims and make use of superlatives. There is an art to writing this style of copy as you do need to keep it from sounding like it is super hyped up.

Imaginative copy is a style in which you may ask the audience to imagine ways to painlessly lose weight, or how it would feel to be a successful entrepreneur. Imaginative copy usually starts with words such as "pretend for a minute," or "imagine." Basically, the copywriter is painting a vivid picture of achieving the perfect life using the product.

Finding the right style is important for the copywriter and it will depend largely on the target audience. It's essential to do all your research before you start writing the actual copy.

Chapter 18 Copywriting Techniques

The power of words can change a company's future. This might be a strong claim, but after reading this, you will understand the reason for this statement. It is the use of effective copywriting techniques that offer value to customers.

Speaking from personal experience, this writer asserts that having a love for words is crucial to copywriting. Continuing education and experience can play their part, but when it comes to copywriting, it would not be possible to satisfy a client without it.

Start right away by telling yourself that in order to create value with words, you need to use effective copywriting techniques. These are full of a talking and connected language in which, along with the application of an SEO strategy, you get carried away by the rhythm of the sentences, the light and non-resonant sounds, breathing between commas and periods, all capable of giving effect to a thought.

The skill of mixing all these elements together is not easy to acquire at all. Writing may be for everyone but doing it to achieve a goal is one of the most difficult aspects of the big and complex world of content marketing. Many vital ingredients need to be present to achieve results through copywriting techniques:

- choose a strategy suited to the target;
- evaluate the right tools to communicate;
- organize useful resources for what is told;
- consider the client as a person, and not as a public.

To all these components, add the most important: the ability to tell by revealing one's own character. Only a company that offers its client something of himself can be appreciated. The customer wants to feel pampered and not deceived by the phrases made (what do you think when you read "industry leader"?). He wants to find out who is behind a brand, to feel part of something beautiful, because it is clean from logic oriented exclusively to the business. Further, the customer wants to bring stories home. It is not because he loves storytelling. Most often than not, he might not be even aware of what it is. He wants to know the stories because they transform a product or a service into something useful and indispensable.

Presenting a company with copywriting techniques

In order to make a company known, it is necessary to choose the right words – words that talk about the business not with the objective of selling but offering added value instead. To accomplish this effectively, copywriting techniques are a big help. These are the tricks that word professionals use to mix strategy and heart together.

How do you do it concretely?

Before the indispensable techniques to show the corporate soul of a brand will be, there is something you must do beforehand.

Approach the screen.

Do not worry, you will only be told to scan each syllable well.

Before writing about a company, listen to what the entrepreneur has to say.

Do not think about the right words. For now, lay aside the thought that you need to put into practice everything you have learned about SEO copywriting. Forget the company's strategies for a moment. Take some time to listen to what the brand wants to tell you.

Translate his message and read what is inside his entrepreneurial heart. Live with the entrepreneur the emotions, and the features that make what he sells unique.

Listen to it several times, take a long breath and put everything in your mind.

Here and now, you are ready to write using copywriting techniques. Now, you can choose the right words. Five essential techniques are suggested:

1. Define a tone of voice that will speak for the company.
2. Capture your attention with an appealing incipit that contains the main keyword of your SEO strategy.
3. It takes care of the simplification and the legibility of the text.
4. Create a link with the reader through words.
5. Share a true story.

The copywriting explained to the client is how important it is to tell oneself online. If you follow this path, it becomes the best way to empathize with the customer who does not need a showcase site that displays a list of products and services. He wants to know and satisfy all his consumer curiosity, to understand, and imagine with his mind. All these are possible, thanks to words.

Company and reader become two characters of a common journey, in which one esteems the other.

A company or an entrepreneur who is presenting and offering himself online should do so without fear and doubt. He must not be afraid of making mistakes. In the event this happens, he admits the mistake and prepares to make improvements. A company grows in small steps together with the words it publishes. It does not insist on being seen for what it is not. It does not self-criticize, nor does it promise the impossible. In addition, it listens to the advice of those who follow its adventures on the web, those who show themselves to be human. If all these can happen, between a web marketing strategy and an essential dose of empathy with the customer, words can create value and lead to a result. This is how the fate of a company will change.

Chapter 19 How to Avoid the Most Common Copywriting Mistakes?

None of us are flawless. As the familiar axiom goes, even monkeys drop out of trees in some cases. What's more, even an expert copywriter may commit an error occasionally. Here are a few slip-ups each copywriter has set aside a few minutes or another.

1. Overlooking your audience. When you are copywriting, you are composing it for somebody. That individual might be your customer; in any case, the audience is the individual you need to act depending on what they have perused. It does a whole lot of nothing to write to fulfill a specific customer if the audience doesn't react to what you have composed. Ideally, you have gotten yourself a customer who knows the audience he is endeavoring to reach.

2. Not knowing your item. When you are endeavoring to expound on something that you don't have any acquaintance with, it appears. Nothing is more terrible than finding out about an item when the creator did not recognize what they were discussing! Few out of every odd composition employment can be in your most academic subject field. However, you should set aside the effort to know something about the item you are expounding on.

3. An excess of detail, or not enough. It is occasionally challenging to realize precisely how much detail to expound on. You need to give the audience enough information to catch their eye, however less information that they feel overpowered.

4. You compose excessively. Individuals today don't have a great deal of time to peruse, so if you cannot catch their consideration with your message rapidly, you will miss out on your opportunity. You must

ensure your first words are, and after that, the peruse will remain to perceive what you need to state to them.

5. You don't make it simple for individuals to do what you need them to do. When you need somebody to purchase something from you, you need to make it simple for them to discover the cost of your item and get it. If you need somebody to buy into your pamphlet, you bring to the table them a simple method to buy in, ideally more than one way. If you genuinely need somebody to accomplish something, make it simple for them to do it.

Five Copywriting Mistakes to Avoid

Keep in mind the significance of good copywriting - in case you're starting a substance advertising system, and you'll have to make an accomplishment of it to accomplish the ideal outcomes.

When your substance does not get the point over, you may lose potential deals and harm your organization's notoriety, which is the reason it's essential to put your copywriting effort in steady hands.

The following are five common copywriting botches that must be maintained a strategic distance from:

1. Exhausting features

'The Father of Advertising' David Ogilvy best aggregates up to the significance of the unassuming feature:

"By and large, fivefold the number of individuals read the feature as the body copy. When you have composed your feature, you have burned through eighty pennies out of your dollar."

If your feature is unfit to attract the peruse, that open door for a deal is more likely than not gone.

A feature ought to be snappy, luring and hard-hitting, and fit for attracting the peruse initially.

2. Highlights without the advantage

A component tells the buyer the item's capacity, while the advantage clarifies why they need it.

Great copywriters present the highlights before utilizing them to persuade a potential purchaser of the item's convenience. A buyer will disregard things that don't straightforwardly profit them.

3. Utilizing the equivalent meta title for each web page

A descriptive, informative copy is significant mostly - yet it likewise needs to get saw, which is the place website streamlining (SEO) comes in.

A Meta title uncovers the name of a webpage and is perused via web search tool robots and guests to the website. To seem higher up the rankings, they must speak to the first and the last second.

When the similar Meta title is utilized for each page, your site won't be appropriately upgraded. This may involve its inquiry rankings, and its capacity to illuminate potential customers regarding your business' items and administrations.

4. Saying excessively... or on the other hand close to nothing

A copywriter must comprehend the peruse and the item. Some copy may involve multiple pages of information. However, others may require a single tweet to get the point crosswise over and accomplish the ideal outcomes.

The significant point to recollect is to be compact. Word economy is central - in all respects occasionally can a 3,000-word article not be diminished to 2,500 or 2,000 words. Succinctness keeps unnecessary information from jumbling your copy.

5. Missing the invitation to act

When you have an 'a snare,' you peruse, and potential client requires a delicate push the correct way. Approach them to agree to accept a bulletin, like your page on Facebook or tail you on Twitter. If you request an activity, the peruse will frequently oblige.

The Top Copywriting Mistakes You Should Avoid Doing Today

Today, content is yet one of the mainstays of a fruitful web or blog website. If your web or blog website dependably has good substance, you build up yourself as an industry or market pioneer or expert, it helps drive more traffic, and it lifts brand introduction or acknowledgment. It likewise helps pull in more deals.

In that capacity, a ton still depends on proper copywriting methods and systems. When you distribute terrible substance, your believability can be adversely influenced, your mood killer and send guests away, and you accidentally dishearten them from purchasing your items or putting resources into your administrations.

In case you're new to copywriting or confounded regarding why your substance is by all accounts pushing guests away, you might submit some grave mistakes that are harming your web or blog website. The following are the top copywriting mistakes you ought to abstain from doing, starting today:

Thinking of exhausting titles and features. As a publicist, remember that regardless of whether you have the best substance if your claim or feature is awful, nobody is going to tap on or read it. Moreover, another oversight publicist often makes attempting to be over-the-top and excessively unique. Even though innovation is an unquestionable requirement, it is additionally vital that you don't go over the edge. You'll finish up confounding and notwithstanding baffling your readers when you think of too preposterous features.

You promise a ton of things. The good substance is something that ought to convince readers to make a move. Nonetheless, encouraging a lot of can have adverse outcomes. Readers today can make sense of when they're being deceived and will leave without delays if your cases are excessively preposterous. Regardless of whether your group of onlookers trusts your cases, these guarantees can be a tremendous disadvantage for you since you will have inconceivable desires to satisfy. When composing the content, dependably speak the truth about what you can offer. You can zest these offers a bit however never go too far that you'll lament doing it.

You are speaking a lot about yourself or your image. A great deal of web and blog locales still have this issue today. The lion's share of the substance is for the most part about materials about themselves, their group, and the organization. As a marketing specialist, you need to comprehend that consumers visit your web or blog website to discover answers or answers for their inquiries and issues, not to find out about you. Ensure that the focal point of the web or blog website ought to be your administrations and what you can offer to your guests or end-clients.

You are stuffing an excessive number of languages in your substance. In conclusion, the regular client won't think about the business language you use. The utilization of such many words can erode a customers' patience and break your transformation rates. A consumer needs to comprehend that you can meet their prerequisites and can help tackle their issues productively. They don't have to realize that you are a virtuoso who knows the intricate details of the business you are in.

Chapter 20 Copywriting Ethics: Staying True to Your Values

We have covered quite a lot about copywriting so far. By now, and if you have followed everything we have looked at, you should become at least a good copywriter. However, what about instances where you want to get better. What do you do then? Like many other professions, copywriting has some ethical rules meant to make you a better, happier, and content copywriter. Becoming a successful and happy copywriter, whether as a freelancer or within an organization, is indeed hard work.

Often, many freelance copywriters set unrealistic goals. This then creates tremendous stress on the individual. To be a success at copywriting, only one simple rule applies: success at work follows happiness.

If you are familiar with the law of attraction, you know what it states: we attract what we project. If you project positivity, you will be more successful in copywriting and other pillars of your life. You will also be productive, motivated, energetic, and resilient. To add to this, you must adopt an ethical approach to copywriting.

You can use the surprise and delight strategy to stay true to your values and be a happier copywriter.

What then is the surprise and delight strategy? The surprise and delight strategy state the following:

Define your success

If you are to achieve copywriting success, you must state what the success looks and feels like to you. Nobody will tell you or define for you a measure of your success. Rather than try to follow strategies from the so-called gurus, concentrate on defining your goals and success indicators.

Defining your success is the cornerstone to achieving them. Some pertinent questions you can use to define your success are:

\# How much money per month, do you want to make from copywriting?

\# How much free time do you require?

\# How many hours per day, will you work?

\# Which field of copywriting excites you?

\# Do you love telling stories or writing technically?

Not defining your goals and success measure will create a sense of instability. However, with defined success measures, once you achieve a goal, you can set a more ambitious one. Moreover, failing to define your goals and measure of success will hinder your insight: you will not be able to know when you achieve the goals or success. Create happiness and stability by defining what you aim to get from copywriting.

Pursue and aim to achieve the clients and consumer expectations

Most of what you will do as a copywriter is please others. On one end, you will struggle to please your boss (clients who hire you), and on the other end, please the consumer with compelling copies. From the client's side, secure a brief of the project. After reading the brief, explain to the client what they can expect from you.

Make sure that the expectation you project is one you can deliver.

In addition, since most clients are not copywriters (the whole reason behind hiring you) the briefs will have some deficiencies. Work with the client and advise them on how you can improve on their goals and help them achieve their objective and goals. On the consumer side, the expectation is a compelling copy offering a solution to a problem.

On top of this, you also must manage your own expectations. If you start from a low point and aim high, you will end up stressed, burnt out and frustrated. The opposite of this statement is also something you must consider. If your expectations and goals are not challenging, you will be burnt out, stressed, and easily frustrated. To this end, you should aim to create challenging but realistic objectives.

You can do this by stating how many copies you intend to create in a day and measuring this against your productivity. Do not give clients instant expectations (I will create your awesome copy in just a few hours). If you do this, you are likely to deliver the work in haste and thus make mistakes. On the other hand, if you offer yourself some leeway, you can exceed your expectations and impress the client. Therefore, be kind to yourself. Give a less stringent deadline but also make it challenging. The trick is to push yourself without driving off the cliff.

Adhere to the rules of ethical freelancing

To put this simply, ethical freelancing dictates the following:

Be truthful to yourself and your clients

Treat every client as you would like him or her to treat you.

Meet the client's expectations as well as your own expectations.

Ethical freelancing is what will set you apart from a million other copywriters. Ethical freelancing also means giving every copy the very best you have to offer. Today, value addition drives the copywriting business. While clients look for the very best people who can add some value to them and their companies, giving each copy your best guarantees your readiness to challenges and shows the client your real value. This then means you must go out of your way to define yourself and the core values driving your copywriting business.

That is the surprise and delight strategy. It will keep you sane, happy, and productive. It will also guarantee you returning clients. Clients who give you work with a smile on their face and a guarantee of your competence to deliver outstanding work.

Chapter 21 Essential Questions for Your Copy

When we talk about setting the target audience, we always think on the basic that we learn through life.

Which professional? Which income and social class? And so on...

However, knowing only this doesn't help on copy. We need more details.

More than that, we also need to understand how our audience's mind works. So, today I use a survey of 7 essential questions for you while you set your target audience!

Let's see which are they...

Who's going to buy the product?

Set who you want to reach. Gender, age, profession, income... all that you are used to, and everybody talks about in every marketing book.

It's important to have a set profile, which you can also give a name to guide yourself. The more accuracy you have, the easier is to be assertive on the communication.

Which is the buyer's personality?

Remember when we talked about copy motivators? Knowing the personality of your audience will help you to be more accurate on the motivators that you'll use.

Let's suppose that you work with an audience that wants to lose weight, but it's frustrated with many fail attempts.

One of the copy motivators can be "save money", because probably these people have already spent much money on fail diets.

You can also perceive which determination is part of the person, because, even if this person is frustrated, he or she keeps trying.

And all of these will help you when you are writing a text or a video script.

Why does anyone need your product?

Be honest and understand that this question is extremely natural and common in your audience's mind.

Depending on what you sell, people don't even know the reason why they need it. It happens with supplements, as chondroitin.

This substance is very used for people who have arthritis and arthrosis, but not all people know it. Many times, it's necessary to let very explicit the reason why someone needs what you sell.

I notice that it's hard for some people. They get angry and impatient: "How come you don't know for what my product is made for?!"

Not always it's supposed to happen. It's our job in copywriting to inform the person to persuade his or her to buy it.

Why does someone need the product now?

That's another thing that you may know about your target audience: how can you generate urgency in their buying decision?

What you can do for this person not to let to buy it tomorrow or next week?

For example, the person understands that he or she needs to speak English if he or she wants to achieve a higher position in the company.

But, sometimes, this person postpones the decision of enrolling himself or herself in a school. Which arguments can you use for this person to avoid postponing this?

- The end of the year is coming! Set as a goal of the next year learning a new language;

- Surprise your boss! In 4 weeks, you can attend to meetings in English;

- The unemployment rate is increasing. Do you want to take the risk of losing your job and not having English in your curriculum vitae?

And so on! The more urgency the person has, the better for you.

What's the main concern of the person who wants to buy it?

Knowing the main concern of your audience, you can use stronger arguments.

But it's important to go beyond the surface...

There's a technique called "3 Why's". In this technique you question 3 times the reason why the person wants a specific change.

For example:

- I want to lose weight!

- Why?

- Because I want to get thinner.

- Why?

- Because I'm feeling ugly.

- Why?

- Because I can't get a boyfriend.

Soon, you figured out that her main concern wasn't health, but relationship. You got that it doesn't matter for her how are the health levels, but if men will feel that she's attractive.

That's why the product doesn't sell. Frequently, we work with the wrong concern/motivation.

What exactly does the product do for the customer?

Be specific and, beyond that, deliver solutions that your audience is looking for.

If the person wants to lose weight to attract men, don't be ashamed to define this as one of the product benefits.

Being "politically correct" or saying something nicer won't get you more customers.

For example, cars. There is a popular belief that car attracts women.

Then, when a youngster buys a roadster Audi, in 90% of the cases he is single.

Audi didn't need to advertise it saying that this vehicle would help him with women, and the seller on the dealership hasn't said this many time to convince the customer.

So, what does your product really do for your customer?

Decreasing the cholesterol level isn't attractive. Saving life and letting the person to know the grandson is. It's all about perspective.

What does motivate the customer to buy it?

At last, what does motivate your customer to subscribe in your lose weight program, for example? This can vary a lot...

Let's say that your audience is made of low-income people. Maybe a sale or a launch voucher be very attractive.

But if your audience is made of high-income people, a great motivation can be a live meeting with you, even if it costs 3 times more.

Another thing that influences a lot here is the personality...

If it is an audience which is desperate for a solution, the faster is the result (do you remember the Kopy Triangle?), the more motivated the customer will be to buy it.

If it's an easy audience, that sees your product as part of a hobby, to deliver something special, as an autographed book, can be more motivating.

In a nutshell:

To understand your audience will turn you more persuasive.

Any copywriting strategy is enough, if you don't answer these 7 primary questions.

Now, let's detail another essential and extremely important issue for you to increase your conversions.

I didn't understand this so well until I saw how experienced copywriters made it...

You'll be surprised too!

Conclusion

So, copywriting means much more than writing texts. Offline and online writing has a multiplicity of purposes and necessarily translates into multiple forms. Seen in this light, web copywriting is and must remain persuasive writing. A writing, therefore, aimed not only at information, but at effective communication.

Copywriting is an instrumental practice and its function remains to influence decisions and to change or reinforce behaviors and opinions. And to do so using precise words and syntax, without forgetting the rhetorical techniques. For me, making copywriting means, therefore, analyze, reason, choose the language most suited to the Brand Identity and shared by the public of a given company. Only later, copywriting is writing. And that's why, before writing texts, I answer 3 questions:

For whom do I write? That is, what is the company or the professional who is communicating with my texts?

Why do I write? So, what is the final goal to be reached with my texts?

Who do I write to? The audience to which the texts are directed, its language, its state in the purchasing process.

To be a copywriter, it is not enough to love writing, to be able to write in current and correct Italian and to be able to do with editing. We need analytical skills, foresight and psychological sensitivity.

Writing this book has been a fulfilling look into the world of professional copywriting. We have the best-kept secrets that can help you, as a copywriter, create magnetic headlines. I hope that I kept the promises I made to you at the beginning of this book. Now I wish I could tell you that by reading this book alone, you will be ready to write viral headlines, but I can't. What you do now will determine if this book will achieve its purpose or end up as one of the numerous reads that you forget as soon as you turn the last page.

As a way of refreshing your memory, let's quickly go over the things we have learned in this book.

First, we looked at the importance of headlines in professional copywriting. We saw that the headline is the chief determiner of whether a reader will open your content or just zoom past it. To drive this point home, we saw that out of every 10 people who come across your posts, 8 just read the headline while only 2 proceed to read the rest of the content. With this statistic, we realize it is very important for us to have great headlines.

With this realization, we proceeded to see how we can improve the efficiency of our headlines by using numbers. We saw the important role that numbers play in headlines. We saw that numbers serve as an anchor to hook in readers because the brain is attracted to numbers and numbers help memory. Generally, we saw that numbers suggest organization and structure and promise something specific. For this reason, numbers endear headlines to the heart of readers, and there is actual proof that headlines with numbers convert into more clicks. From there, we saw how we could practically work numbers into existing headlines to improve effectiveness. Then we saw instances where numbers made headlines more effective. We learned how to improve our headline's effectiveness by 73% by adding numbers.

Besides a lot of updating, study and practice in the field. Practice that exposes you of course also to the risk of making mistakes in the testing phase, although errors to be considered, when you work with the decision-making processes of an audience and rely on responses that can never be predicted.

Lightning Source UK Ltd.
Milton Keynes UK
UKHW020423181120
373567UK00001B/4